I0827974

IMAGES
of America

Fall River Revisited

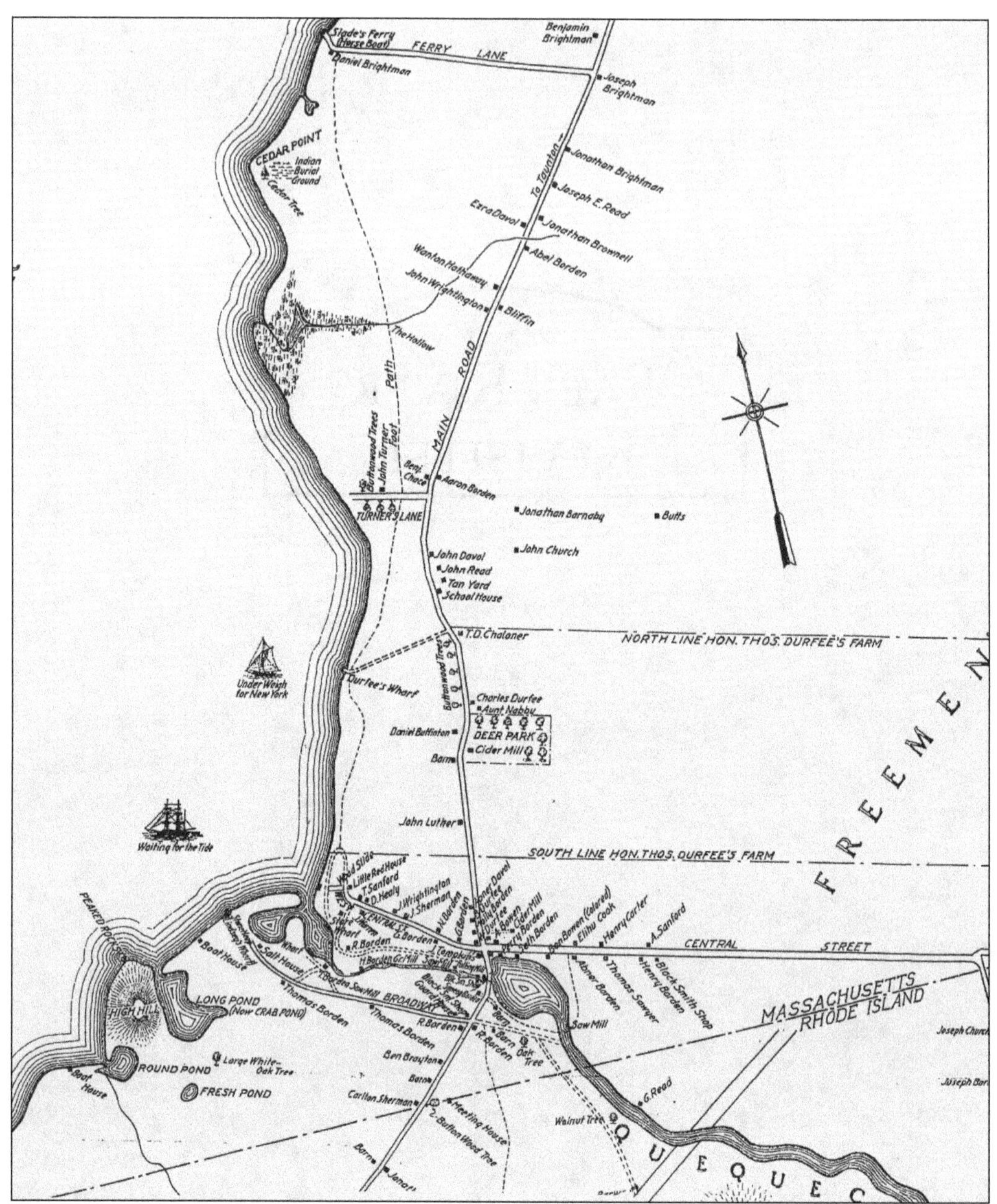

This 1812 map is of the West End of the village of Fall River and the shore of the Taunton River. It depicts the names of the landholders and their concentration along the mouth of the Quequechan River. The following year, the first textile mill was built, ushering in the Industrial Revolution to Fall River. (Courtesy of private collection.)

On the Cover: This photograph of Charles Cavanaugh, a 15-year-old back boy in the mule spinning room at the King Philip Mill, was taken in 1916 by Lewis Wickes Hine (1874–1940). Hine worked as a photographer for the National Child Labor Committee (NCLC) and traveled the country documenting child labor practices. Hine was in Fall River in 1912 and 1916. His work influenced public attitude about child labor and its effects on the young and proved to be influential in the NCLC's fight for more rigorous child labor laws. (Courtesy of the Library of Congress.)

IMAGES
of America

FALL RIVER REVISITED

Stefani Koorey, PhD,
and the Fall River History Club

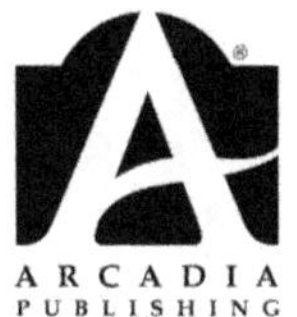

Copyright © 2012 by Stefani Koorey, PhD, and the Fall River History Club
ISBN 978-1-5316-5088-9

Published by Arcadia Publishing
Charleston, South Carolina

Library of Congress Control Number: 2011936164
For all general information, please contact Arcadia Publishing:
Telephone 843-853-2070
Fax 843-853-0044
E-mail sales@arcadiapublishing.com
For customer service and orders:
Toll-Free 1-888-313-2665

Visit us on the Internet at www.arcadiapublishing.com

To Michael Brimbau, whose interest in Fall River history inspired my own, and to Harry Widdows and Kat Koorey, who accompanied me on this journey

Contents

ACKNOWLEDGMENTS

A book of this scope could not have been undertaken without the help and support of many people. My heartfelt appreciation is extended to each person who allowed me the privilege of looking through his or her family scrapbooks and personal collections. I especially enjoyed the stories that the images triggered and will forever value those all-too-brief strolls down memory lane.

Many of the images contained herein were contributed by members of the Fall River History Club, which is comprised of 40 or so kindred spirits who gather every month at the Fall River Public Library to hear informal talks and share their interests in the rich history of this city. They include (in no particular order) Kenneth M. Champlin, Bill Goncalo, Jay Lambert, George Petrin, Bob Kitchen, John Friar, Alan Amaral, Marc Belanger, Alfred Lima, Mary Ann Wordell, Everett Castro, Joe Carvalho, Jim Mullins, Leonard Rebello, Tom and Deb Athearn, Barry French, Phil Silvia, Brian Curt, Jack Faria, Tom and Karla Moran, Dave Jennings, David Greene, Debbie Kelley, Russell Castonguay, Rick Burt, Nancy Aruda, Gail and Tony Caprio, Tom Skibinski, Jim and Connie Soule, Dave and Sandy Dennis, Rebecca and Jim Cusick, Marc Dion, Walter Mitchell, Paul Pietraszek, Annie Pietraszek, Michael Brimbau, and Anne-Marie Grillo.

The Fall River Historical Society has been most gracious in allowing me access to the collection of P.D. Borden, former city engineer for Fall River, which contains hundreds of images of the city taken of what appears to be every possible location. In addition, the society has granted permission for me to select from its extensive image collection of the Cotton Centennial celebration of 1911, and chapter three of this book is comprised of the society's contribution entirely. Curator Michael Martins and assistant curator Dennis Binette deserve much more than thanks for their assistance in the research for this book, and for their help I am deeply indebted.

And, of course, a debt of gratitude goes to P.D. Borden for collecting so many photographs of this city and for having the foresight to label each one, preserve the albums, and then donate them to the Fall River Historical Society for posterity and history's sake. They have proved invaluable in this work. May his efforts be a lesson to us all.

On a personal note, I would like to thank those friends who put up with my hibernation during the writing of this book. They include Nicole Sylvia, Dipti Sharma, Ian Garrett, Onsloe Brimbau, and Shannon Brimbau. A thanks also goes to Paula Costa Cullen who recommended me for this project.

A thanks also goes to my acquisitions editor, Lissie Cain, who is always supportive and an expert at keeping me on task to meet deadlines. Your kindness has not gone unnoticed.

INTRODUCTION

In 1911, Fall River, Massachusetts, was the number one producer of cotton cloth in the United States, and second only to Manchester, England, in the world. In its heyday, Fall River boasted 43 corporations, 222 mill buildings, and 3,800,000 spindles, producing two miles of cloth in every minute of every working day in the year. These companies employed Portuguese (mainly Azorean), Irish, French Canadian, and English laborers who immigrated to the city in order to secure work in the mills that flanked the Quequechan River. Other immigrant populations that have made Fall River their home and secured a place in the history of the city include Italians, Poles, Russians, and Jews. In addition to its rich mill history, Fall River's story also includes two famous murder mysteries involving Sarah Cornell and Lizzie Borden. Lizzie is perhaps Fall River's most (in)famous native, and the gruesome nature of the murders of her father and stepmother in 1892, followed by her acquittal the following year, endures in America's psyche. She has become the iconic ax-wielding malcontent, even though there is no evidence to paint her as this monster. And if you have the courage, you can spend the night in the murder house, which was turned into a bed-and-breakfast in 1997.

The city of Fall River is essentially a collection of neighborhoods, each possessing a rich cultural heritage and notable architecture. The city boasts of three Frederick Law Olmsted parks, an abundant natural water supply, a deepwater port, seven miles of waterfront, and 12,000 acres of forest set aside in perpetuity as the Southeastern Bioreserve. Fall River possesses an eclectic collection of locally owned and operated restaurants that offer a broad range of culinary styles, the world's largest historic naval exhibit at Battleship Cove, and the first public building constructed over a federal interstate highway. Fall River rests on a massive ledge of granite, a batholith, that was, incidentally, once the source of one of the city's industries. Famous Fall River natives include Emeril Lagasse, George Stephanopoulos, Joe Raposo (composer for *Sesame Street*), Jerry Remy, Victoria Lincoln, E.J. Dionne, Morton Dean, Greg Gagne, Gladys Hasty Carroll, and children's author Nancy Cote. Fifty miles south of Boston, 183 miles northeast of New York City, 18 miles southeast of Providence, Rhode Island, 14 miles west of New Bedford, 18 miles north of Newport, and a few short hours from Cape Cod, Fall River is perfectly located on the South Coast of Massachusetts.

In an odd turn of events, while gathering images for this volume, I was concurrently running for mayor of Fall River. I had a rare opportunity to engage residents in sharing their memories of the city that they love. And as I listened to their stories of Cherry & Webb, McWhirr's, Camara's Grocery, the great conflagration of 1928, the old city hall, the sounds of the textile mills in full operation, the "falls" of the Quequechan River, and hundreds of other familiar sights that are no longer in existence due to urban revitalization and economic downturns, I was inspired by the indomitability of Fall River's spirit as evidenced in her people.

While I was not fortunate enough to win my race for mayor, I have taken with me a deep understanding of just how bittersweet it can be to live in a community that does not resemble in sight, sound, or feeling the city of one's youth. Fall River today is not the Fall River of its past for many of reasons. The textile mills put this city on the map of the world. Their decline in production began with a shift of manufacturing to the South, where the cotton was grown and harvested, and then overseas, where cheap labor finished them off. Fall River's motto is "We'll Try." To some, this might seem to be a weak way of expressing an attempt at success. Those who do not understand the history of the origin of this motto mock it and rally for it to be changed to something more action-oriented. It is important to note, however, that these words symbolized something significant to a generation that had just witnessed a massive fire in 1843 that destroyed a great deal of their downtown and residential areas. As a stunned and saddened populace gathered around the smoldering rubble of their once vibrant Main Street, it was somehow able to summon up the strength of will that only a resilient people can know and claim, then and there, that people would start anew with hope and determination to restore their city. When placed in its historic context, then, "We'll Try" is essentially a valiant motto of perseverance and one that cannot be improved upon by changing its wording.

Antiquarian booksellers will tell you that Fall River is one of the most collected of New England's cities. Early books about Fall River's history always fetch top dollar, and every Thursday night at the Fall River Elks Lodge at the Sowersby's Auction, one is bound to find a historical gem or at least a story or two from residents who are reminded of their childhoods as they peruse the tables resplendent with artifacts, antiques, and doodads. No matter where Fall Riverites roam, they harbor a deep appreciation for the city of their birth and feel connected once again by owning a piece of her. Perhaps this is what drives the book and collectible market for Fall River items.

Like other cities in the nation, Fall River is currently experiencing an economic crisis. Its unemployment rate is almost double that of the commonwealth, one in five of its residents is living in poverty, and its school system is faltering, creating a bleak outlook for the foreseeable future. Partly due to the lack of money to effectively run a city of 88,000, Fall River is probably no different than other communities that once depended on a manufacturing economy, only to lose out to lower wages and cheaper manufacturing costs. Essentially a one-industry town, Fall River is endeavoring to reinvent itself in the 21st century. And if the past is prologue, the renaissance of the city will be something to behold.

One

The Immigrant Influx

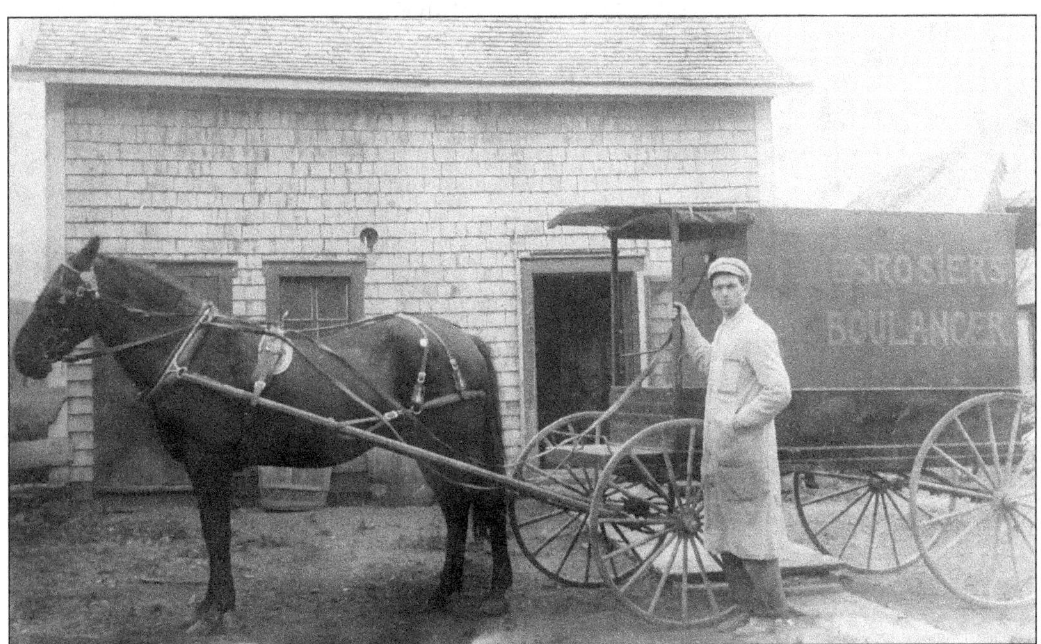

As a young man, Andre Desrosiers (pictured here around 1910) worked for his father Octave's bakery on Myrtle Street in Fall River, as did his brothers Romeo and Joseph. Each of Andre's four sisters (Marie Anne, Marie Blanche, Marie Luce, and Marie Enath) attended Thibodeau Business College. Octave emigrated from Canada and settled in a predominantly French Canadian neighborhood in Fall River's South End in the King Philip Mill section. (Courtesy of Dennis Binette.)

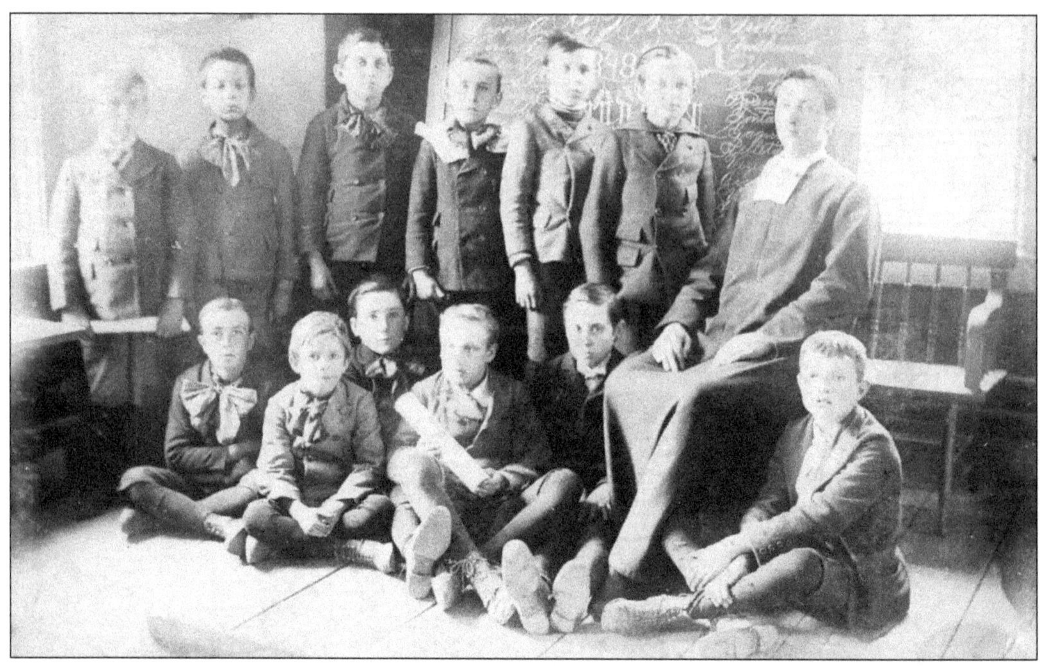

The Notre Dame parish, located in the Flint section of Fall River, was created in 1874 and was mostly comprised of French Canadians. After the first wooden church was destroyed by fire in 1893, a new magnificent granite church, designed by Louis G. Destremps, was built. In 1982, it too was destroyed by fire. This image depicts a class at the Notre Dame School in 1898. (Courtesy of Kenneth M. Champlin.)

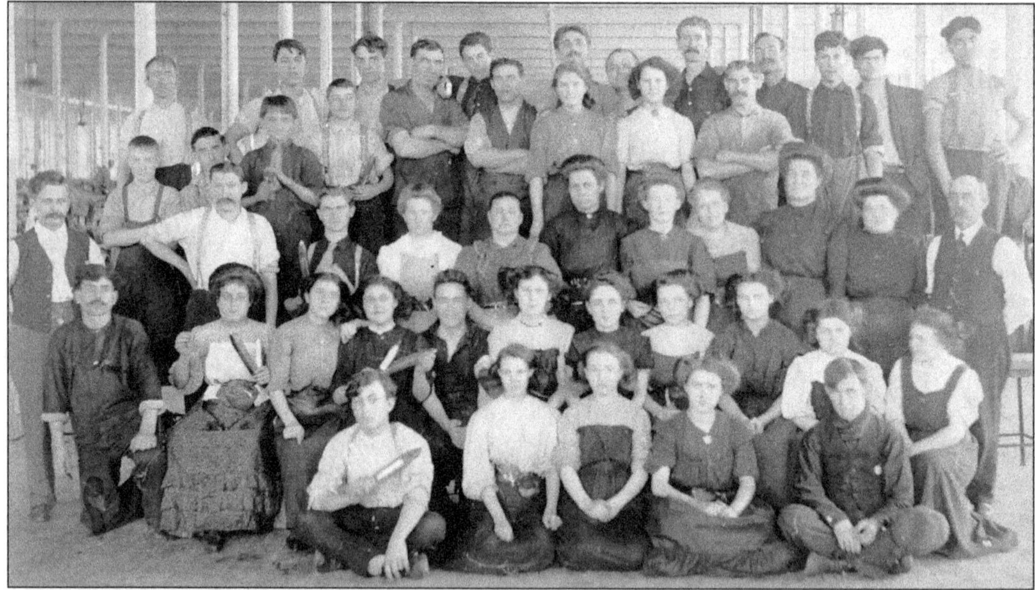

Photographed around 1908, Bernadette Parent (sixth from left in the second row) entered the mills at the age of 15 or 16 and worked as a spinner, one of the least skilled jobs of the mill operatives. Born in Quebec in the late 19th century, she later married Patrick Hughes from Brownsville, Texas, whom she met when he was in Fall River during his service in the US Navy. (Courtesy of Kenneth M. Champlin.)

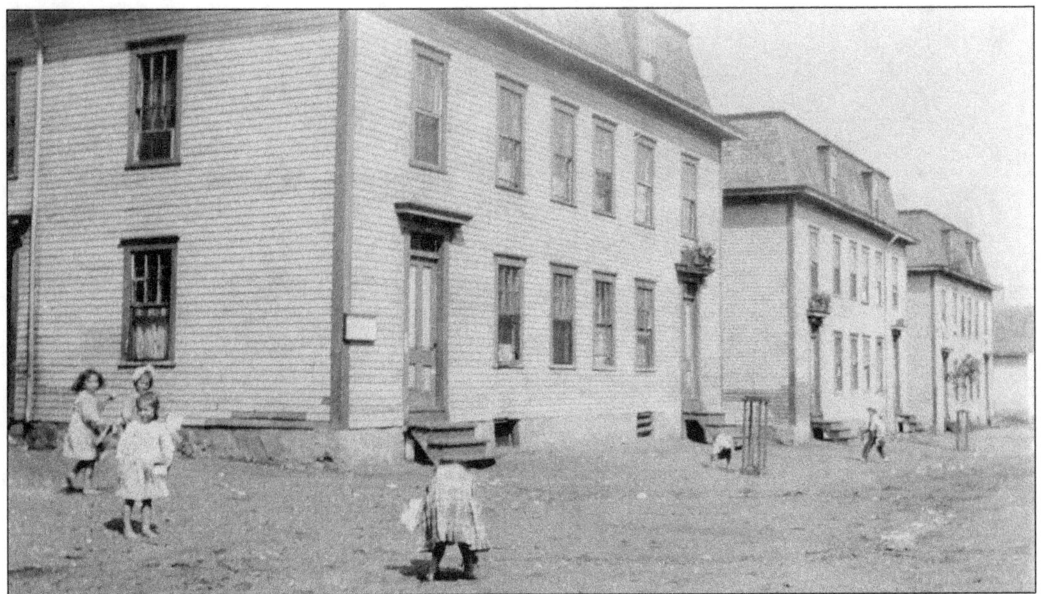

Early tenement houses, built by the mills, were the mandatory living quarters of the operatives. Typically, they were overcrowded and clustered adjacent to the mills so that the workers could be in walking distance to work as well as in earshot of the bells that called them. These tenements had no plumbing, no city water, and no electricity. Outhouses were in general use in these working communities until the 1920s. (Courtesy of Kenneth M. Champlin.)

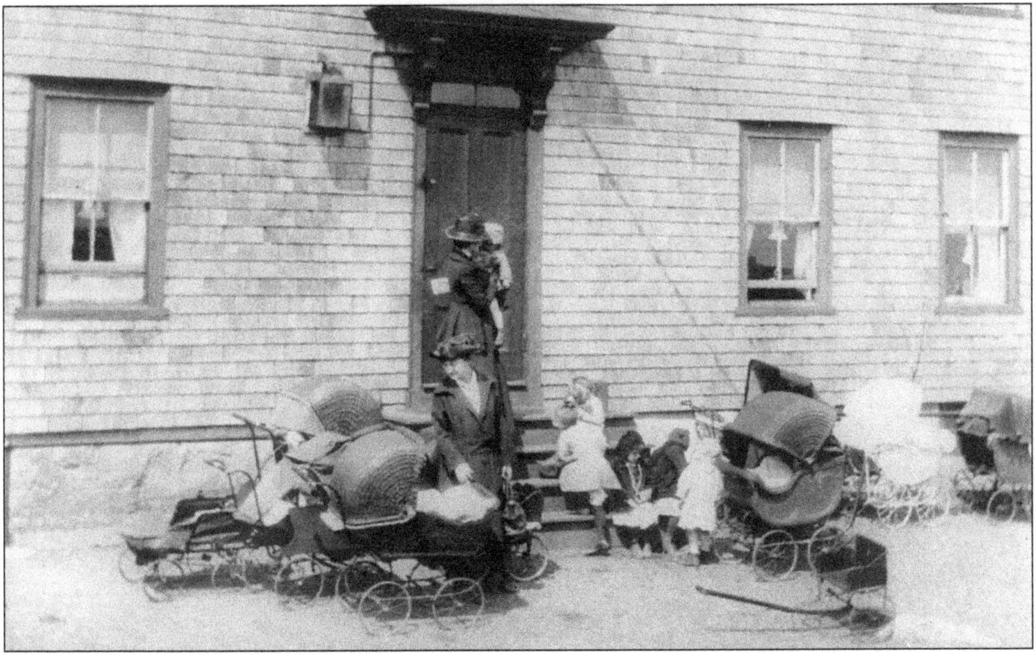

The King Philip Settlement House, located in the South End of Fall River, was opened in 1913 by the District Nursing Association in response to a high infant mortality rate in the tenement community surrounding King Philip Mills. The facility had a prenatal and well baby clinic, and about 80 to 100 mothers and babies visited each week, obtaining health care from Dr. Hicks and nurses Elizabeth Barrette and Margaret Parker. (Courtesy of Kenneth M. Champlin.)

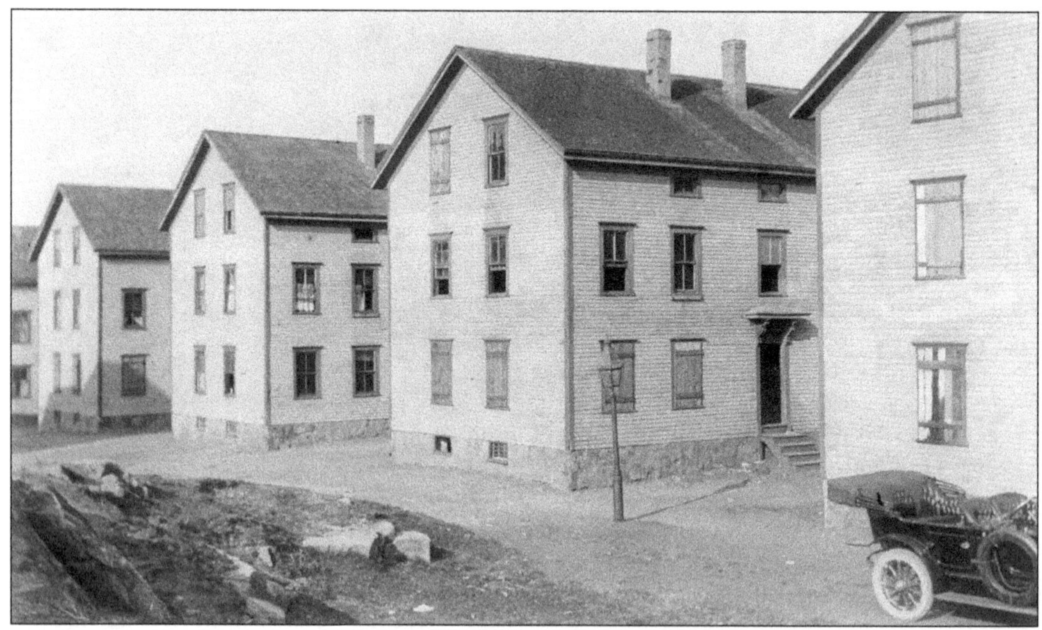

These Fall River tenement houses are typical of those constructed by the mills. The King Philip Mills Nos. 1 and 2 were built in 1871. At that time, a routine workday was 14 hours, from 5:00 a.m. until 7:00 p.m., repeated six days a week. Children became mill workers at age eight, by which time it was determined that they had developed the necessary stamina. (Courtesy of Kenneth M. Champlin.)

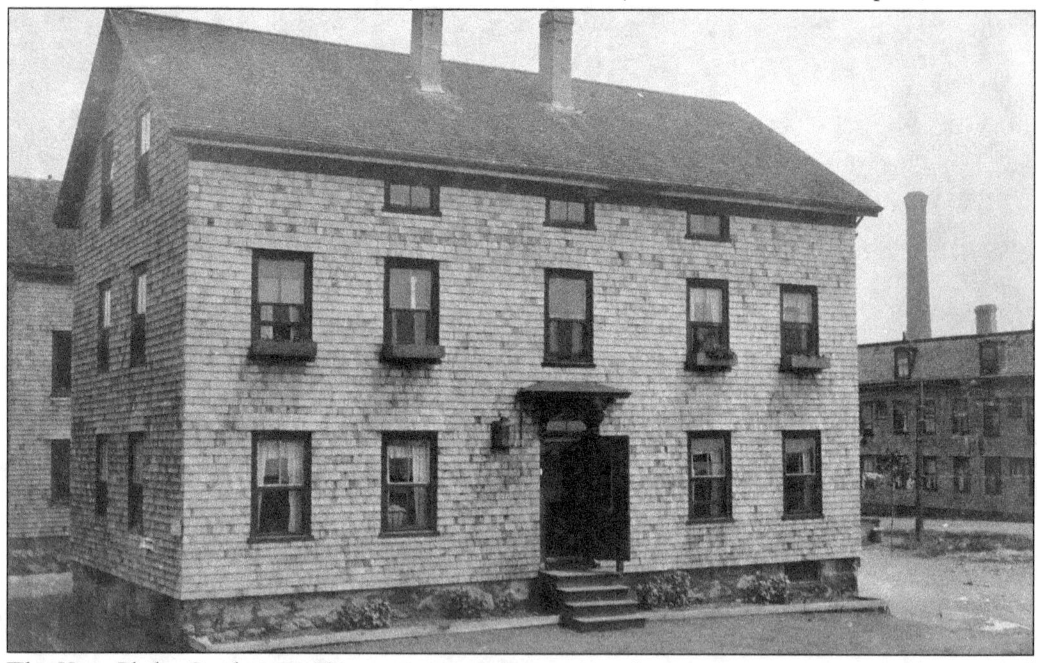

The King Philip Settlement House was part of a nationwide progressive movement that started in Chicago in the 19th century. Providing assistance to immigrant families, such facilities were popular for their showers and baths, as none of the tenement housing had indoor plumbing. The prices were 5¢ for an adult and 3¢ for a child, and included a bar of soap and a clean towel. (Lewis Hine photograph, courtesy of the Library of Congress.)

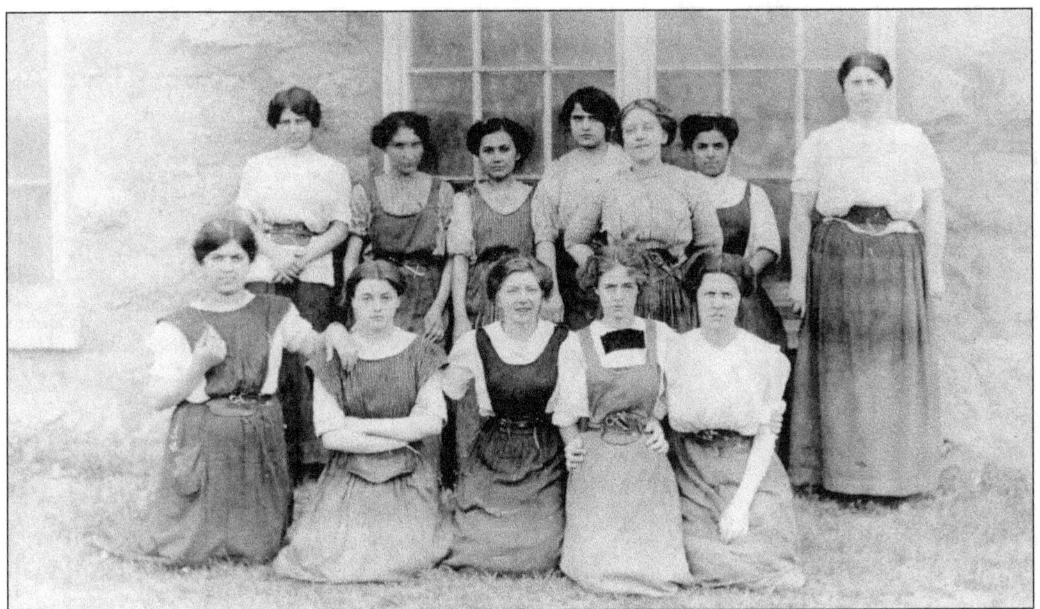

Often, an entire family would be employed in the same mill. Pictured around 1920, Bernadette Parent (first row, right) and her sister Marilese (second row, right) worked as spinners at a mill in the Flint section of Fall River. The cases around the women's waists hold their scissors. By 1900, more than one-third of the population of Quebec had immigrated to the United States to work in New England's mills. (Courtesy of Kenneth M. Champlin.)

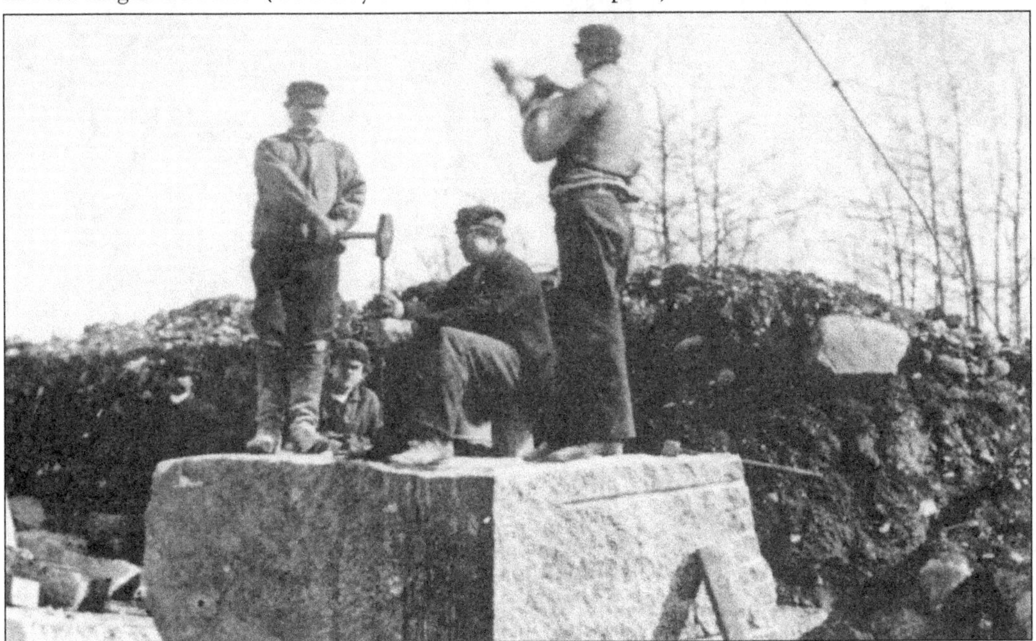

During one of the glacial periods, glaciers moved through the area and carved out the landscape of the region, pushing tremendous amounts of stone and volcanic rock with them. Fall River rests on a massive ledge of granite, a batholith, once the source of one of the city's industries, which was mainly worked by Italian immigrants who came to this country as skilled tradesmen. By 1900, 44 percent of the city's working Italians were self-employed. (Courtesy of private collection.)

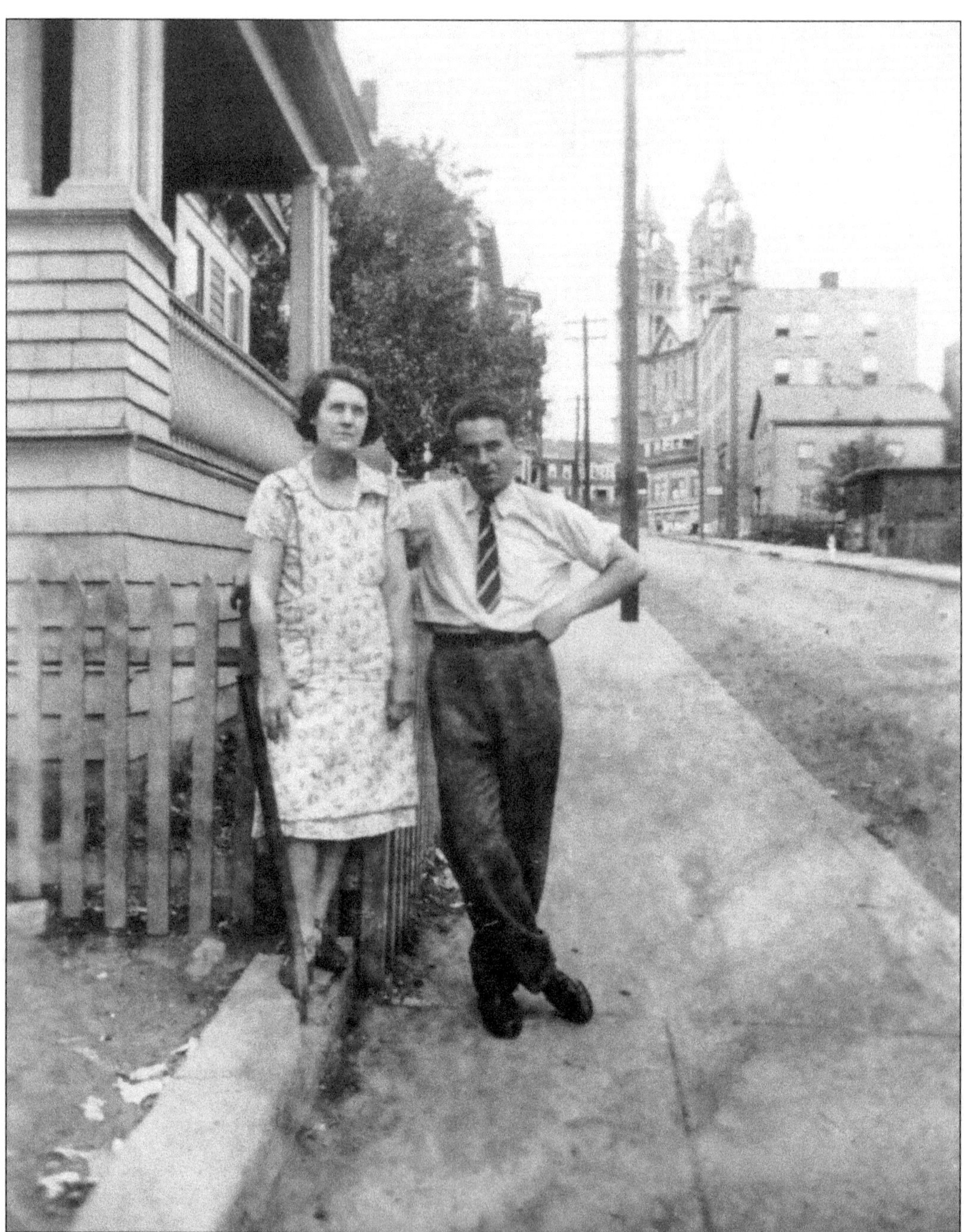

Mill operatives primarily rented apartments their entire lives, mainly because the mills in which they worked were not located in single-family neighborhoods. Without the financial wherewithal to own their own transportation and, in the early days, the requirement by mill owners that their workers live in company tenements, these workers rarely lived outside of the mill's environs. Here, shortly after World War II, Bernadette Parent Hughes stands with her son-in-law Edward R. Champlin Sr. in front of the triple-decker where she lived on Boutwell Street in the Flint section of Fall River. The omnipresent spires of Notre Dame Church can be seen in the background. (Courtesy of Kenneth M. Champlin.)

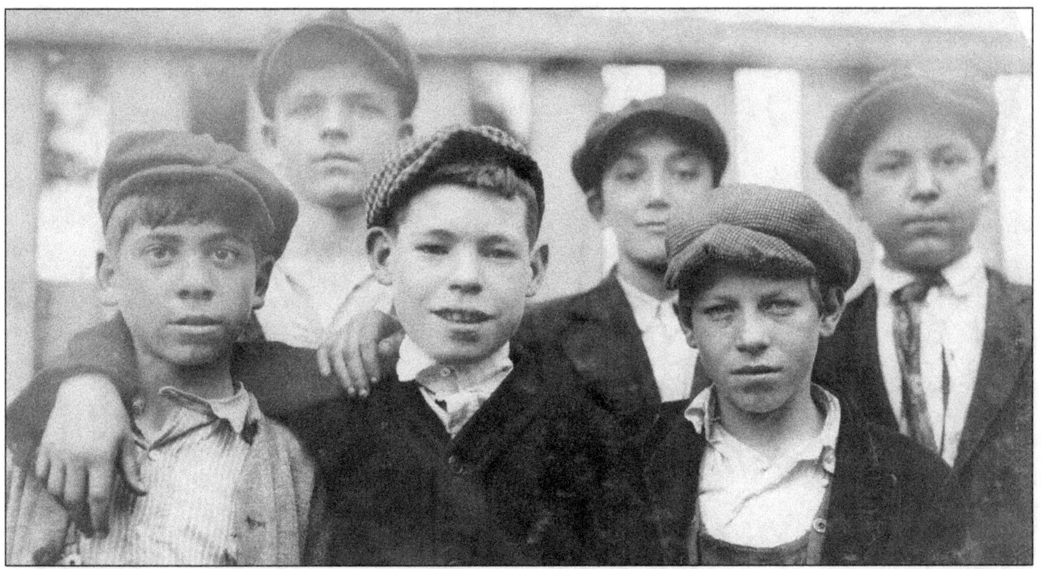

In 1900, Fall River had a higher percentage of foreign-born inhabitants than any other large city in the United States. Of that number, 36 percent were Canadian, 27 percent British, 13 percent Irish, 15 percent Azorean/Portuguese, and 3 percent Russian, with many being Jews fleeing the pogroms. This image from 1916 is of a group of 14- and 15-year-old drop wire boys and sweepers who work at the Granite Mill No. 2. (Lewis Hine photograph, courtesy of the Library of Congress.)

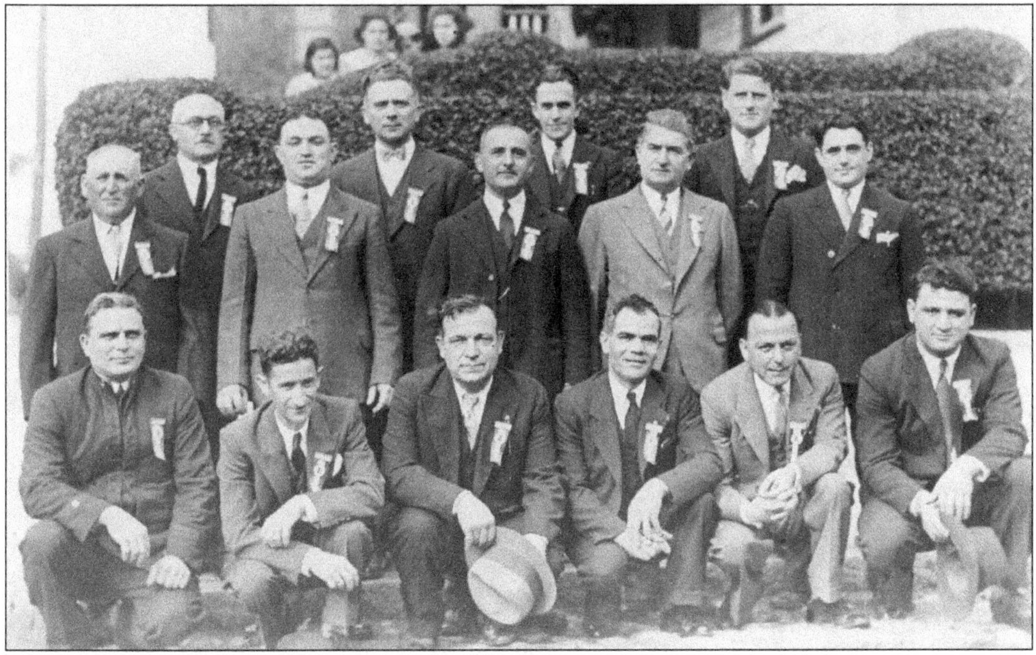

In 1910, Columbus Day was made a legal holiday in Massachusetts. Festivities on this day include parades, concerts, and fireworks. Organizers were members of the city's Italian clubs, the most prominent being the Italian Association of Fall River, formed in 1897. This photograph is of the Columbus Day Committee around 1936. Those identified are (first row) second from the left, Ernest Barsi, and far right, Fred Dagata; (third row) second from the right, Peter Pieroni. (Courtesy of Alan Amaral.)

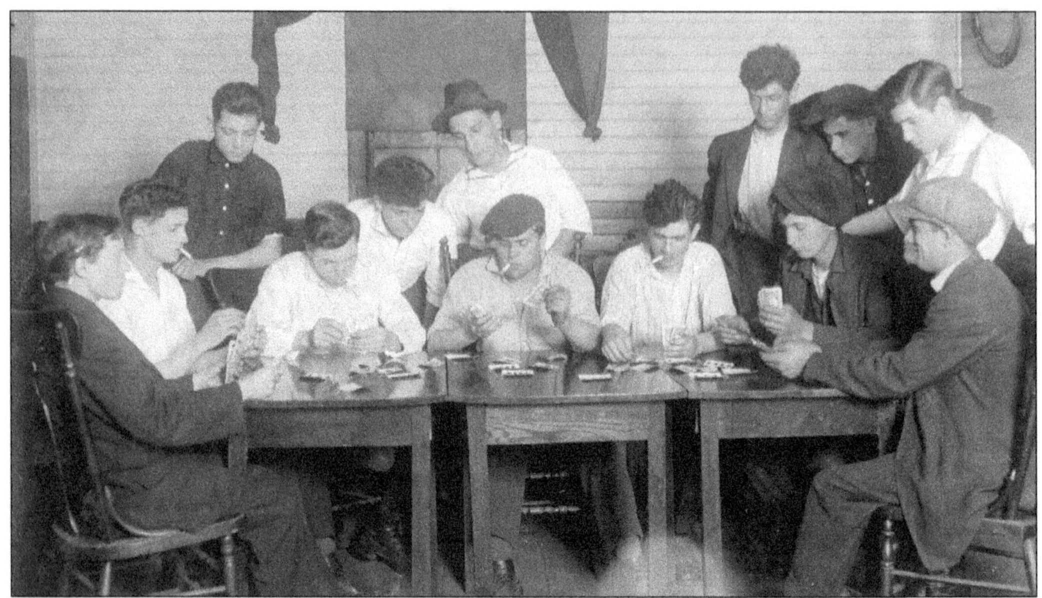

The Azorean Portuguese immigrants, much like the French Canadians who came to call Fall River home, did not, as a group, assimilate into the American culture. Instead, they maintained their own language, religion, and customs. This group of Portuguese mill workers, ages 15 to 25, is enjoying an evening's recreation. (Lewis Hine photograph, courtesy of the Library of Congress.)

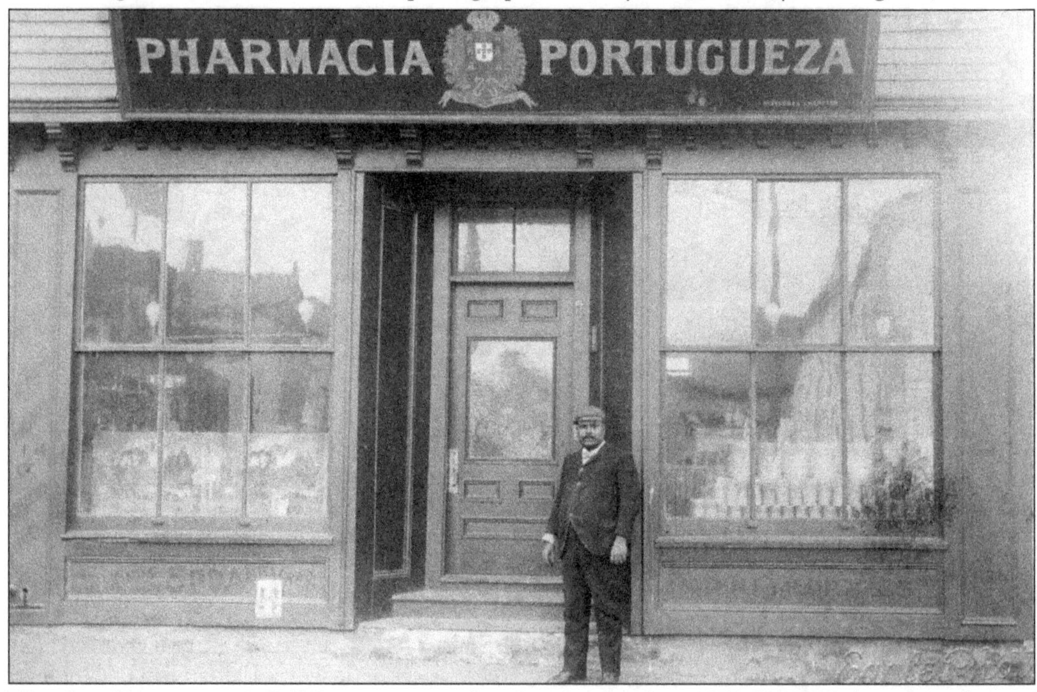

The first Portuguese in Fall River were said to have arrived in 1855. In 1890, large numbers of Portuguese immigrants, mostly from São Miguel, began to arrive to work in the city's cotton mills. Within 30 years, one-fifth of Fall River's population was Portuguese. By 1924, Fall River boasted three Portuguese clubs, three newspapers, four banks, five benevolent associations, and seven Catholic parishes. (Courtesy of private collection.)

In 1919, it was noted that Azorean Portuguese families in Fall River were often large, with eight or more children, and sometimes between 12 and 15. Because of these numbers, there was a period of poverty before the children were old enough to work, necessitating older siblings to begin working in the mills as early as age eight. This Portuguese spinner is at work at the American Linen Company in 1916. (Lewis Hine photograph, courtesy of the Library of Congress.)

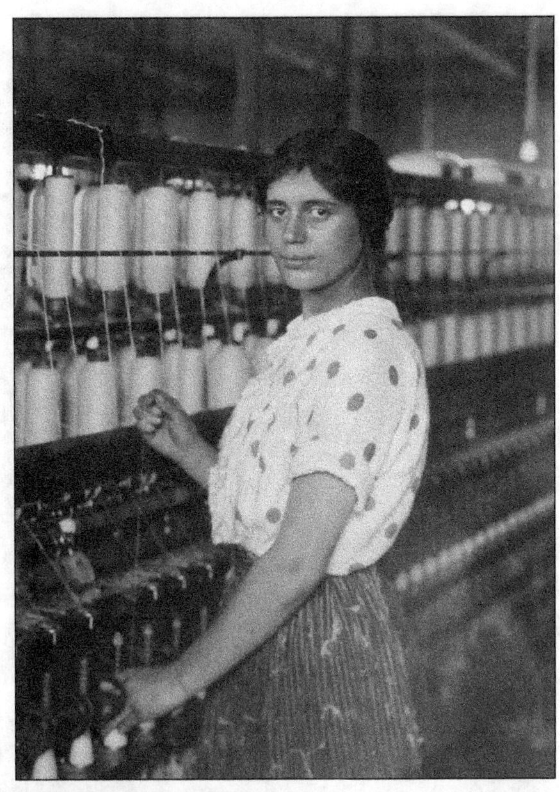

From 1890 to 1914, more than one-half of all immigrants to the United States were Italian, accounting for one-third of all arriving stonecutters and one-half of all arriving barbers and hairdressers. In Fall River, most of the workforce at three different granite quarries was comprised of Italian immigrants. This 16-year-old Italian ironworker is attending a carving class at the King Philip Settlement House in June 1916. (Lewis Hine photograph, courtesy of the Library of Congress.)

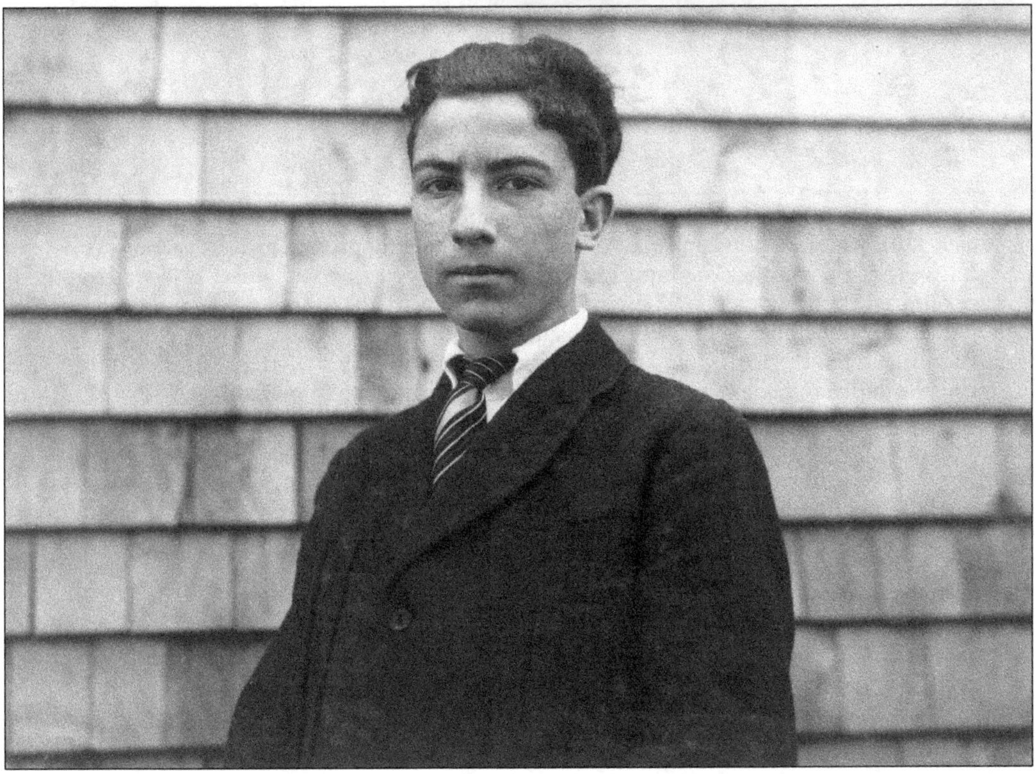

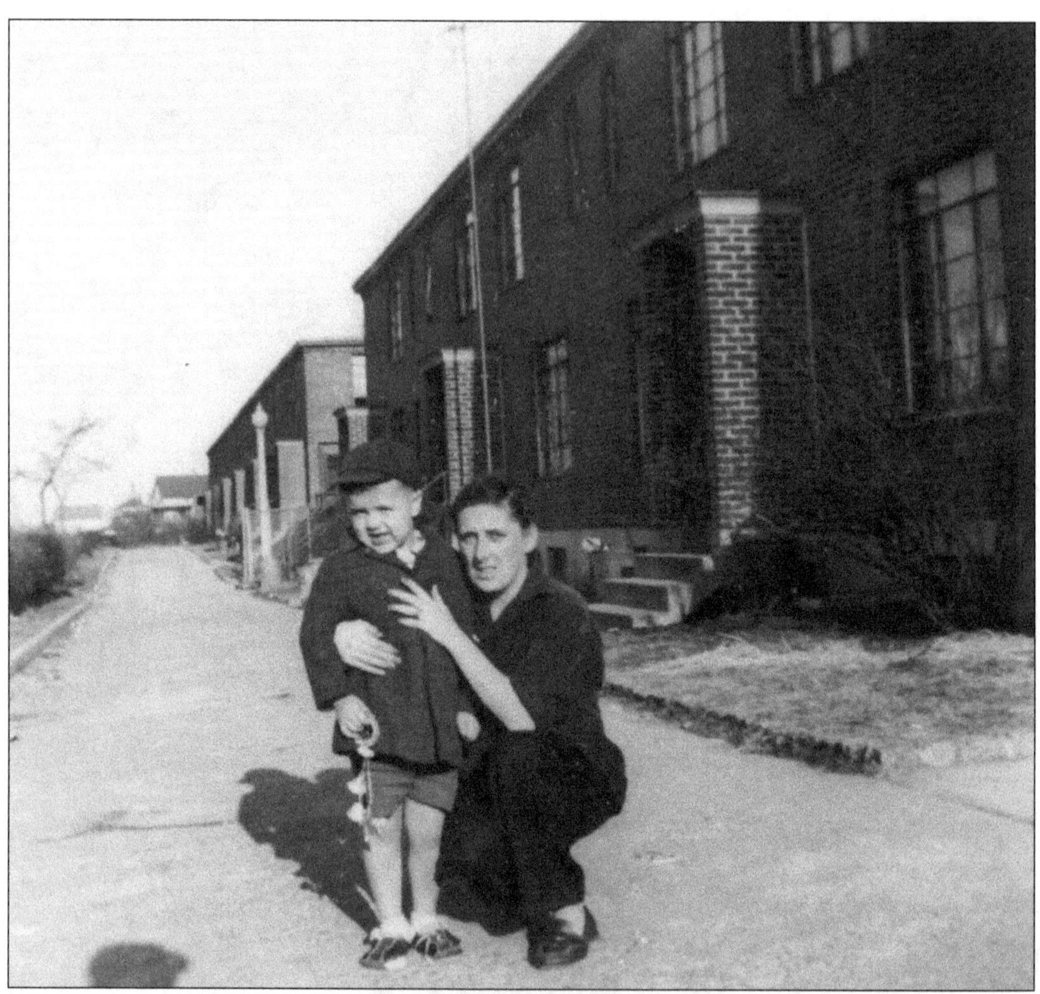

As a boy, Ken Champlin (pictured here with neighbor Irene Radcliffe) lived from 1952 to 1958 at Sunset Hill, which at the time was a new federal housing project for low-income veterans. Champlin says, "I remember the rats. The thing that was odd about Sunset Hill was that coal furnaces heated the apartments. There were coal bins in the basement, and you had to pay for your own coal. I remember fights over the coal. I distinctly remember the bins, shoots, and coal trucks coming down the road. The buildings were steel frame construction. Not like tenements, but more like duplexes. Side by side like row houses. And there was a playground with a fountain/shower type of thing. It was a circular area of asphalt with curved spouts coming out of ground. When the water was on, it would stream out of the spouts and meet in the center. It was how we kept ourselves cool in the summer as kids. It was an okay place to live, I guess. After this place, we moved to a six-family tenement in the North End." (Courtesy of Kenneth M. Champlin.)

Two

Cotton Textile Manufacturing

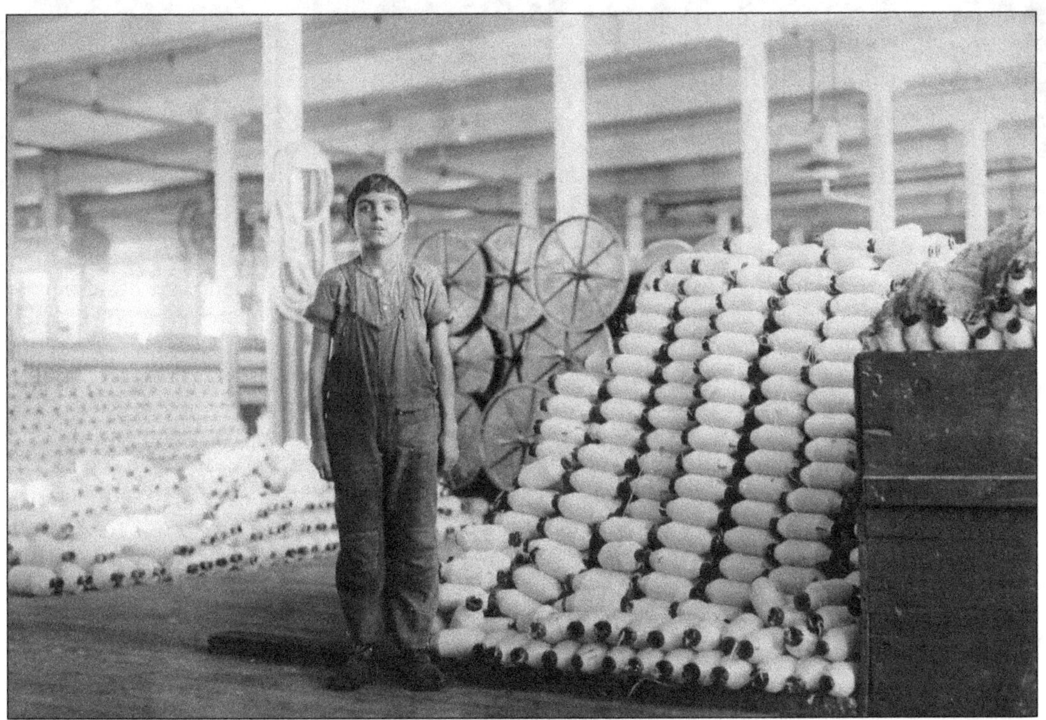

At the time this photograph was taken in January 1912, Manuel Miranda had been a doffer in the card room of the Cornell Mill for six months, removing filled bobbins from spinning machines and replacing them with empty ones to receive the product. When asked his age, he replied, "I'm goin' on 16," noted the photographer, "but didn't say when he would reach it." (Lewis Hine photograph, courtesy of the Library of Congress.)

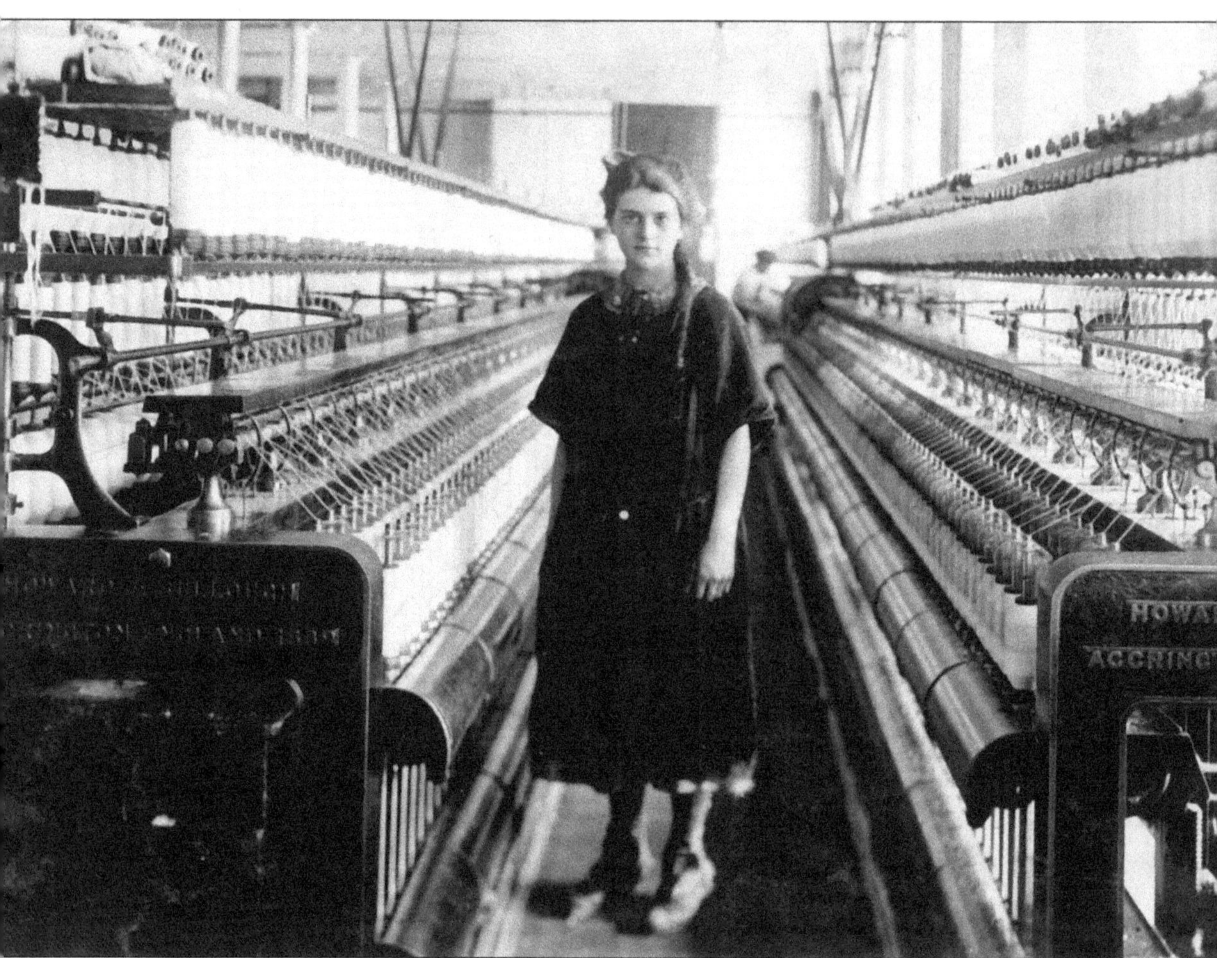

Prior to 1812, most family farms were self-sustaining and provided for their own basic needs, including the manufacture of clothing, mostly made from the wool produced from their own sheep that they then spun into yarn on foot-powered spinning wheels, then weaved into cloth on hand looms. Because removing the seeds, leaves, and stems from raw cotton was so labor-intensive, it was not economically viable as a raw material for cloth. The inventions of the cotton gin in 1793 by Eli Whitney, with which greater volumes of cotton could be cleaned with less human toil; the sewing machine in 1847 by Elias Howe; and the straight needle and foot treadle in 1851 by Isaac Singer all worked to help usher in this country's industrial revolution and put Fall River, and cities like it, on the map. (Lewis Hine photograph, courtesy of the Library of Congress.)

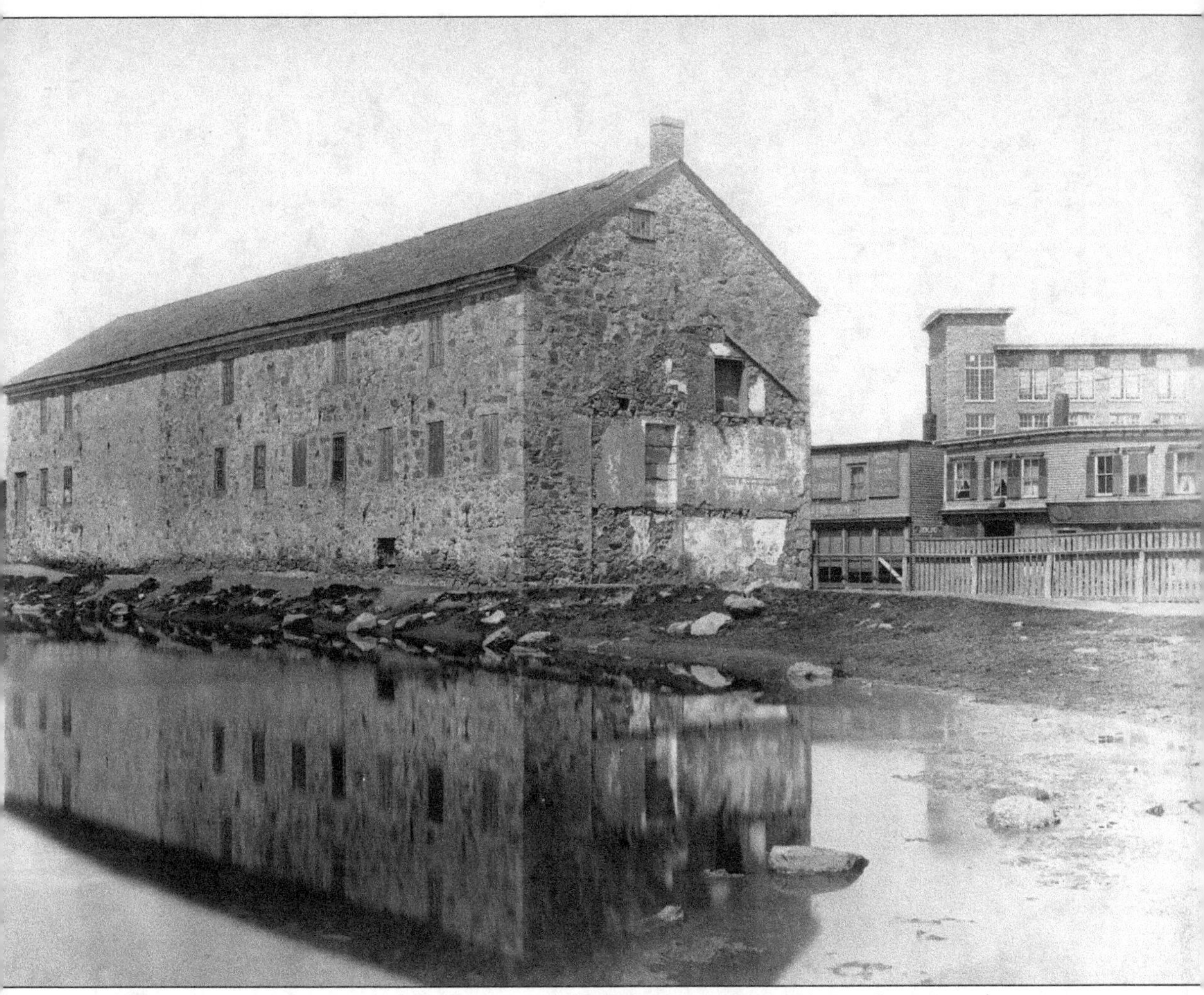

Fall River's first cotton-spinning mill was started in 1811 by Col. Joseph Durfee, a Revolutionary War veteran who took an active part in the Battle of White Plains. It was built on a stream and pond, now the intersection of South Main and Globe Streets at Father Kelly Park. It operated as a cooperative—the cotton was imported from the South, distributed to the farm families for the intensive task of picking it, then sent to the mill to be spun into yarn, and returned back to the farmers to be woven into cloth. Finally, the cloth would again be given to the mill for finishing and made ready to sell. The first three cotton mills in Fall River were cooperatives. It was only in 1821, with the organization of the Pocasset Manufacturing Company, built on the second falls of the Quequechan River by Samuel Rodman of New Bedford, that the cooperative model ceased to be used. (Courtesy of private collection.)

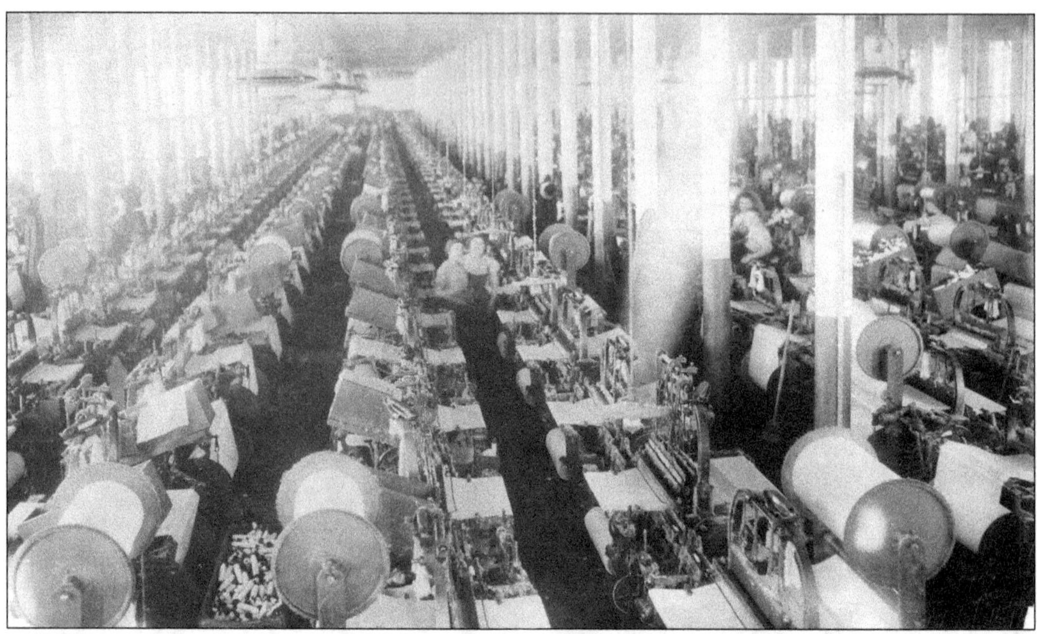

Fall River was ideal for cotton textile manufacturing because the climate was similar to the English textile region of Lancashire, with higher relative humidity and more even and milder temperatures. This is the weaving room at the Cornell Mill. The photographer notes, "The looms started up with deafening clatter" immediately after the image was taken in January 1912. (Lewis Hine photograph, courtesy of the Library of Congress.)

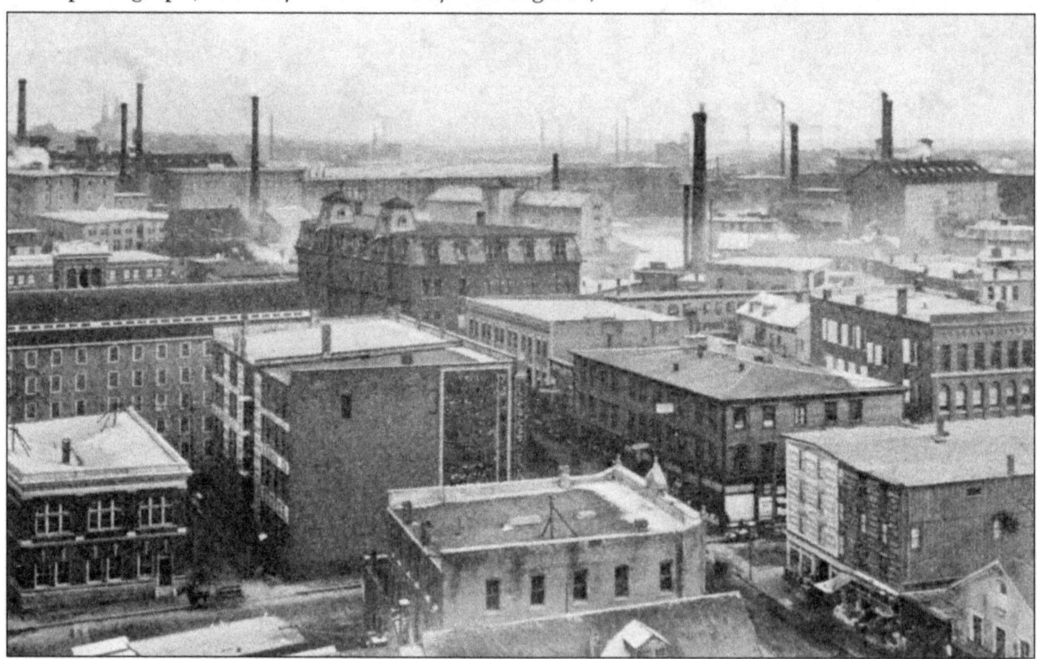

Some mills in Fall River only manufactured thread, like the Kerr Mills, while others bleached the fabric white, like the Fall River Bleachery. Still others, like the American Printing Company, printed the white cloth. Chase Mill, located on Rodman Street, conducted all operations on one site. (Courtesy of private collection.)

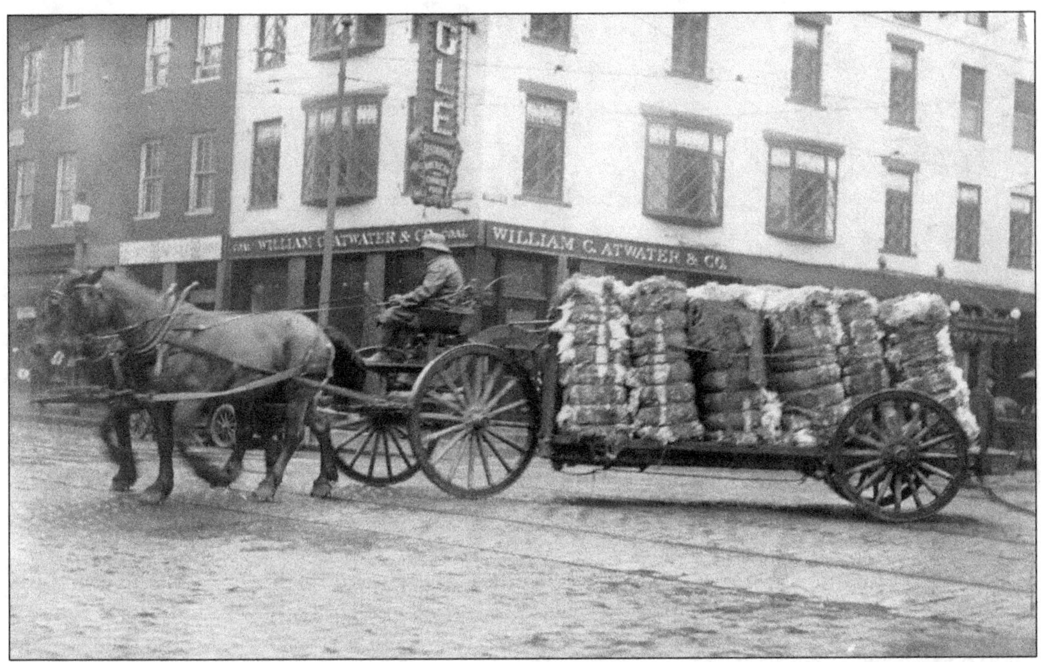

Fresh off the boat from the Southern states, these bales of cotton are on their way to the mill in this image from 1916. Even though by this time the Model T had been on the market for eight years and Fall River had a trolley system, cotton was still transported through the streets of the city by horse- or mule-drawn wagons. (Lewis Hine photograph, courtesy of the Library of Congress.)

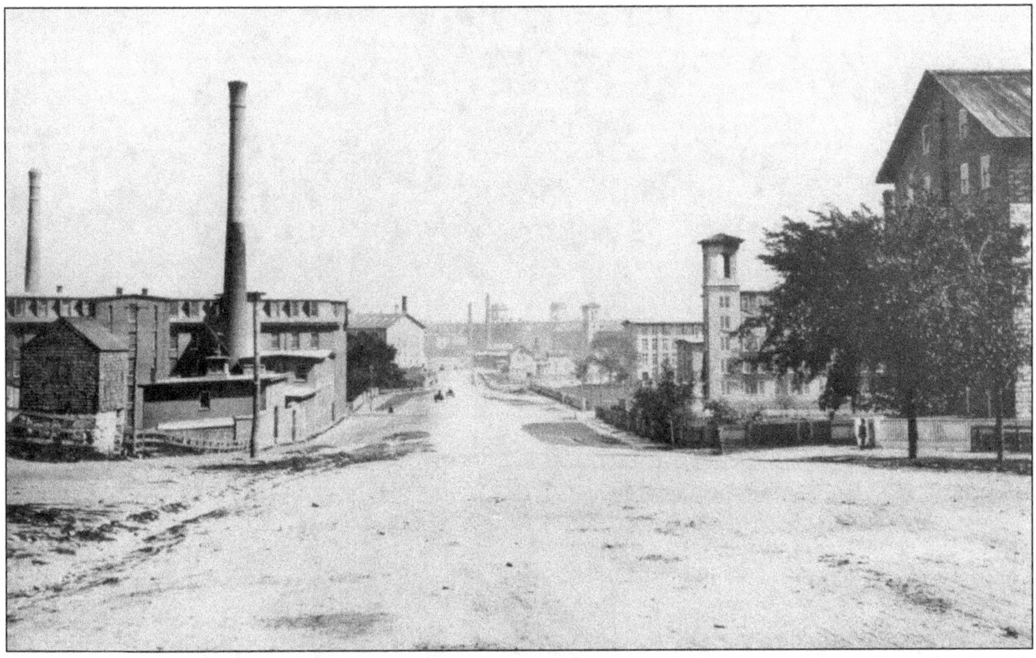

Looking north on Eight Rod Way (now Plymouth Avenue), one has a view of six mills—the Davol, Union, and Durfee Union Mills on the left and the Richard Borden, Crescent, and Merchant Mills on the right. The Richard Borden Mills burned down in November 1981. (Courtesy of the Fall River Historical Society.)

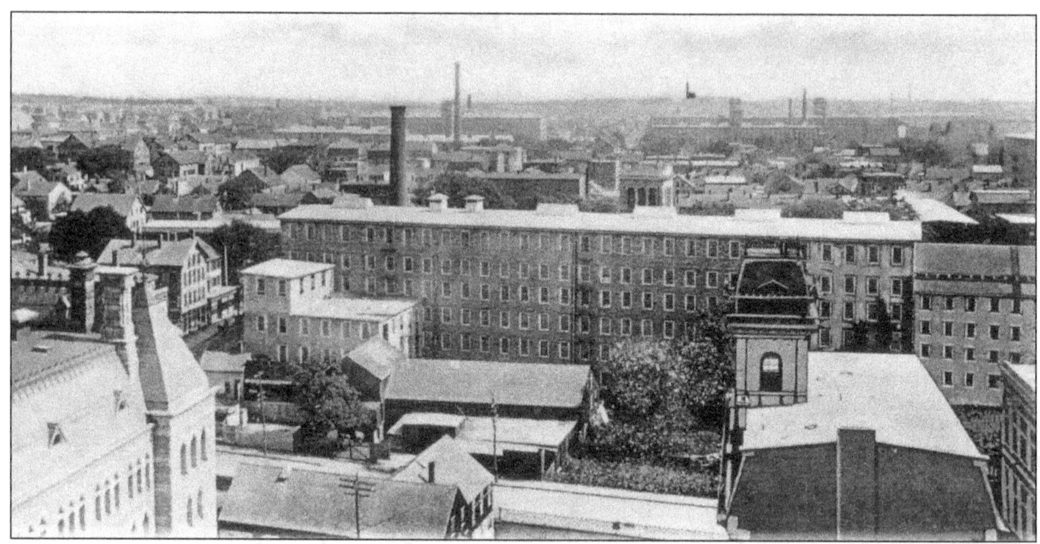

Essentially a one-industry town, Fall River became, in 1911, the number one manufacturer of cotton textiles in the United States, and second only to Manchester, England, in the world. By 1910, Fall River's full growth had been reached, with 43 corporations, 222 mill buildings, and 3,800,000 spindles, producing two miles of cloth in every minute of every working day of the year. Shown above, the view east from city hall depicts just how integrated the mills were to the downtown area. (Above, courtesy of private collection; below, Lewis Hine photograph, courtesy of the Library of Congress.)

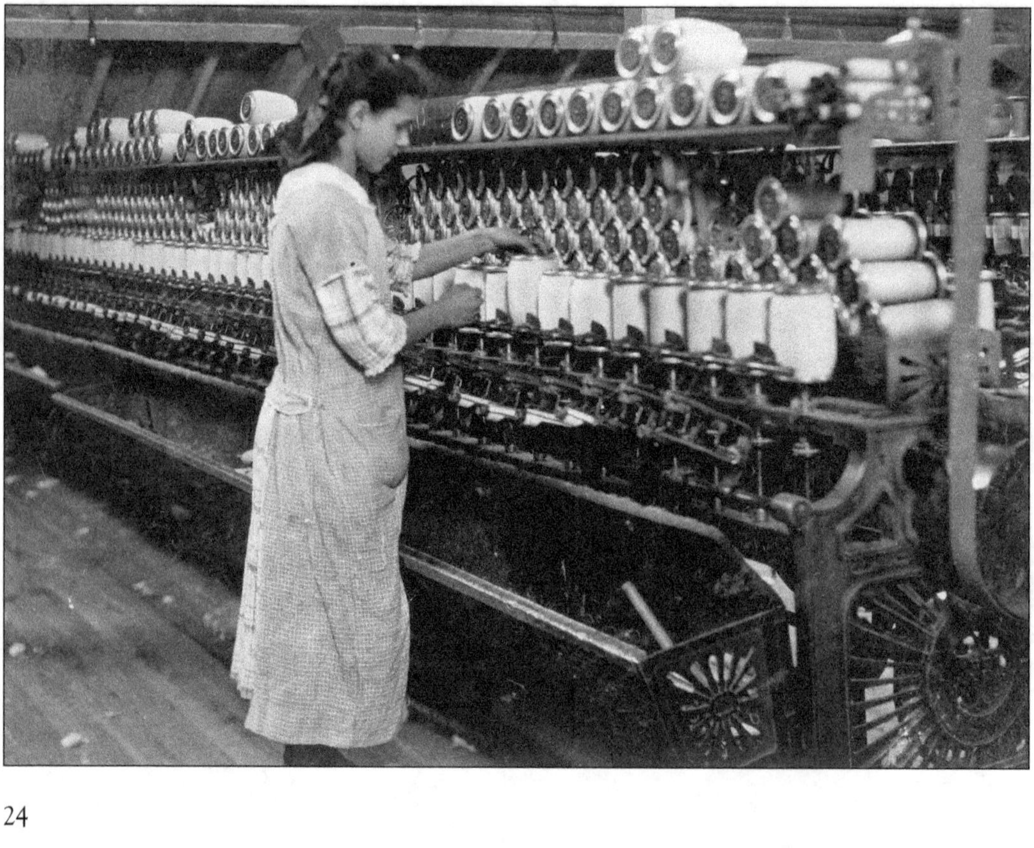

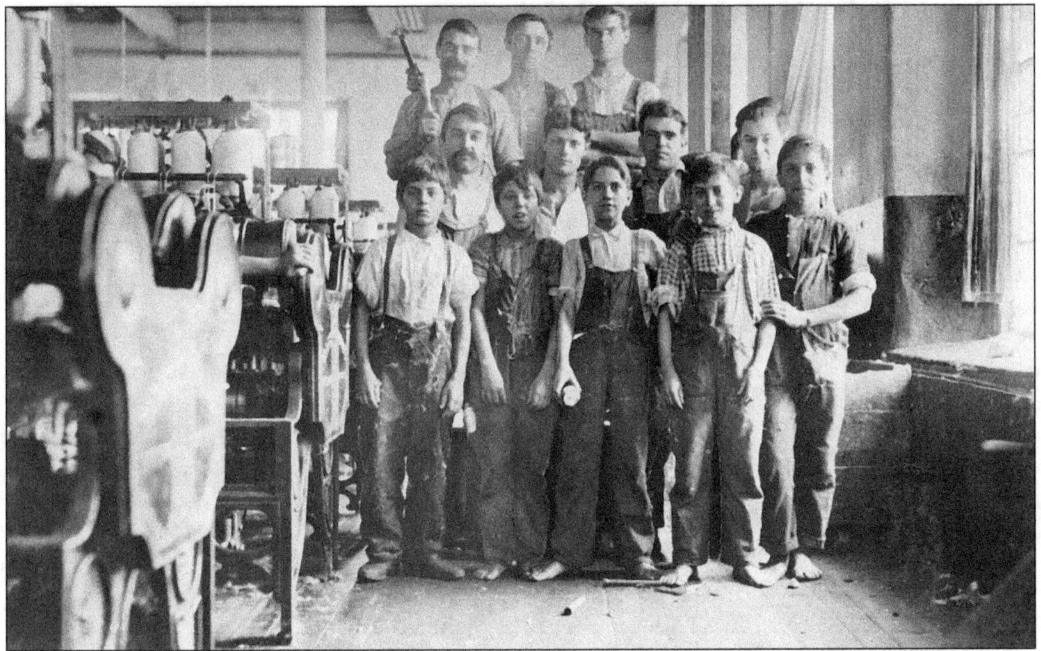

Of these young doffer and spinner boys working in the Seaconnet Mill, the youngest are, from left to right, (first row) Manuel Perry, John E. Mello, and Manuel Louis. When interviewed by the photographer, "none could write their own names. The last [front row, far right] couldn't spell the street he lives on. They spoke almost no English." (Lewis Hine photograph, courtesy of the Library of Congress.)

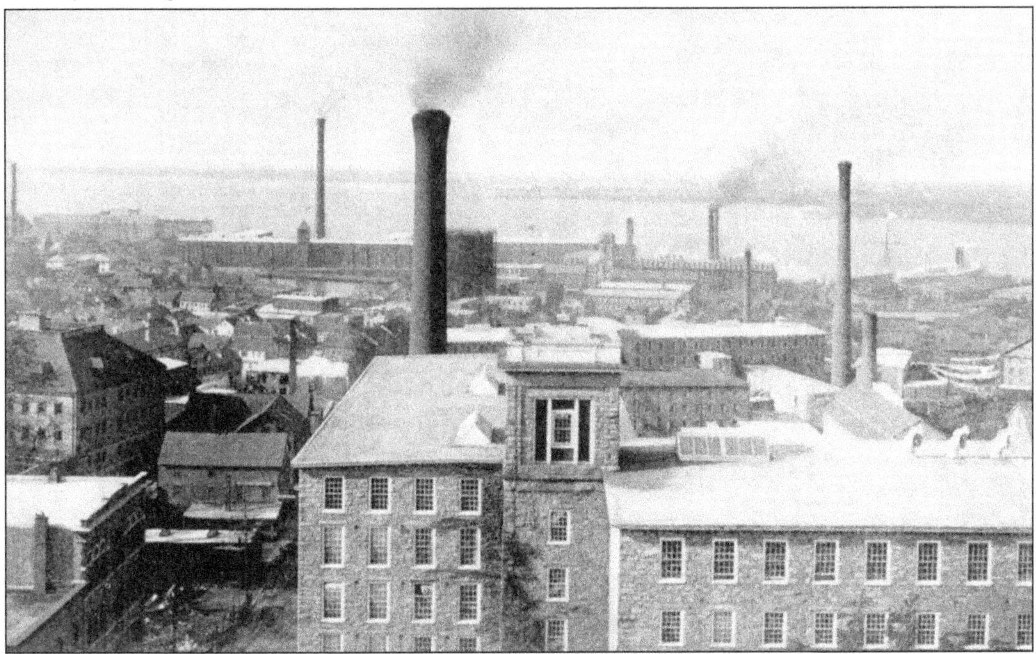

In 1927, it was remarked that "industry is the presiding goddess of Fall River; an idle man could no longer live there than a beetle in a beehive." This view is from city hall toward the Taunton River and Mount Hope Bay. (Courtesy of private collection.)

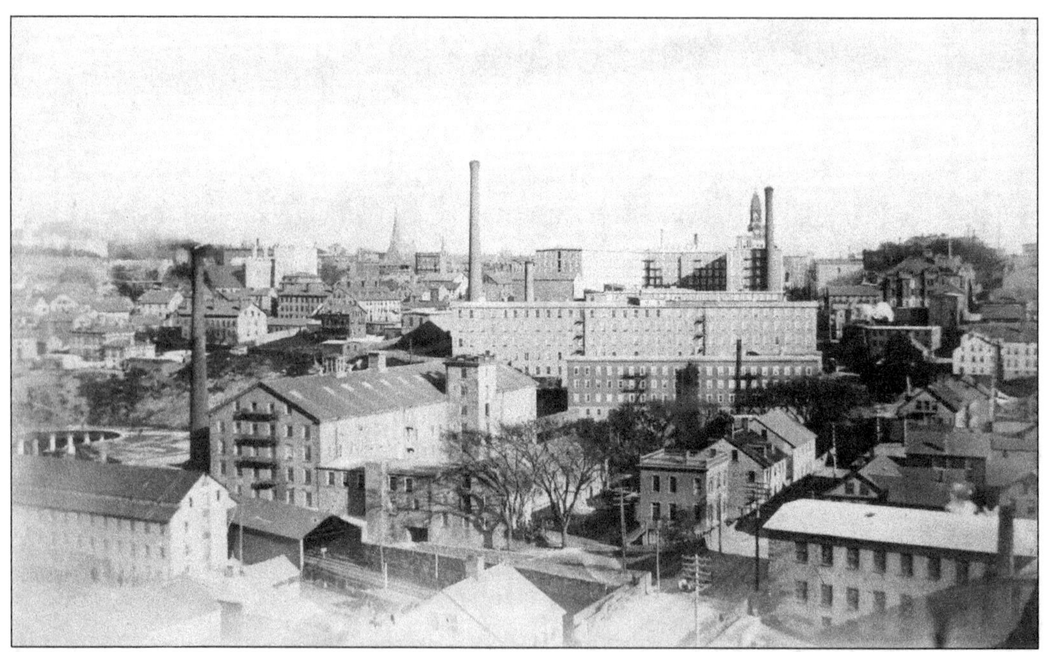
Fall River granite was used in constructing all of the granite textile mills in the city. Often, the granite would be quarried directly from the site of the new mill. This view is easterly from Pocasset Street and northerly from Canal Street. (Courtesy of the Fall River Historical Society.)

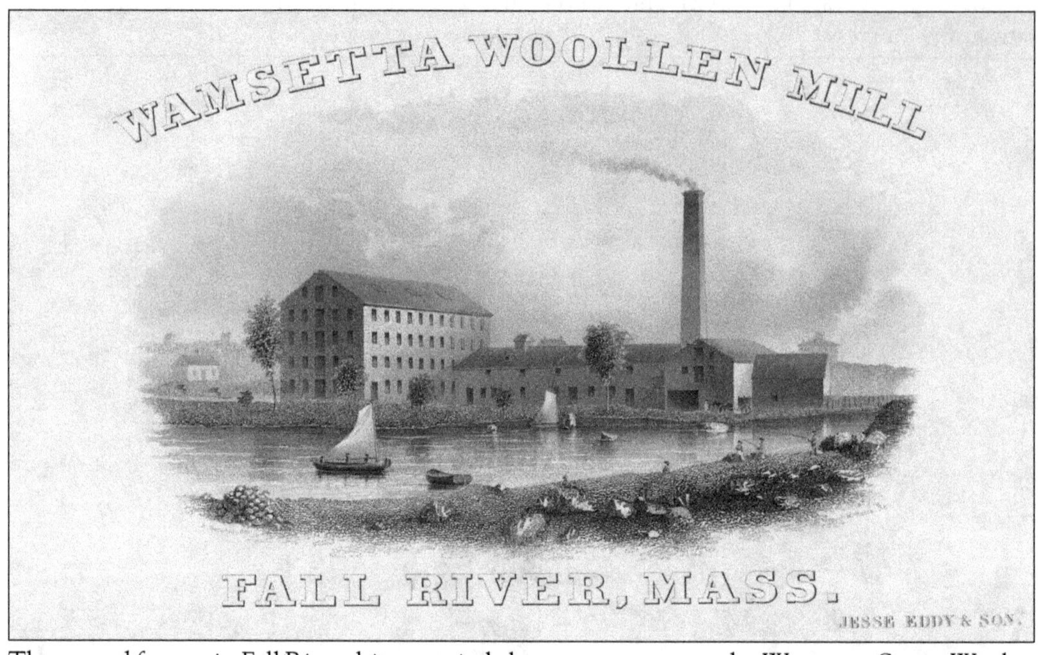

The second factory in Fall River driven entirely by steam power was the Wamsutta Steam Woolen Mills, located on the upper Quequechan River near Pleasant Street, next door later to the Durfee Union Mills. This mill used the river for making the steam and condensing it after passing through the engine. It was built in 1849 but is no longer in existence, torn down, most probably, to make way for Interstate 195. (Courtesy of the Fall River Historical Society.)

SO THAT YOU DON'T FORGET

Don't Waste Anything, Material, Supplies or Time.

Ideas. Mention that bright idea you had just now to your overseer and see what he thinks about it.

Won't You Keep That Waste Off The Floors? It's worth money and the cleaner it is the more money it's worth. You wouldn't let nickels or dimes or quarters lie around, would you?

Do A Good Week's Work And Get A Good Week's Pay. Be known as the best hand in the mill at your kind of work. The best hands get the best pay so it's up to yourself. Don't think you aren't noticed—you are.

Keep Your Machinery Running Every Possible Minute. If every machine in these mills stopped needlessly at some time or other in every hour for only three minutes the plant would produce 7,000 lbs. weight of finished cloth per week less than it ought to do. When a machine is unavoidably stopped do your best to get it started again immediately; stoppage means loss.

Don't Think That Your Effort Won't Count. It will if everybody gives a hand.

We All Ought To Pull Together!

Won't You Help?

THE MANAGEMENT OF THE
POCASSET MANUFACTURING COMPANY

Employees in the mills were urged to "work together" for the betterment and safety of all, as detailed in this 1916 poster from the Pocasset Mill. The Pocasset Manufacturing Company began operations in 1822 and was the third mill on the Quequechan River. Founded by Samuel Rodman of New Bedford, with $100,000 in capital, the Pocasset Mill, located west of Main Street, did not, in its early days, manufacture textiles, but instead provided space for rent for small businesses to engage in the textile industry. In the ensuing years, four more mill buildings would be constructed. By 1877, the Pocasset Mill employed over 550 people and owned 54 tenements to house its operatives. In operation until 1926, the Pocasset Mill complex was destroyed in 1928 by fire that started in one of its empty structures. (Lewis Hine photograph, courtesy of the Library of Congress.)

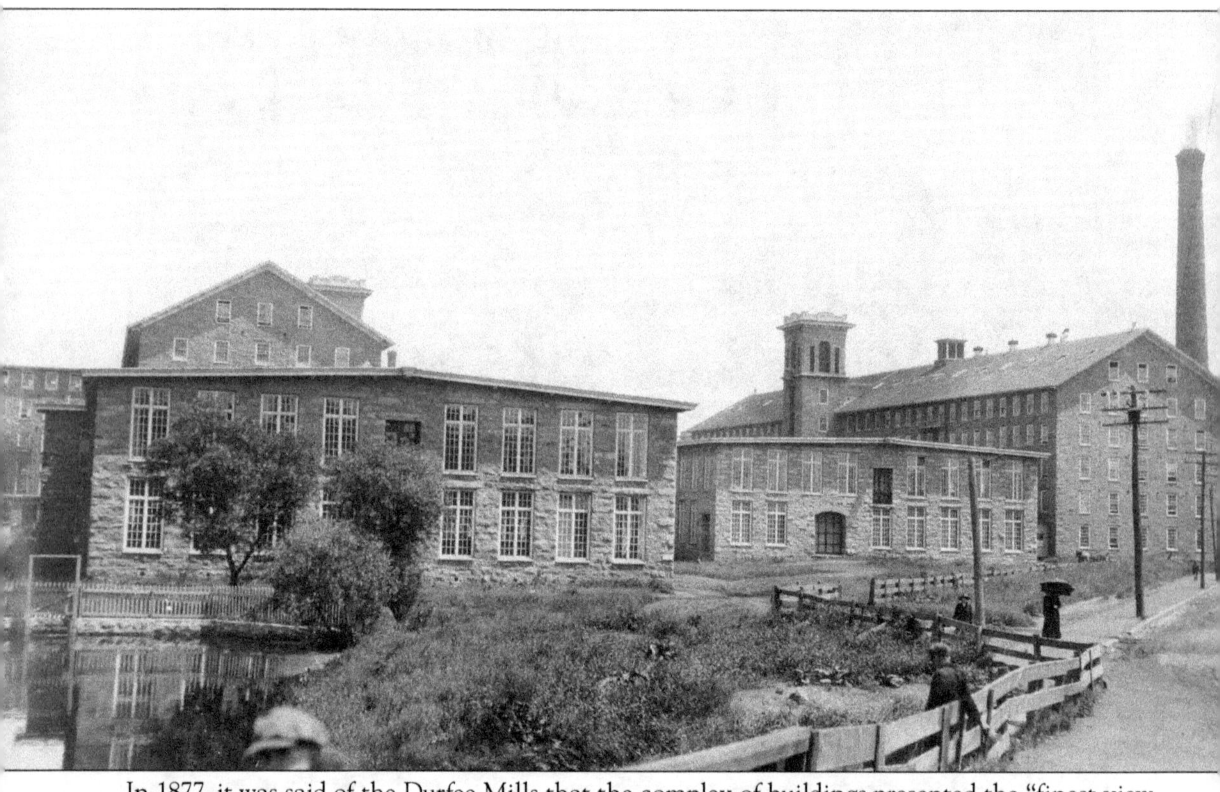

In 1877, it was said of the Durfee Mills that the complex of buildings presented the "finest view to the eye that seeks something like artistic effect." One might argue that this view of the back of the Durfee Mills in 1916 belies that statement. As the largest and most successful textile-manufacturing firms in Fall River, Mill No. 1 began operation in 1866 and Mill No. 2 in 1871. The two mill buildings are 5.5 stories in the Italianate design, with seven-level center towers. Located on Plymouth Avenue and Pleasant Street, the structures were built of granite quarried on-site and were the first mills constructed using portable steam engines to hoist the granite into place. All of the original major structures are still standing. (Lewis Hine photograph, courtesy of the Library of Congress.)

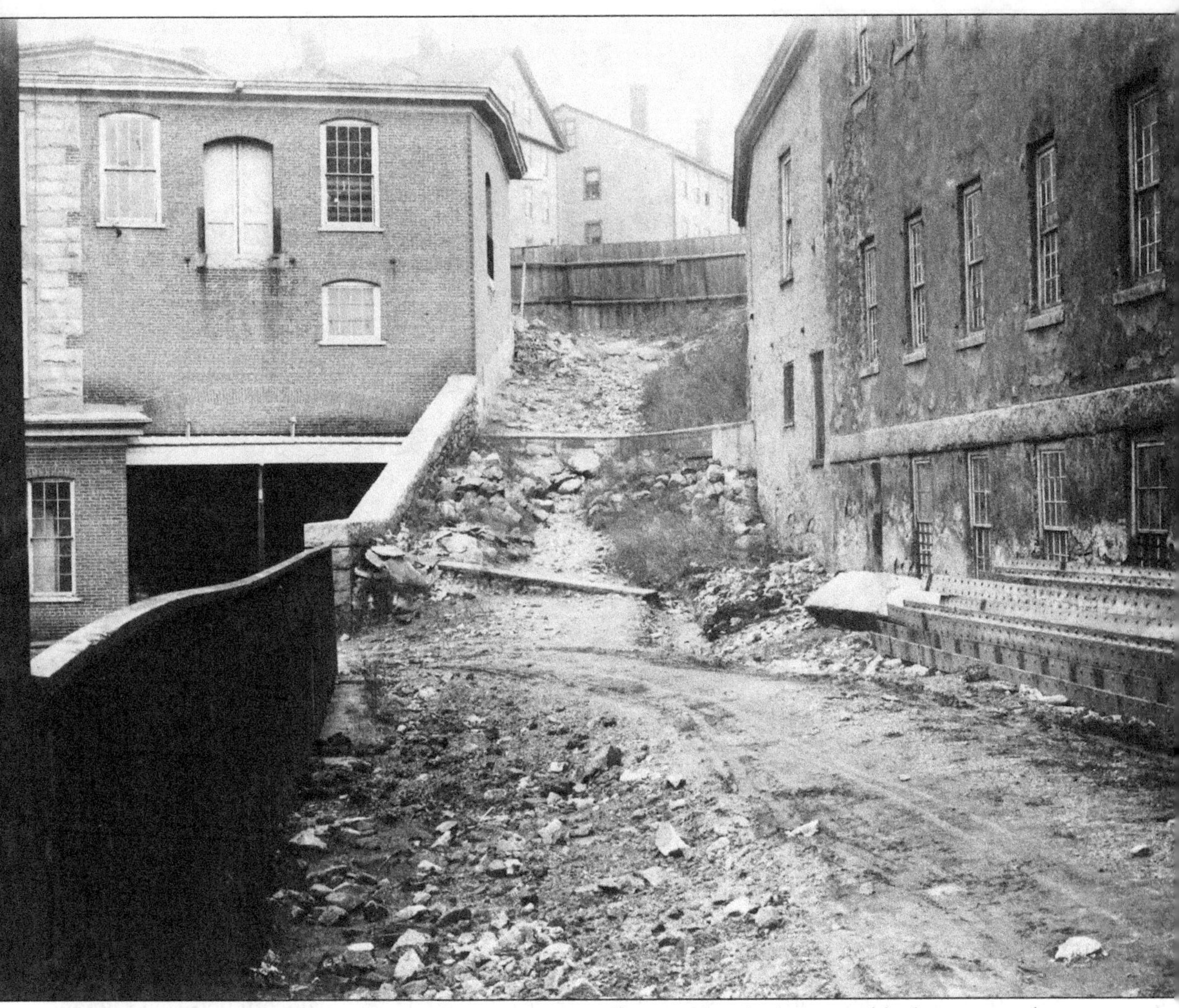

The Pocasset Manufacturing Company was eventually comprised of two sizable factories—the Quequechan Mill (1826), with 16,392 spindles and 492 looms, which manufactured print cloth; and the Pocasset Mill (1847), for the manufacture of "sheetings and shirtings," with 9,000 spindles and 224 looms. Both mills were constructed of stone and were five stories high, with the Quequechan 319 feet long and 48 feet wide and the Pocasset 208 feet long and 75 feet wide. The Pocasset Mill, considered to be "of phenomenal size, for its day," was run by a Corliss engine and three turbine wheels. According to Henry Fenner, it was "the first mill to be erected in which details had been carefully worked out, before beginning construction, as to the location of machinery, shafting and belting, a plan which resulted in a great saving over the old methods." This view is of the north side of Pocasset Street, between the White and Quequechan Mills. (Courtesy of the Fall River Historical Society.)

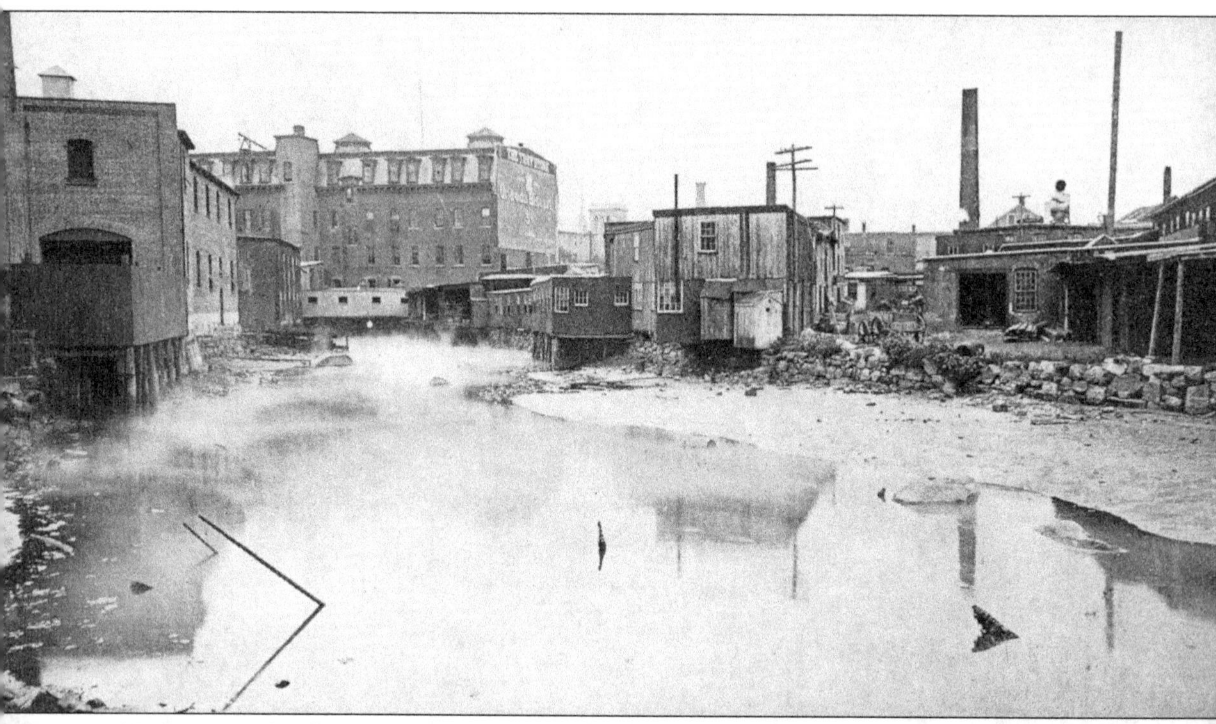

No history of Fall River would be complete without the mention of what industries (mills, laundries, and manufacturing) have done to the Quequechan River in their attempts at attaining economic prosperity. This view is looking downstream from 100 feet below the Fall River Laundry in 1909. At times, the heated water discharge from the mills would raise the river's temperature to over 120 degrees, effectively killing any living thing in its waters. In addition, the mills along the Quequechan built their privies to overhang the river, and raw human waste was emptied into it daily. These companies had little concern for the environmental impact of their abuse on the natural habitat of the river. The fronts of the mills might have looked pleasing to some, but the backs of those same mills showed just how invasive the textile industry was to Fall River's natural resources. Right up until the Quequechan River was forced underground to make way for Interstate 195, residents were exposed to horrific odors, and the visual reminders that human sewage was still being pumped into the waters. (Courtesy of John Friar.)

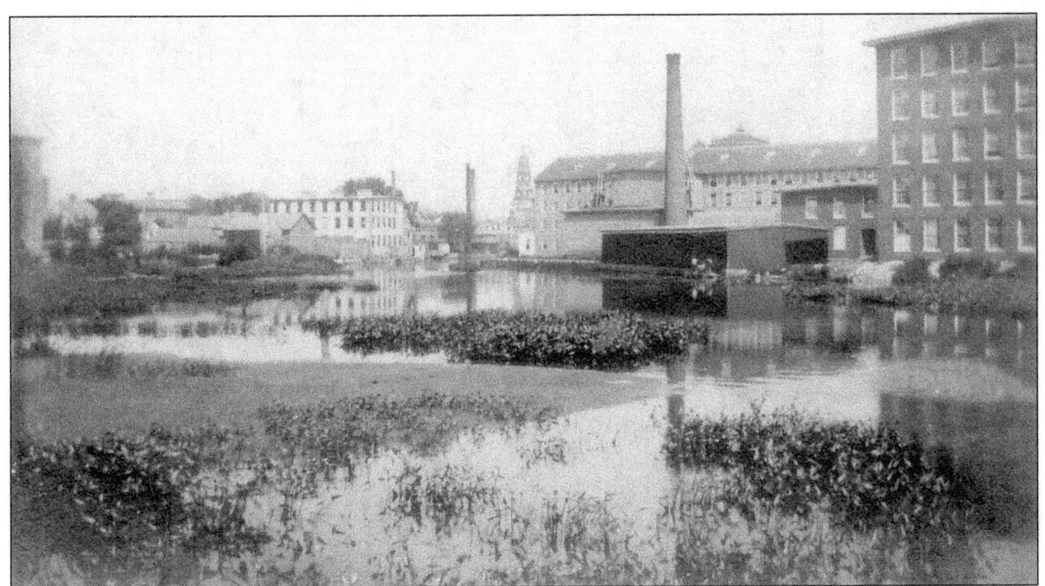

This tranquil scene of nature in harmony with industry was not the reality of life along the Quequechan River. The 1915 report of the Watuppa Ponds and Quequechan River Commission found "a strikingly large amount of pollution" from industrial runoff and sewage. "It is evident," the report concluded, "that the Quequechan River, for the greater part of its length, is nothing more nor less than an open sewer carrying dilute sewage." (Courtesy of the Fall River Historical Society.)

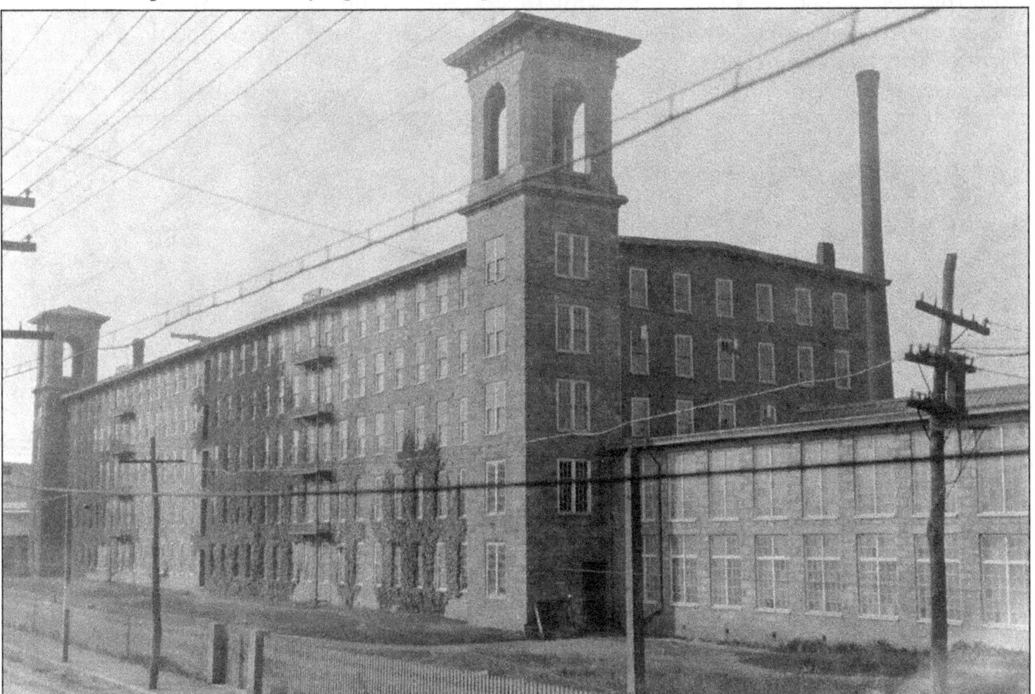

The Richard Borden Manufacturing Company began operations in 1873 on Eight Rod Way, the present-day Plymouth Avenue. It produced 12,000,000 yards of print cloth annually. The entire complex was destroyed in a spectacular fire in November 1981. (Lewis Hine photograph, courtesy of the Library of Congress.)

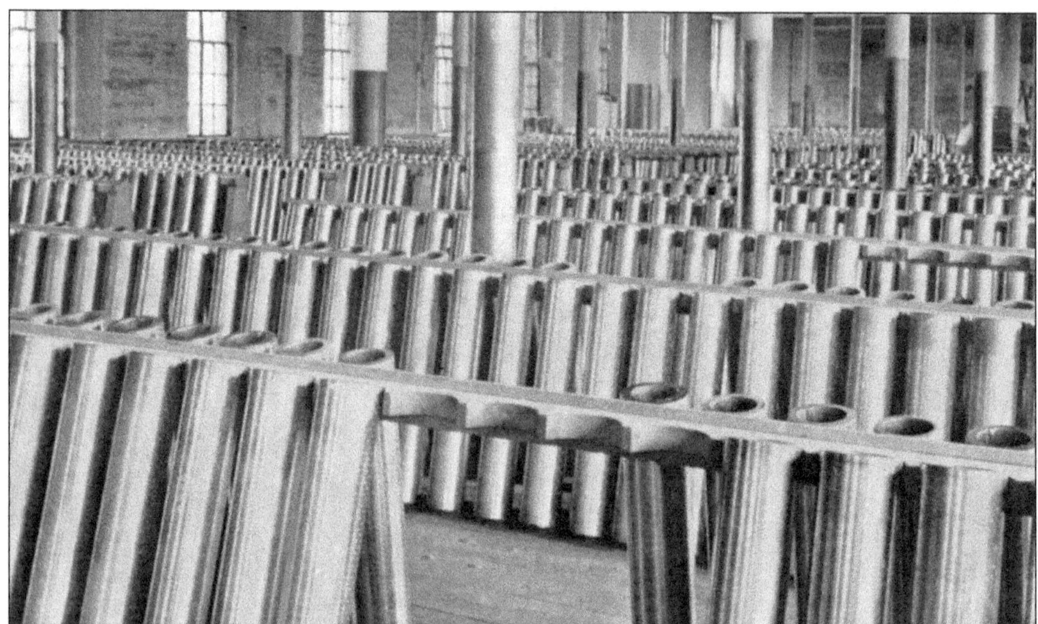

Until 1832, the printing of cloth was done by hand or block—each a time-consuming process. In block printing, a length of cloth was spread out on a table, and wooden blocks that had been inked would be pressed onto the cloth and then struck with a mallet to insure an impression. Then the cloth would be rolled over drying rollers, and the next section would be impressed. Adding more than one color necessitated many runs through the blocking and drying process. With the invention of etched copper rollers and then yard-wide rollers, the process of printing fabric became mechanized, and thus profitable. (Both, courtesy of Marc Belanger.)

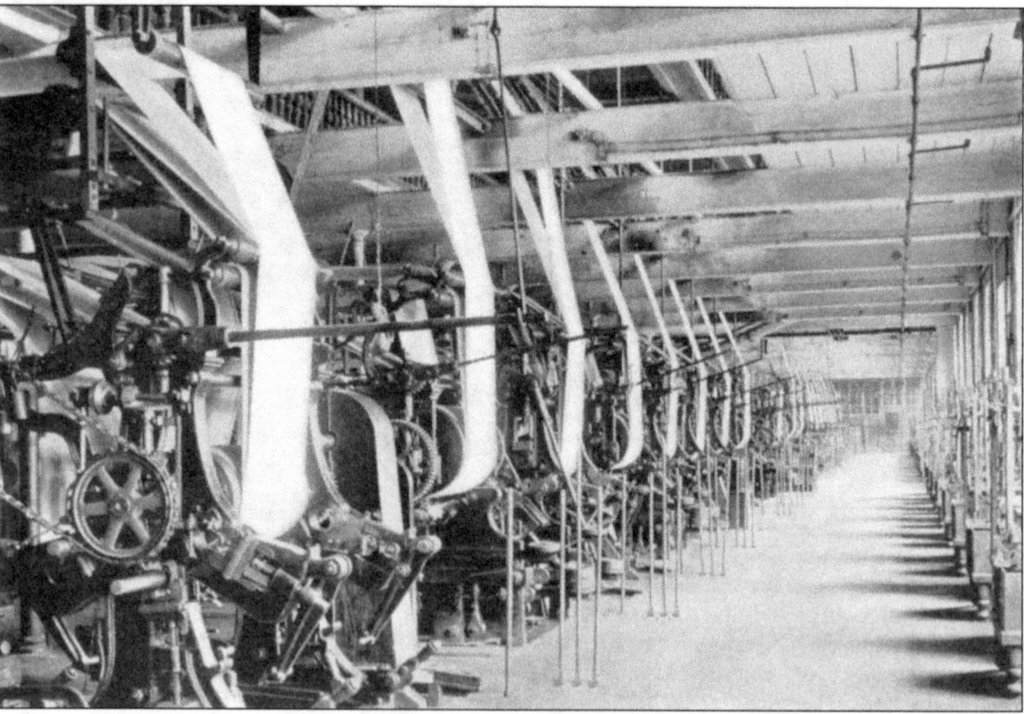

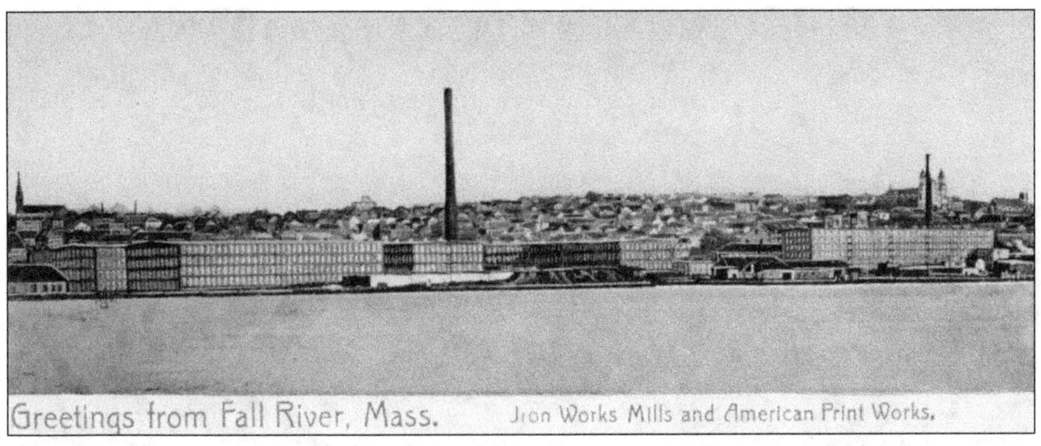

Established in 1835 by Holder Borden, the American Print Works grew to be the largest cloth printing company in the United States. With a dock on Mount Hope Bay and railroad tracks extending to the site, the American Print Works was in a perfect location to receive raw materials and get its product to market. Closing its doors for good in 1934, the huge complex was sold to Firestone Tire & Rubber Company. Two large blazes—one in 1941 and the other in 1973— destroyed most of the buildings. The image above is the American Print Works from the Somerset side of the Taunton River. The image below shows what the impressive entrance to the American Print Works, at the west end of Anawan Street, looked like. (Both, courtesy of Marc Belanger.)

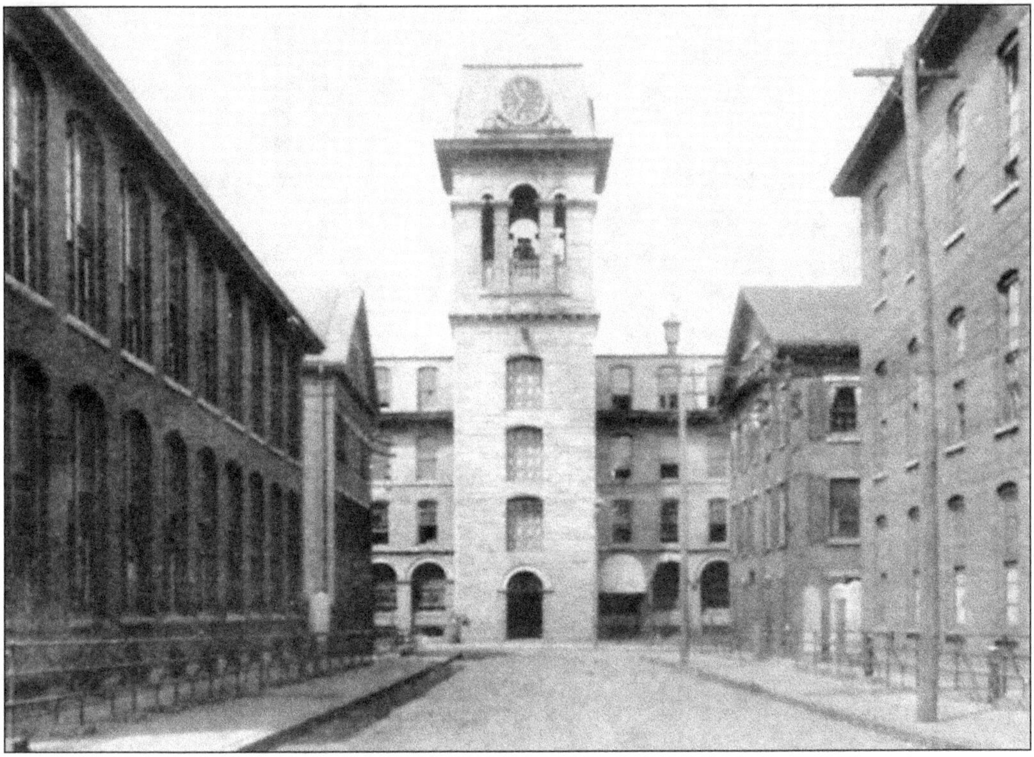

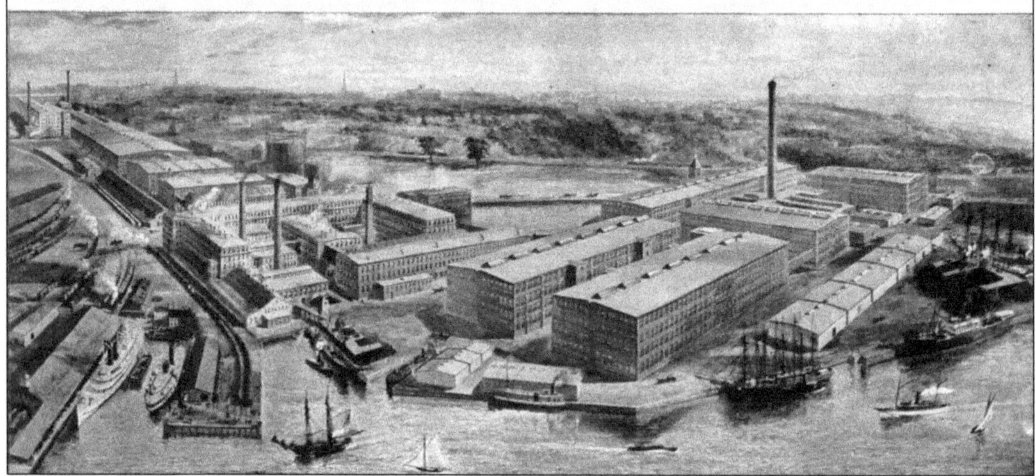

As the largest print works in the United States, the American Print Works boasted seven mills, 29 printing machines, 10 engines, and 115 boilers using 1,600 tons of coal a week and creating 17,750 horsepower; it employed 6,000 operatives. Weekly, its bleaching and printing production yield was 100,000 pieces, while its cloth woven yield was 78,000 pieces. To accomplish this, the company used 1,500 bales of cotton per week and ran 459,000 spindles. (Courtesy of Marc Belanger.)

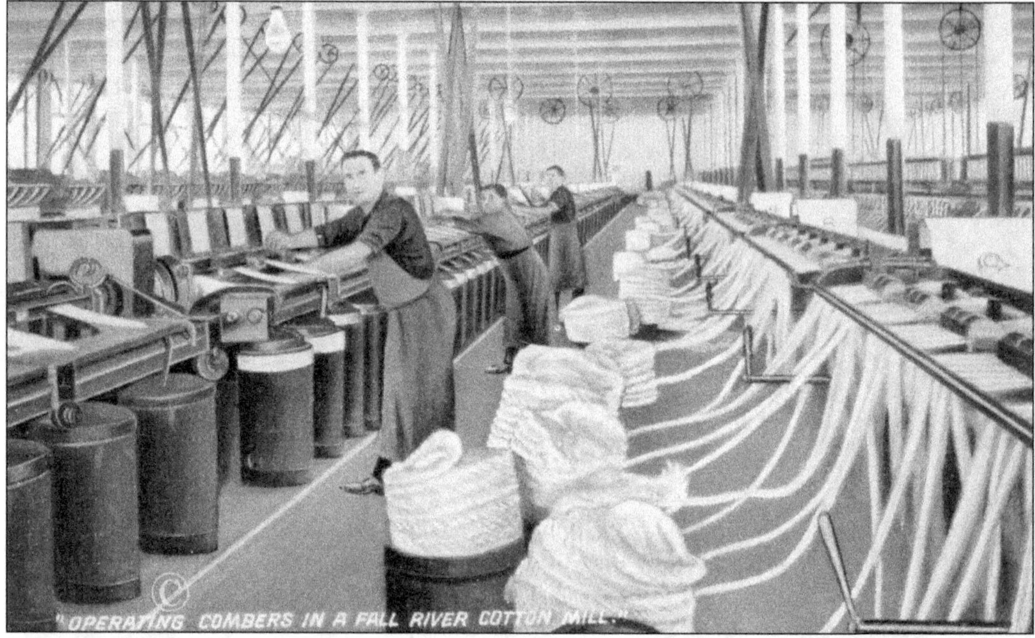

Combing is part of the process of transforming raw cotton into textiles. Combing further cleanses the cotton fibers to remove the short, undesired ones—those too short for the combed yarns. Combed yarn is preferred to carded yarn because it is used in higher-quality fabrics and thus fetches a higher price. (Courtesy of Michael Brimbau.)

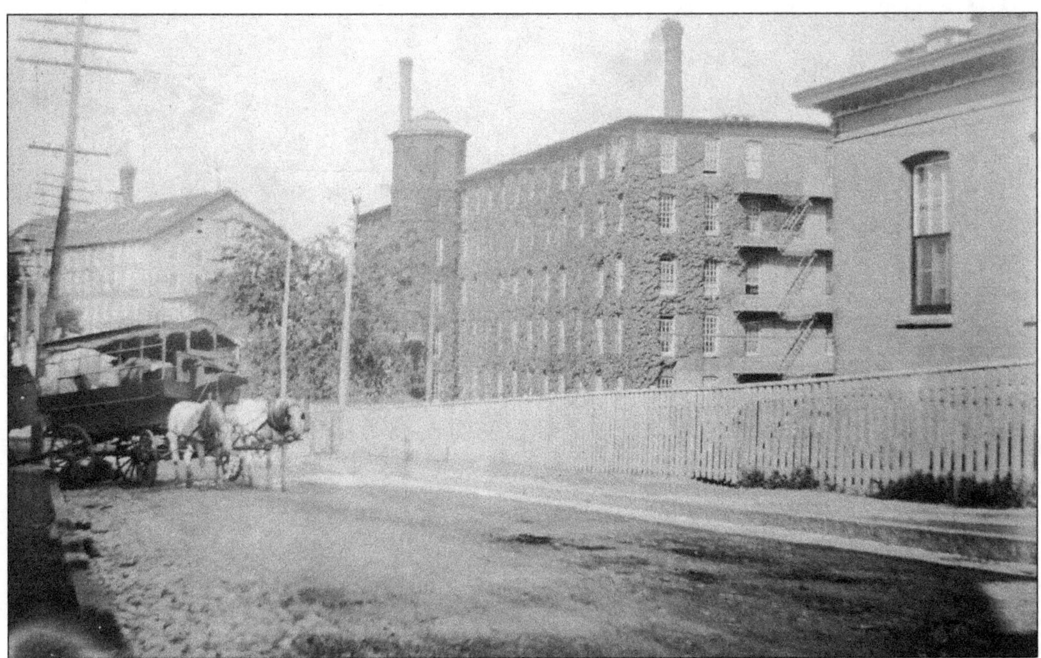

The Luther Mill was built in 1870–1871 as part of the Robeson Mills. In 1903, the Luther Manufacturing Company purchased the company and began operations immediately. This was a particularly attractive brick mill with an octagonal stair tower. It was torn down in 2001 to make way for a gas station. (Courtesy of private collection.)

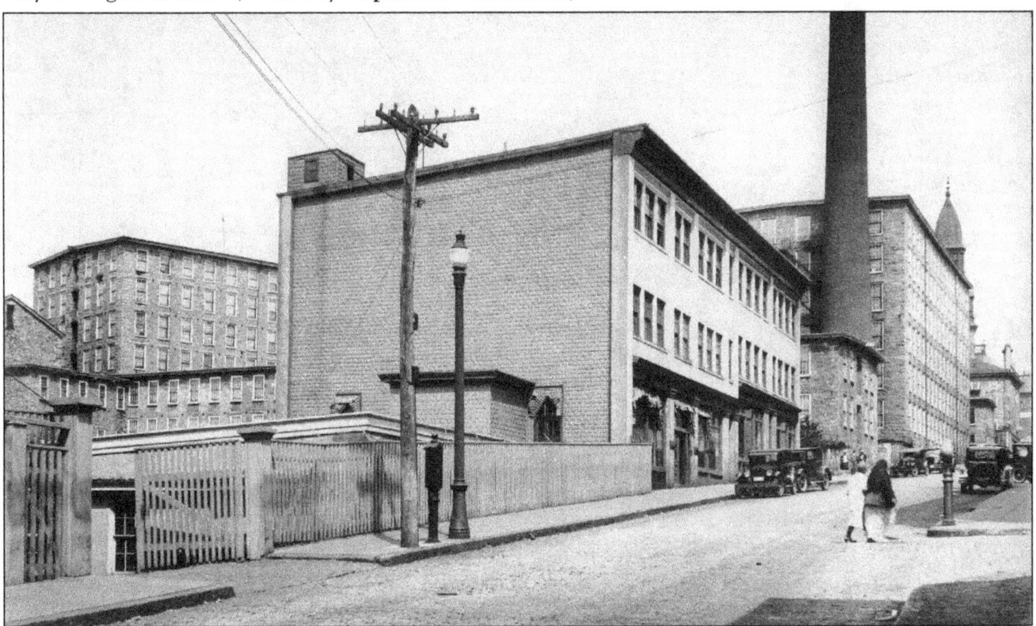

Because of its reliable flow of water, granite bedrock, and location next to a navigable waterway, Fall River was able to manufacture cotton textiles at 13-percent lower costs than the inland Merrimack River centers of Lowell and Lawrence, Massachusetts, and Manchester, New Hampshire. This view of Pocasset Street is facing easterly from Camden Street. (Courtesy of the Fall River Historical Society.)

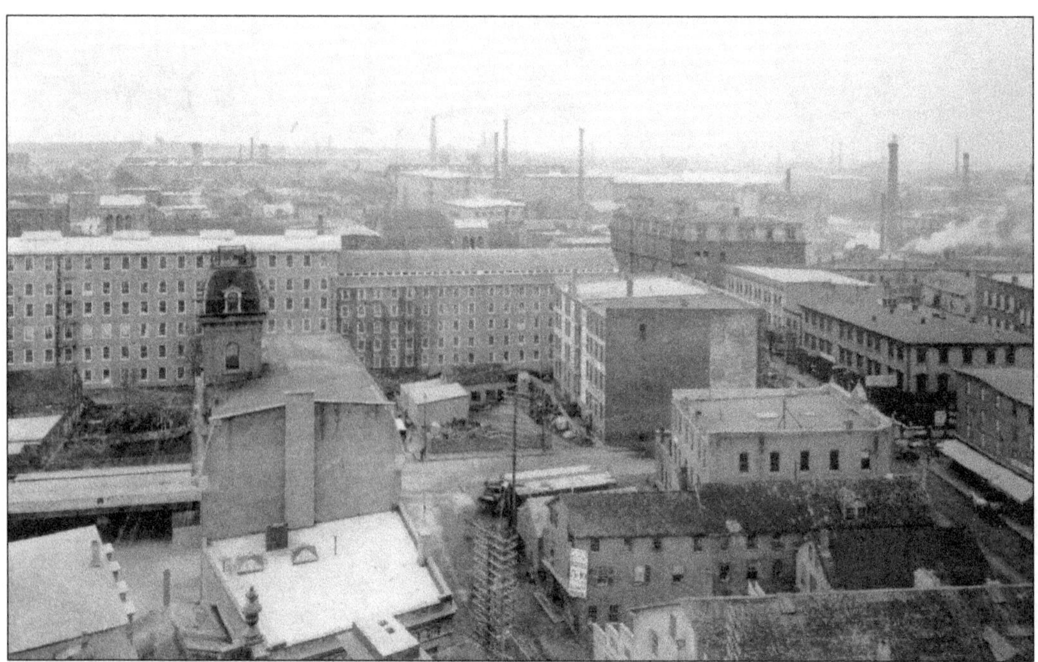

Buildings made of Fall River granite include the old city hall, the old Granite Block, St. Mary's Cathedral, St. Patrick's Church, Notre Dame de Lourdes Church, the Slade School, the lower section of the old B.M.C. Durfee High School, the Fall River Public Library, and the Bank Street Armory. (Courtesy of private collection.)

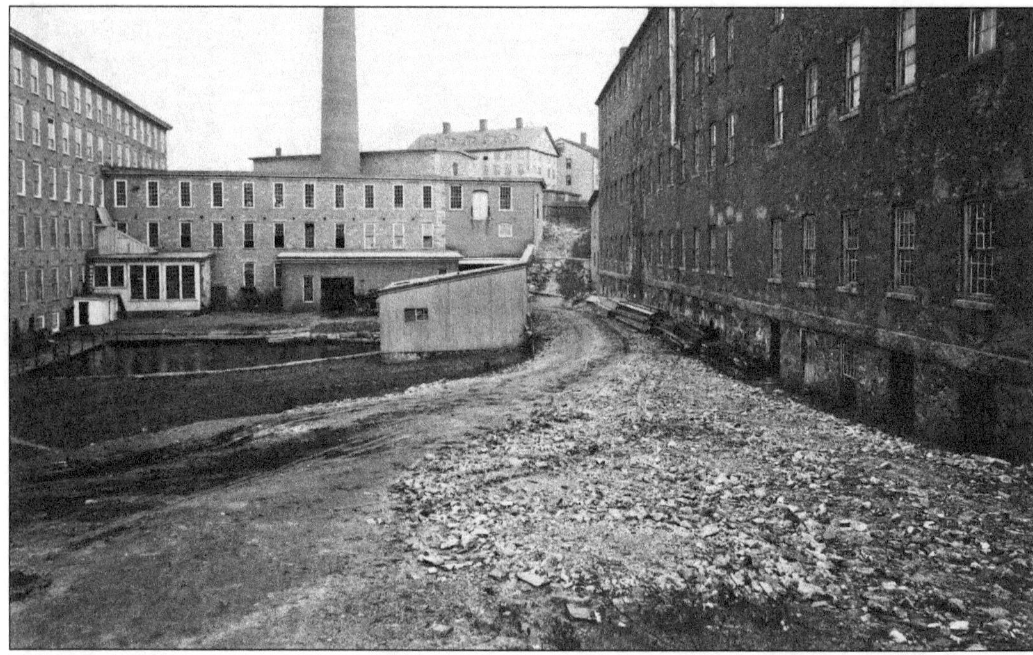

This is a view up Camden Street, north of Pocasset Street. To the left is the Fall River Manufactory, and to the right is the Robeson Print Works. Camden Street no longer exists, having been replaced by the ramps for Interstate 195. Camden was impassible in its midsection, and that condition can be seen clearly at the center of this photograph. (Courtesy of the Fall River Historical Society.)

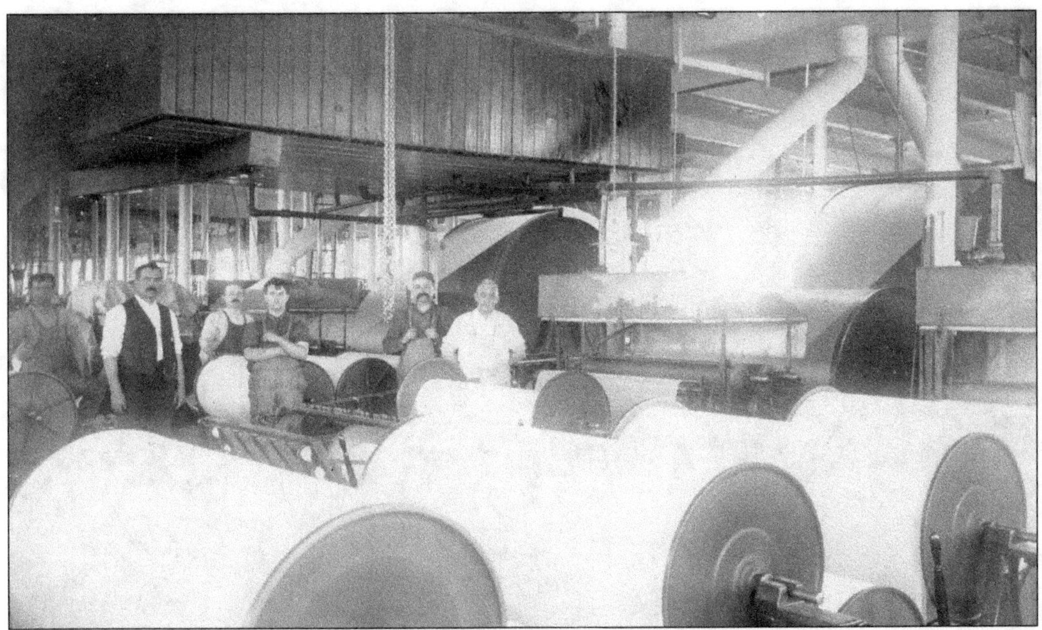

The image above is of workers in the warper room of an unidentified mill in Fall River. Cloth is woven on a loom, which is an apparatus that holds warp threads in place while filling threads, or wefts, are threaded between them. A warper room is where the warp, which has been wound onto large spools, goes to be placed on large racks that are then wound off on "warper beams," the number of threads on which determines the number of threads to the inch in the cloth. The warp is not strong enough to stand the strain of weaving and has to be strengthened by sizing and goes to the "slasher room," as seen below, where it is marked into "cuts" for the guidance of the weavers, who, as the mark in the cloth is reached, cut it off from the loom. (Both, courtesy of Kenneth M. Champlin.)

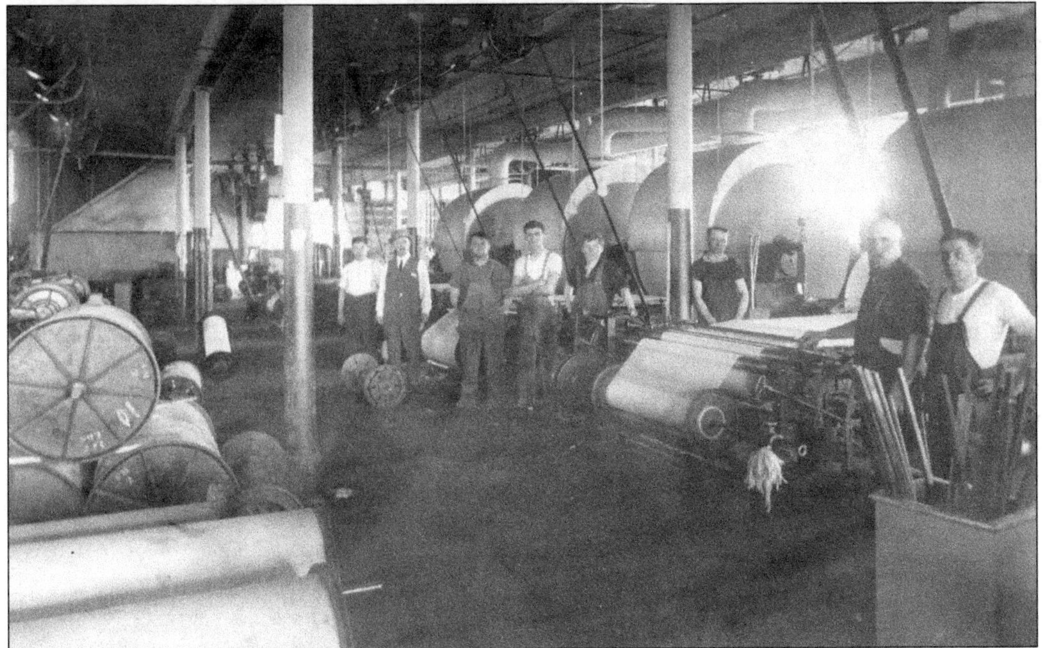

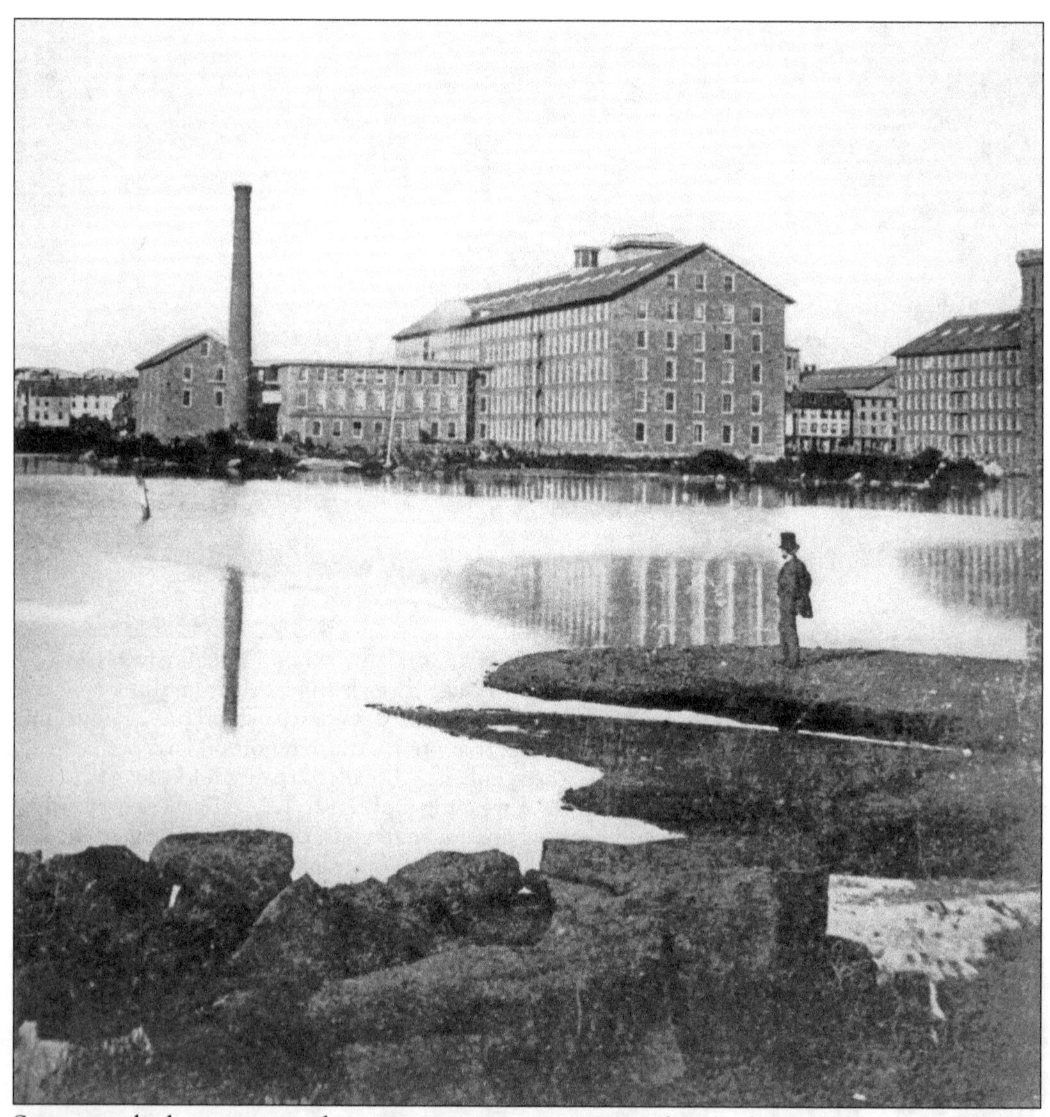

Some men look at a river and see nature at its most spectacular. And some, like David Brayton, see opportunity for financial success. The David Braytons of the world built America into an industrial power, the likes of which people may never see again, and without them, Fall River may not have prospered in the 19th and early 20th centuries. Cotton was king in Fall River, and the only thing that stopped these titans of industry was someone else's desire for financial success with the wherewithal to take it from them. When the South finally figured out how to make the cotton textiles locally and invested heavily in the latest technology, Fall River as the center of cotton textile manufacturing was to be no more. This image shows David A. Brayton on the south side of the Quequechan River, viewing the mills on the north side. (Courtesy of John Friar.)

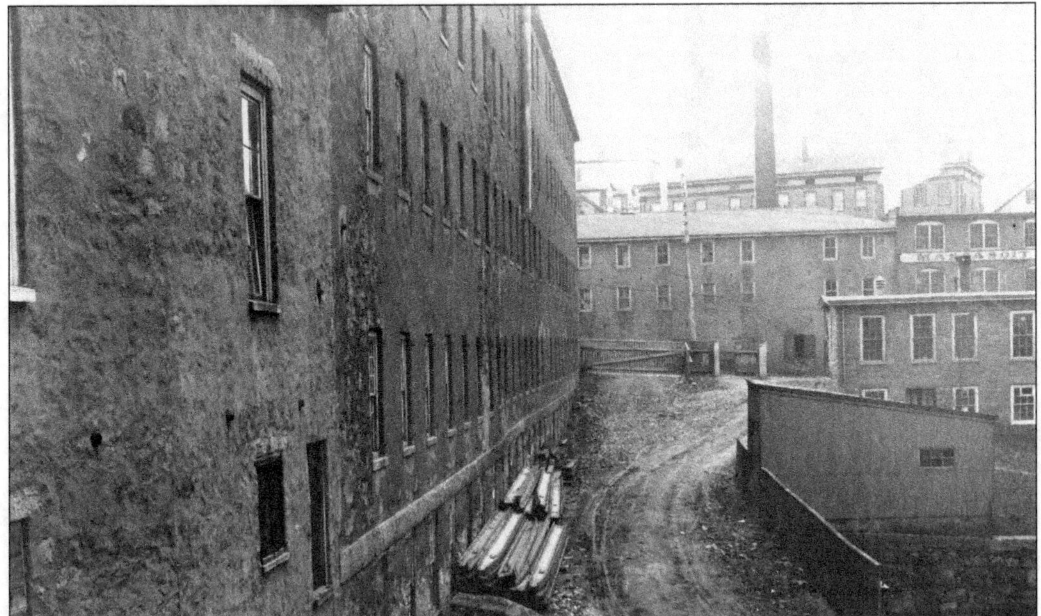

This is another view of Camden Street, north from Pocasset Street, this time between the Quequechan and Fall River Mills. Camden ran from Pocasset to Central Streets, but the middle portion, at its most steep, was impassible, in effect creating two sections with the same name. In the distance, one can see the Massasoit Mill, a stone building constructed in 1826 by the Pocasset Manufacturing Company, which was later called the Watuppa Mill. (Courtesy of the Fall River Historical Society.)

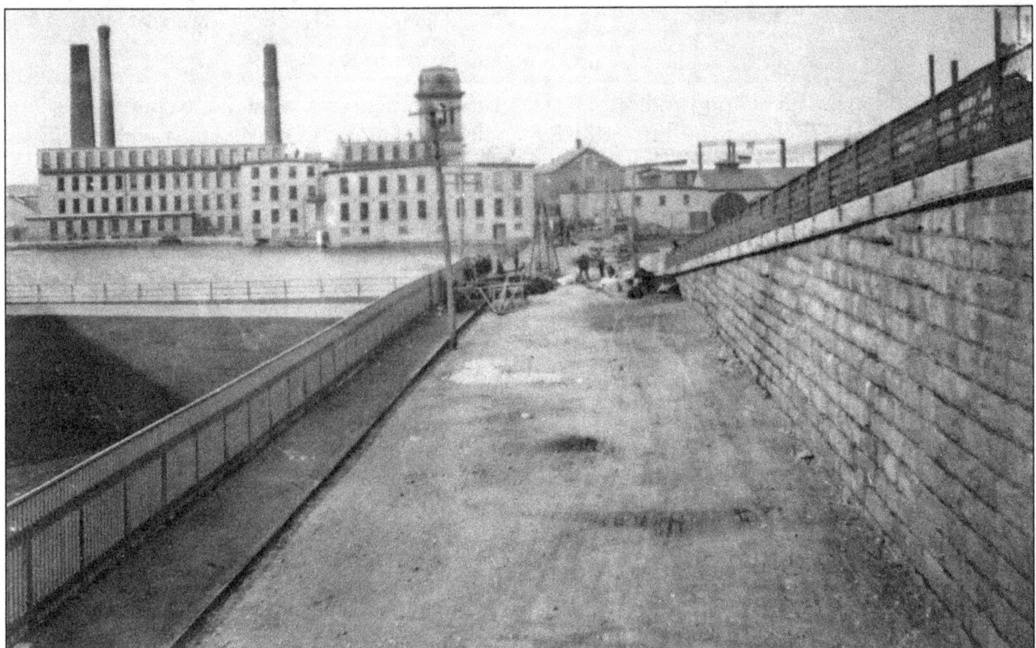

Taken on Water Street from Crab Pond Bridge, this photograph is a side view of the American Print Works complex. Today, the Borden & Remington Chemical Company occupies this site and, as recently as May 2011, has demolished Mill No. 1. (Courtesy of the Fall River Historical Society.)

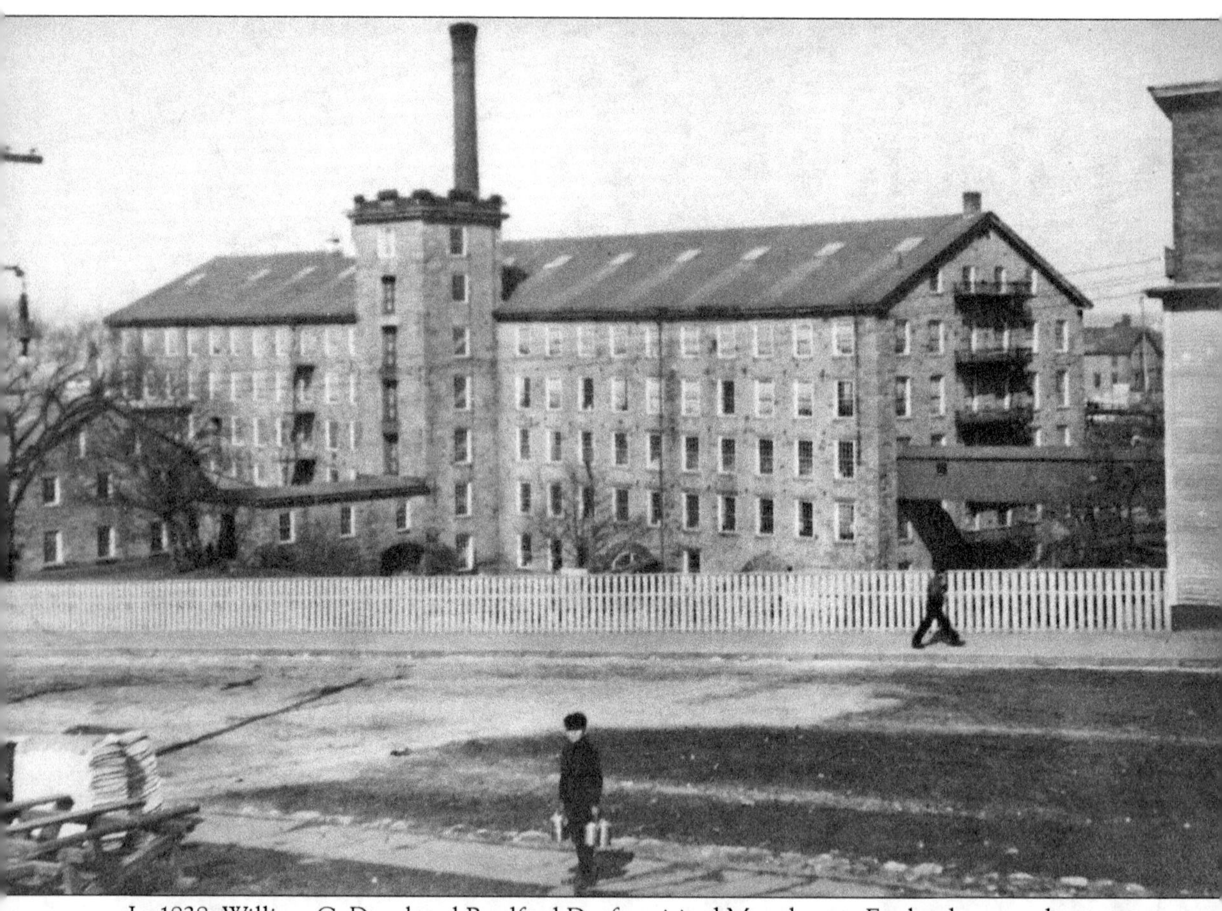

In 1838, William C. Davol and Bradford Durfee visited Manchester, England, to purchase some self-acting mules for their new mill in Fall River. Self-acting mules were the latest technology in textile manufacturing in which the operations ordinarily performed by the spinner were achieved by automatic means. Much to their chagrin, the men were not allowed to remove the new inventions from the country due to restrictions on the exportation of new technology. Instead, they "arranged" to have one of the machines purchased, sawn into small pieces, and sent to France, then on to Fall River. It arrived two years later, was reassembled into a model, and duplicated. In 1846, eight years after their trip, Davol and Durfee installed the "new" mules into their new Metacomet Mill (pictured). Thus, Fall River was the first textile-manufacturing city in the United States to use these self-acting mules. (Courtesy of the Fall River Historical Society.)

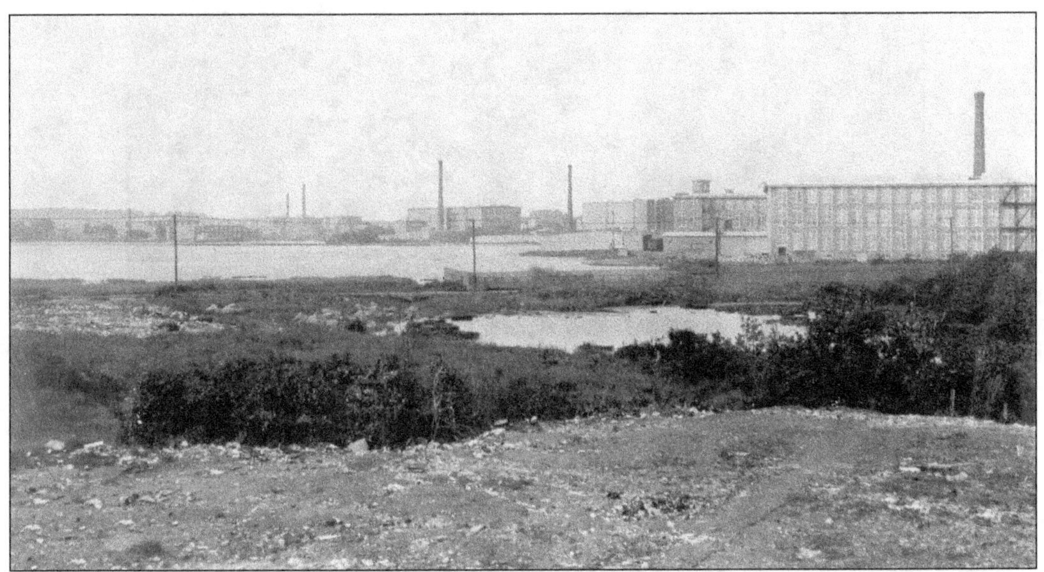

Four mills along the Quequechan River—the Davis, Arkwright, Wampanoag, and Pilgrim—are shown here in 1916, a year in which Fall River was experiencing an economic depression, a downturn that seemed to plague the city every 10 years. (Lewis Hine photograph, courtesy of the Library of Congress.)

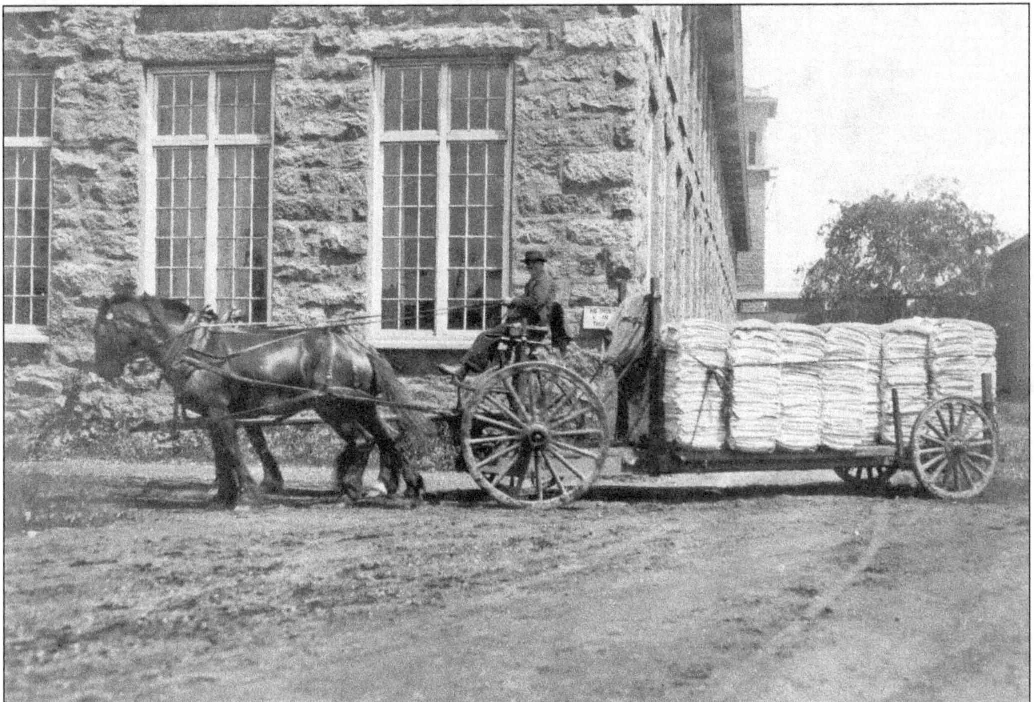

With its overnight delivery service to New York City via freighter, Fall River had a major advantage over inland centers of textile manufacturing, like Lowell or Lawrence. Products, such as those pictured here leaving the Durfee Mill on June 21, 1916, would arrive in the New York Garment District in time for factory and sweatshop workers to turn the cloth into finished garments. (Lewis Hine photograph, courtesy of the Library of Congress.)

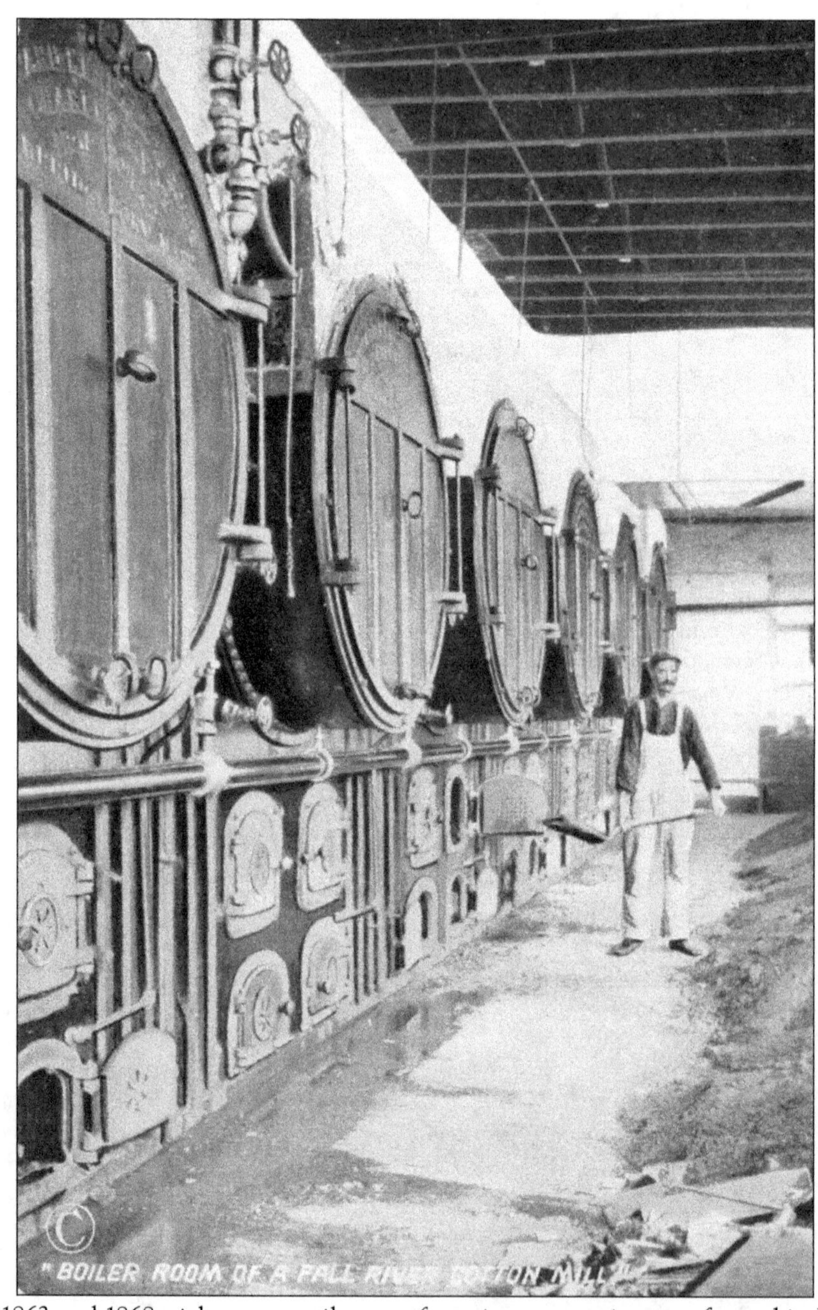

Between 1863 and 1868, eight new textile-manufacturing companies were formed in Fall River, which doubled the city's production capacity to over 500,000 spindles, surpassing Lowell as the largest textile-producing center in the United States. After 1870, there was an even larger surge of mill construction. Between February 1871 and March 1872, there were 15 new textile companies formed, and 22 new mill buildings were constructed. It is documented that Fall River grew faster than any other textile city of its time. Steve Dunwell says, "One out of four new spindles added to New England between 1850 and 1875 was placed in Fall River. The city controlled one-sixth of all New England cotton capacity, and one-half of all print cloth production. Fall River rightly called itself 'Spindle City.'" (Courtesy of Michael Brimbau.)

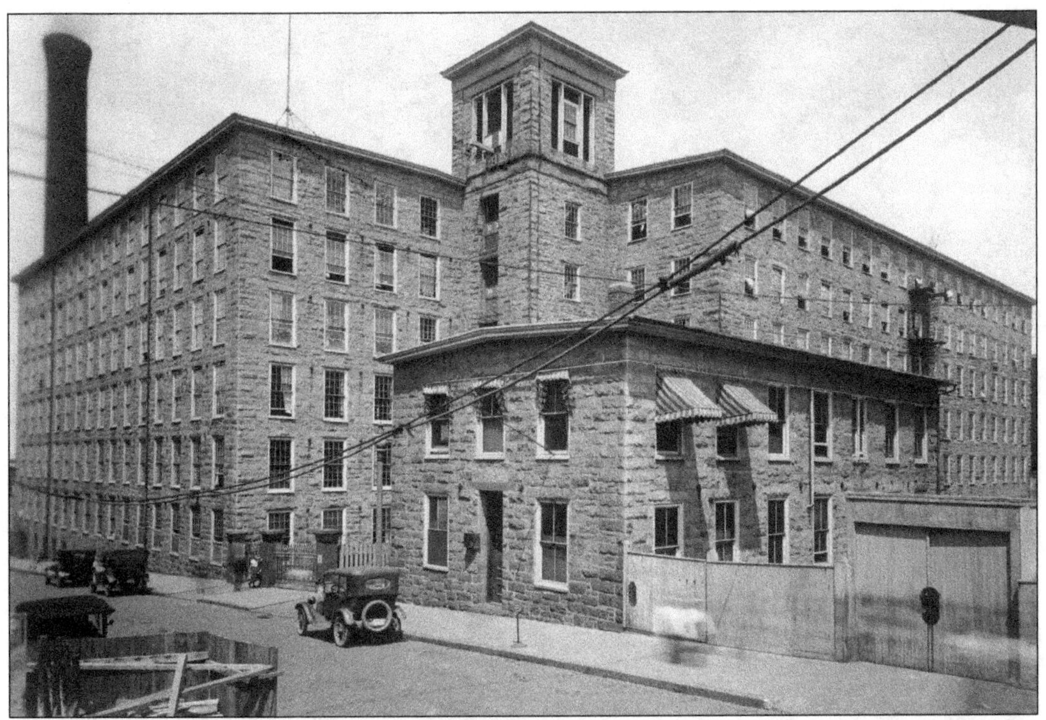

Pocasset Mill is pictured as seen in 1926, two short years before its total destruction in the fire of 1928. (Courtesy of the Fall River Historical Society.)

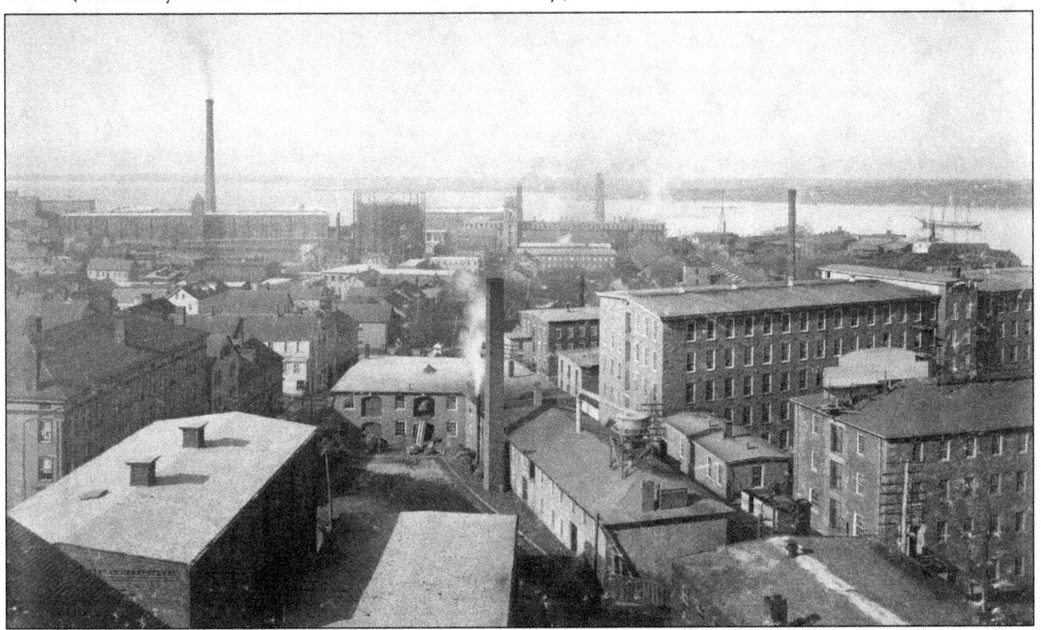

Part of the reason for Fall River's success in textile manufacturing had to do with its geographic placement on the Taunton River and Mount Hope Bay and its location south of Cape Cod. Cargo and people bound for Boston and points north could more easily travel to Fall River than attempt a rounding of the cape, where shoals and storms made for a dangerous and lengthy journey. (Courtesy of private collection.)

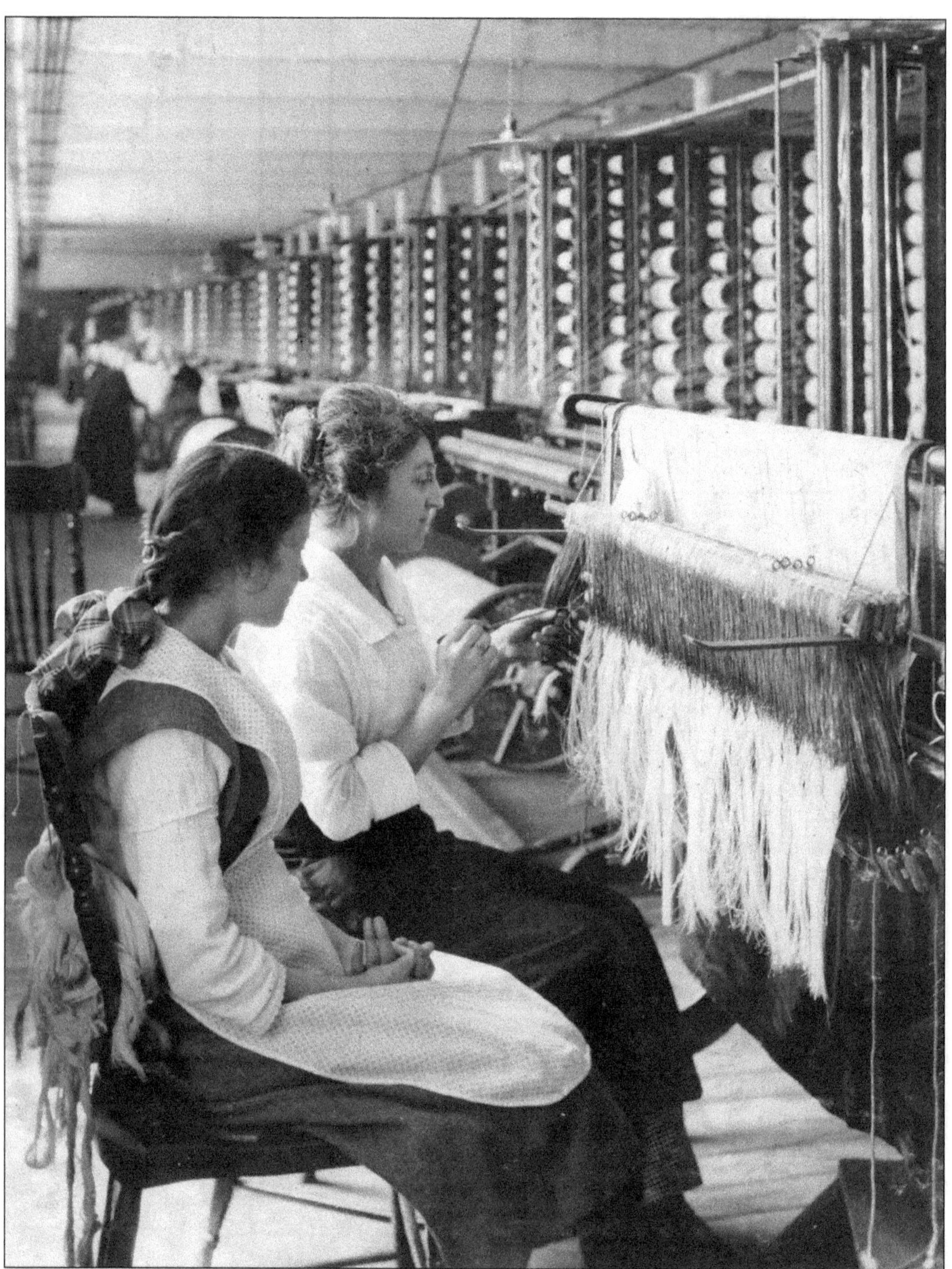

Employed for only a few weeks, 14-year-old Yvette Frappier is seen here in 1916 being trained by a teacher who has been a drawer-in for nine years at the King Philip Mill in the South End of Fall River. According to the photographer's notes, Yvette was the only girl in the department. A drawing-in boy assists girls in attaching warp yarns to harnesses, a harness being the device for holding the warp yarns in a loom. The woman is showing her how to draw the thread through an eye in the harness. (Lewis Hine photograph, courtesy of the Library of Congress.)

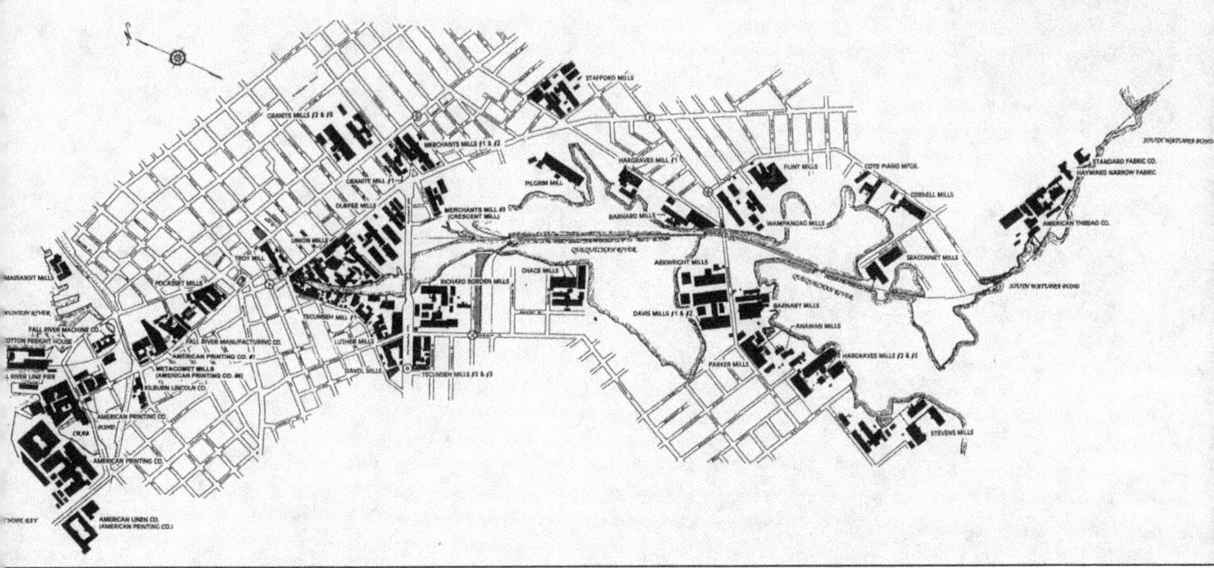

This map shows the location of the textile mills along the Quequechan River in Fall River in 1915. In 1911, Fall River had 111 mills in operation, equipped with about 4,000,000 spindles and 93,000 looms, manufacturing more than 1,057,240,000 yards of cloth per annum, and with some 34,000 operatives employed, according to the *New York Times*. The Quequechan River is two miles in length from the head at South Watuppa Pond to the dam at the top of the falls at Third Street. There were eight waterfalls in the final one-half mile of the river's course. The flow of the Quequechan is 121.6 cubic feet per second, or over 9,841,500,000 gallons per year. The river was placed in a conduit in the 1960s to make way for Interstate 195. The map is placed here so that the mouth of the river, which is in the west, is at the bottom so one can have a sense of scale. (Courtesy of Alfred Lima.)

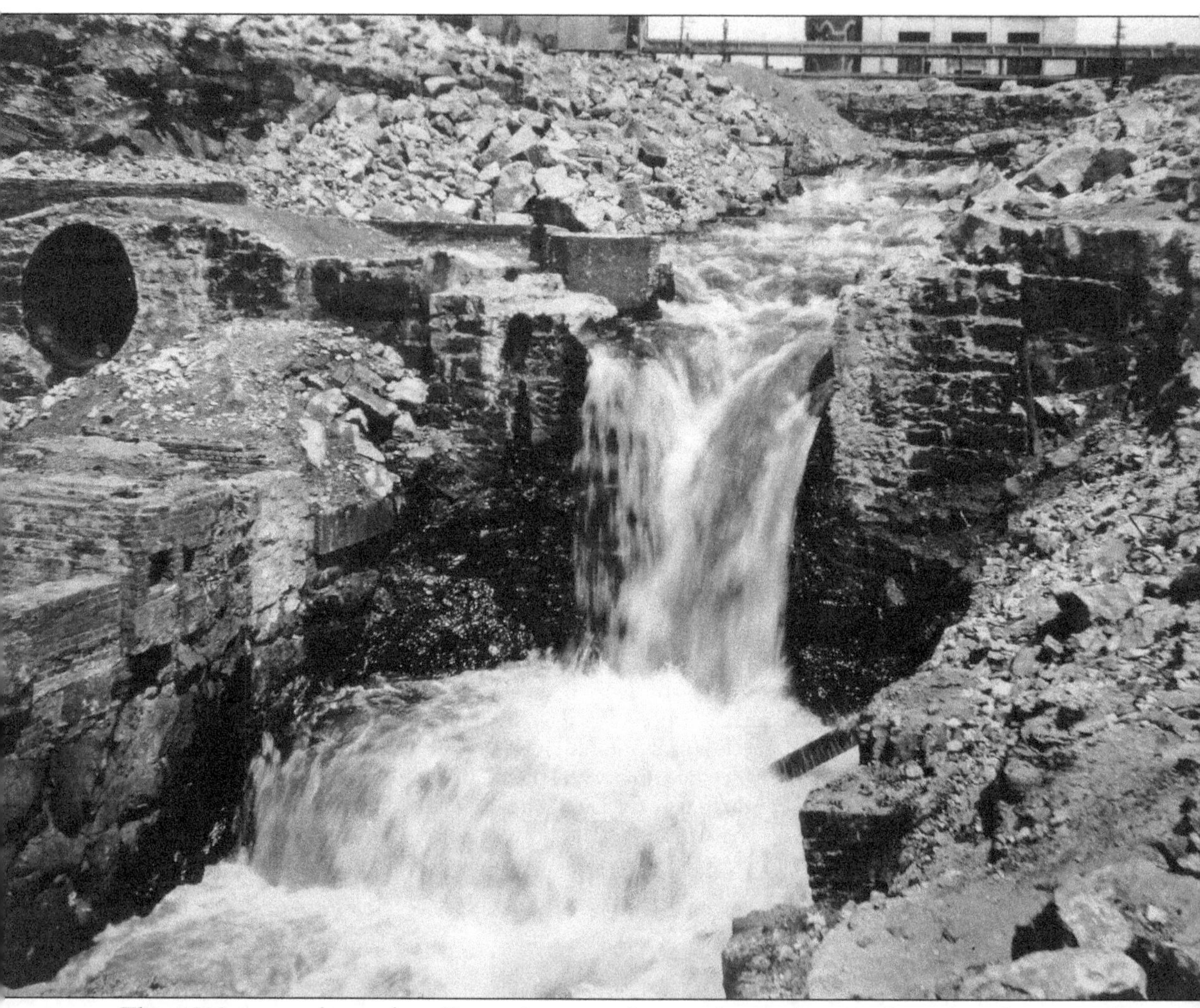

This 1929 image shows the effects of a major fire on the landscape of a city and a river. As the second falls in the Quequechan River, these waters were directly under the old Pocasset Manufacturing Company complex, which burned down, along with the Granite and Durfee Blocks, in the fire of 1928. It was later determined that these mills were the epicenter of the conflagration, as demolition workers were warming themselves on that very cold February day. The fire was declared officially out some two days after it started. The rubble from the Pocasset Mill that is seen here, piled up along the top and sides of "the stream," is what is left of the mill complex, and the waterfall has been exposed for the first time since 1822. (Courtesy of the Fall River Historical Society.)

Three

The Cotton Centennial

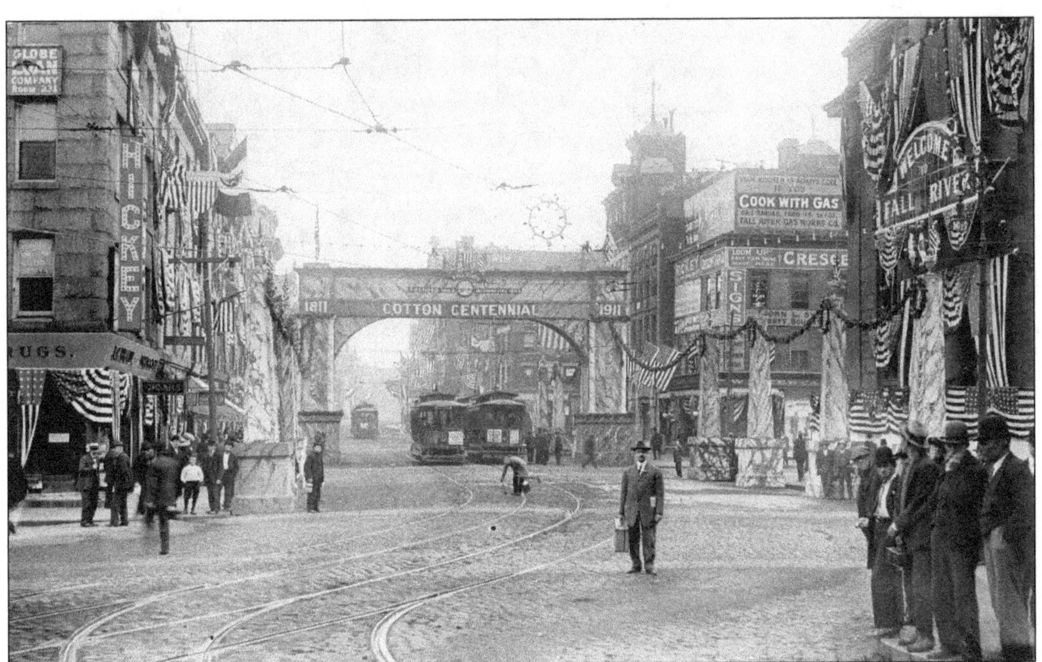

In 1911, Fall River had the world by the tail. It was the leading manufacturer of cotton cloth in the world and had 30 to 35 percent of its population working in the mills. It was time to celebrate. From June 19 to June 24, the city decided to throw itself a party and called it the Cotton Centennial Carnival. But first, citizens would have to decorate the city. (Courtesy of the Fall River Historical Society.)

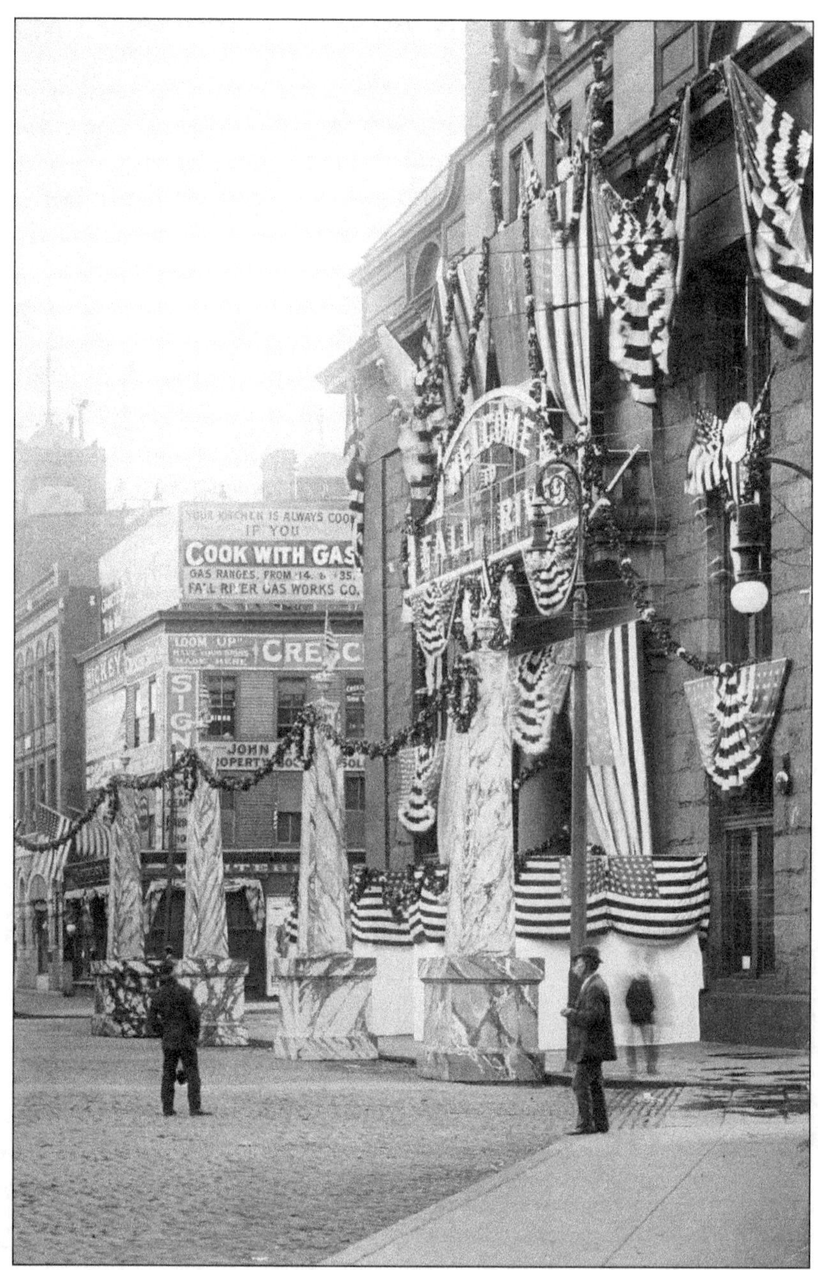

City Hall received a special dressing because it was here that many of the events would begin and end. A dais was constructed on the front steps for the first day's activities of crowning the Queen of the Cotton Centennial. Later in the week, the president of the United States would be visiting and be driven by this same stage. In addition to parades, fireworks displays, a horse show, and concerts, there were special exhibits throughout the week at various city venues: at the armory on Bank Street was a display of ladies handiwork; at Durfee Technical School was an exhibit of goods made in Fall River; at the Music Hall was a history display that included the desk that Col. Joseph Durfee sat behind in the first mill in the city in 1811; and at the Fall River Public Library was a showcase featuring artists from the Fall River School. (Courtesy of the Fall River Historical Society.)

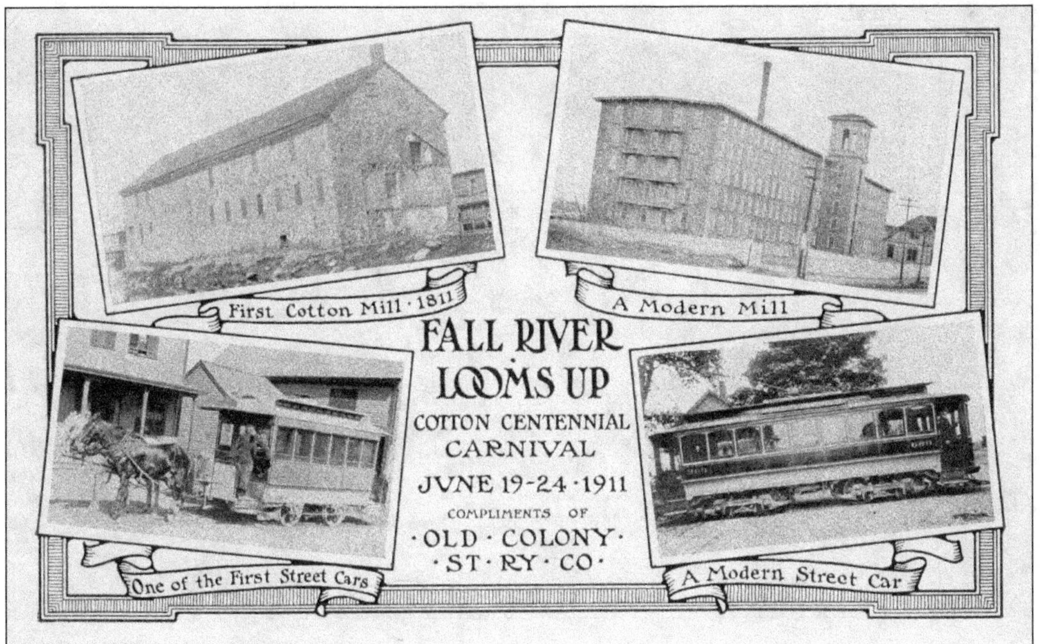

A postcard was issued commemorating the event and to show how far the city had come in 100 years. Images of the old mill and the new, as well as the old form of horse-drawn conveyance versus the new electric trolley, were used to advertise the advances that the Cotton Centennial Carnival was meant to celebrate. (Courtesy of Michael Brimbau.)

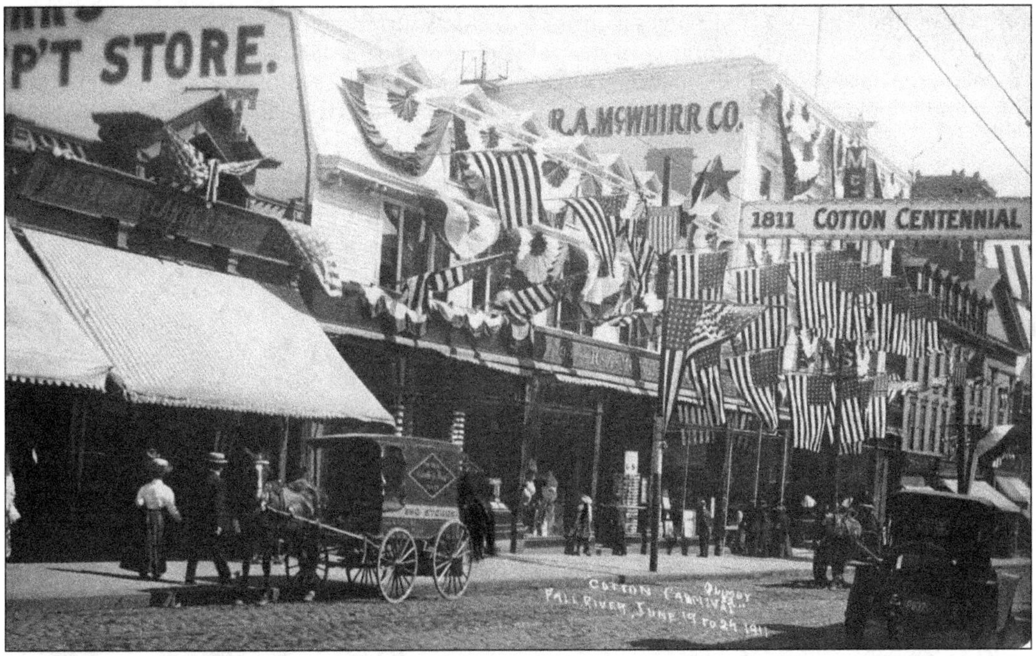

Everything was red, white, and blue, and flags were hung wherever people could find a place to put one. McWhirr's was no exception. Everyone was getting into the spirit of the festivities, and even though rain had been forecast for the first parade day, the city was an exciting place to be, with anticipation running high. (Courtesy of the Fall River Historical Society.)

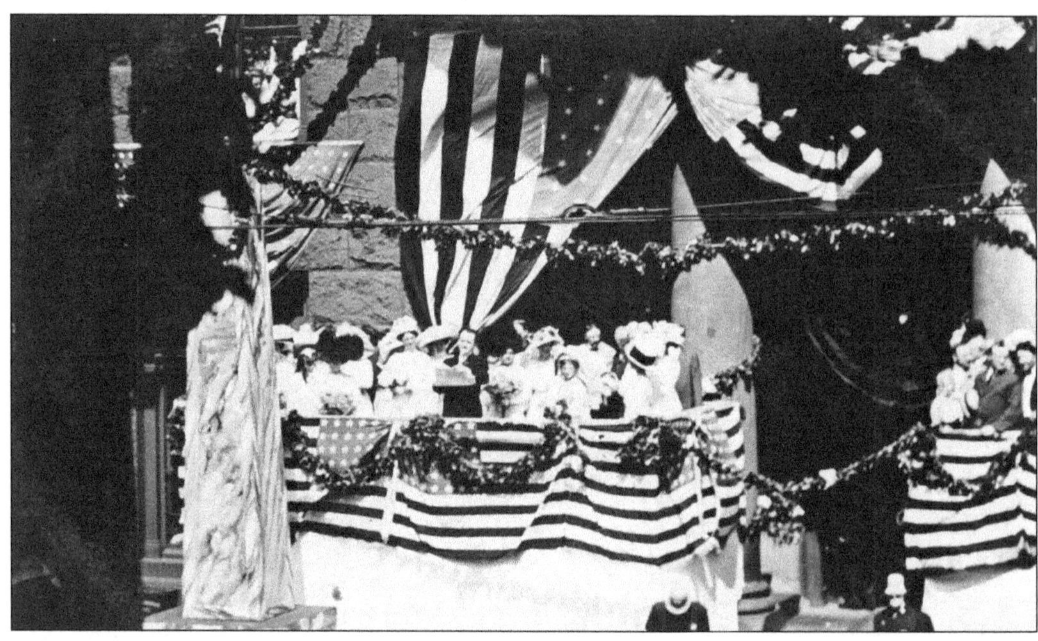

The first day, June 19, saw the crowning of the Queen of the Cotton Centennial, Marion Pierce Hall, who was, incidentally, the daughter of the president of the Manufacturers Association. However, she was not the first choice of the committee—her sister was, but she was shy and uncomfortable with making speeches and declined the honor. The queen had an 18-lady court that accompanied her. With surnames such as Davol, McWhirr, Brayton, and Chace, this grouping of Fall River ladies was representative of the owner class of the textile industry. Before the queen's arrival on the dais, the band Germania serenaded the crowd with several marches by John Philip Sousa and popular songs of the day. (Both, courtesy of the Fall River Historical Society.)

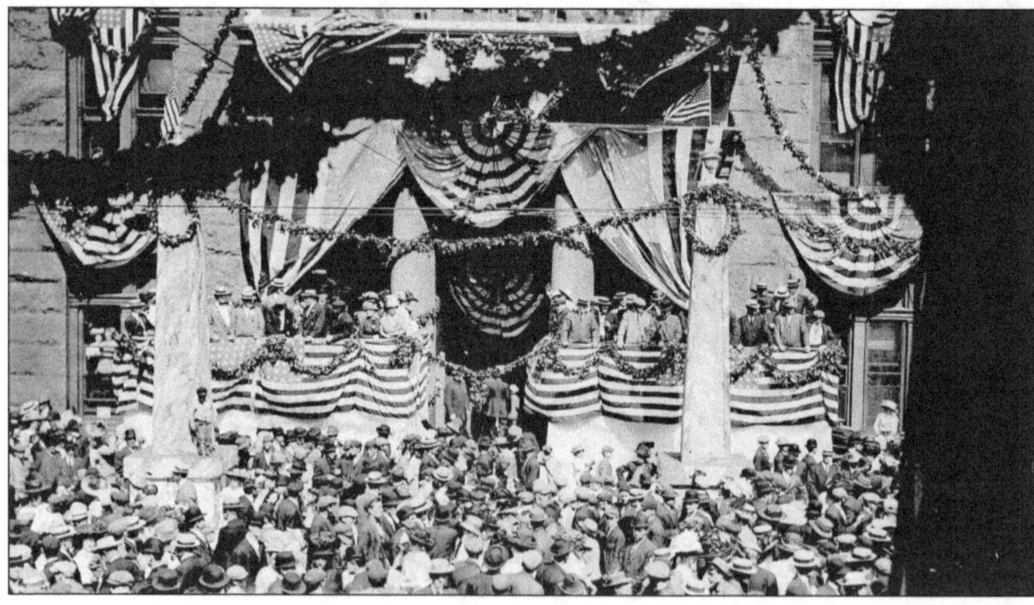

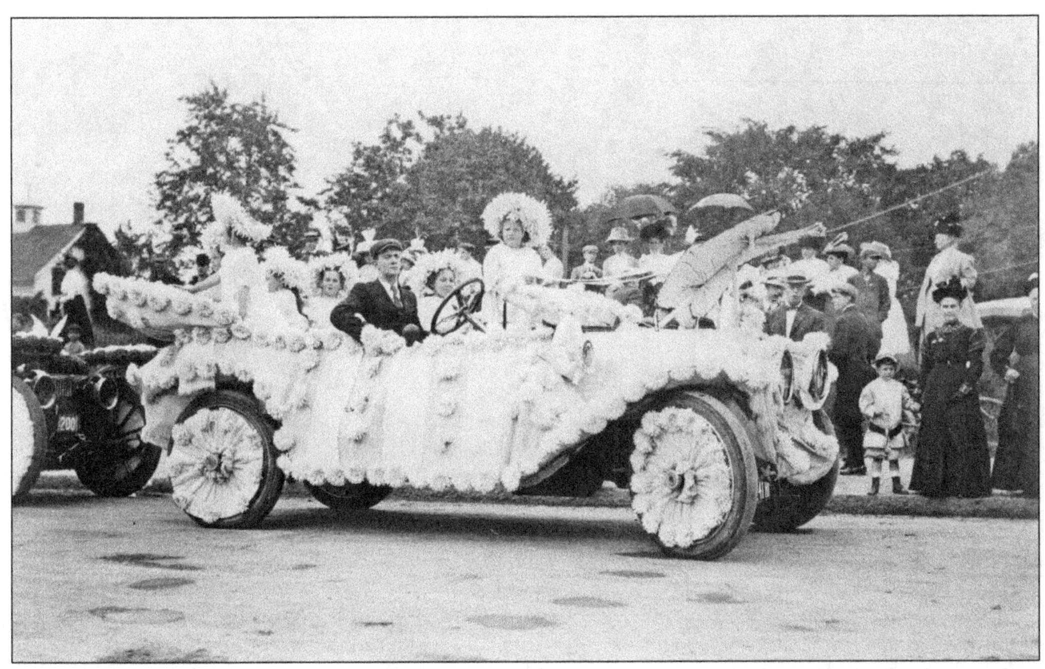

The second day of the Cotton Centennial Carnival showcased those who could afford automobiles to parade them before the city, after much creative decorating. The ladies in the car in the image above are, from left to right, Margaret Waring, Helen Lawton, Helen Hambly, Lorene Humphrey, and Elizabeth West. It is known from correspondence that the butterfly on the front of the car was pink, and the streamers were pink crepe paper with pink trimming. The route this auto parade took was from the Highlands, where these owners live, to the old mill at Globe Street, then back to the Highlands. In this way, it was assured that everyone could enjoy the decorated roadsters. Even the rain could not stop the city from enjoying the day. (Both, courtesy of the Fall River Historical Society.)

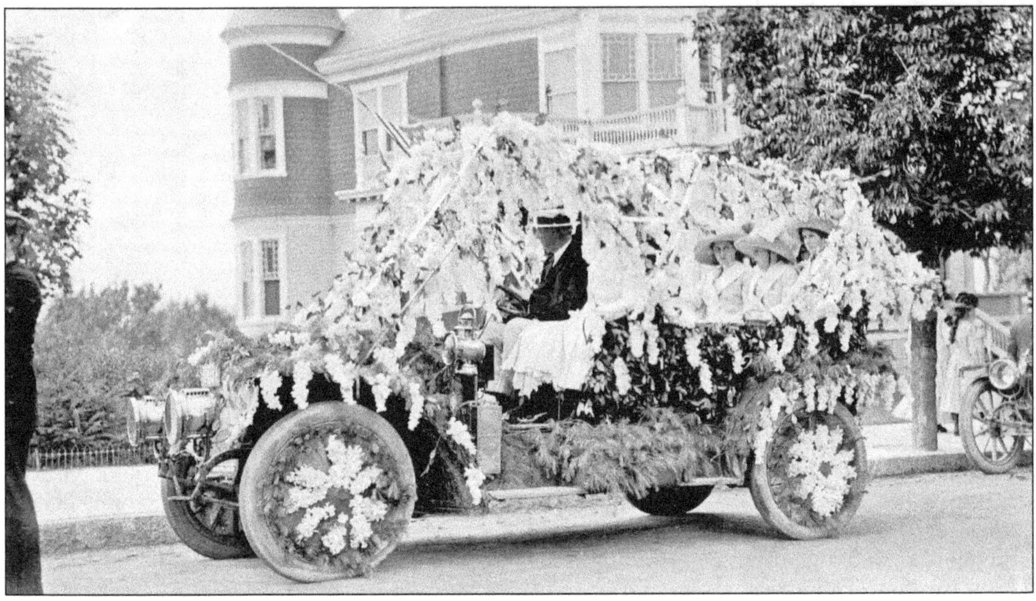

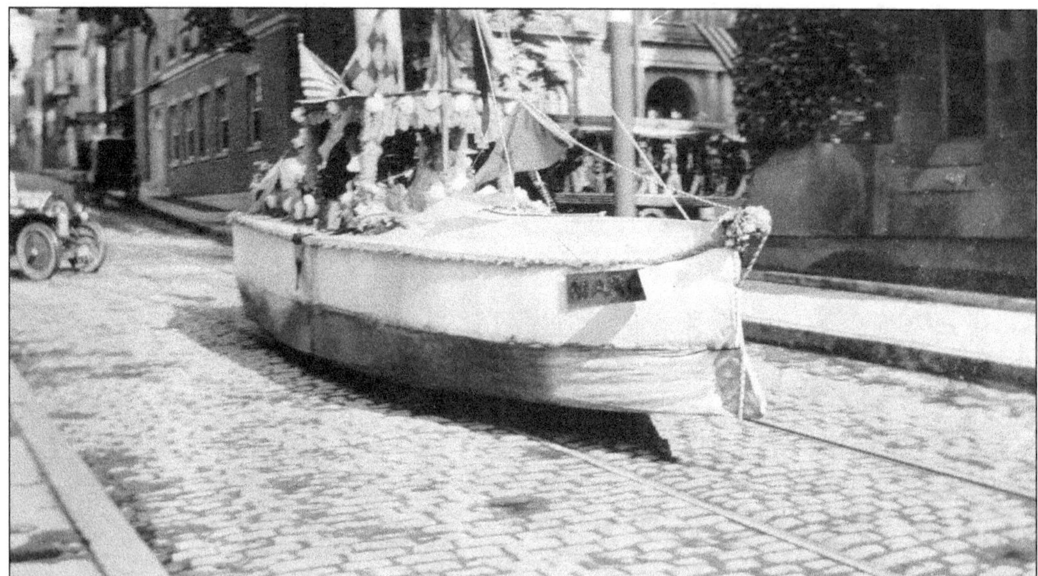

The second day of the Cotton Centennial Carnival was Auto Day, with over 100 automobiles of various types competing in categories according to size. Here is a car, imaginatively decorated to look like a boat, driving past Rock and Franklin Streets. The owners are W. Irving Peirce and Edmund L. Peirce. (Courtesy of the Fall River Historical Society.)

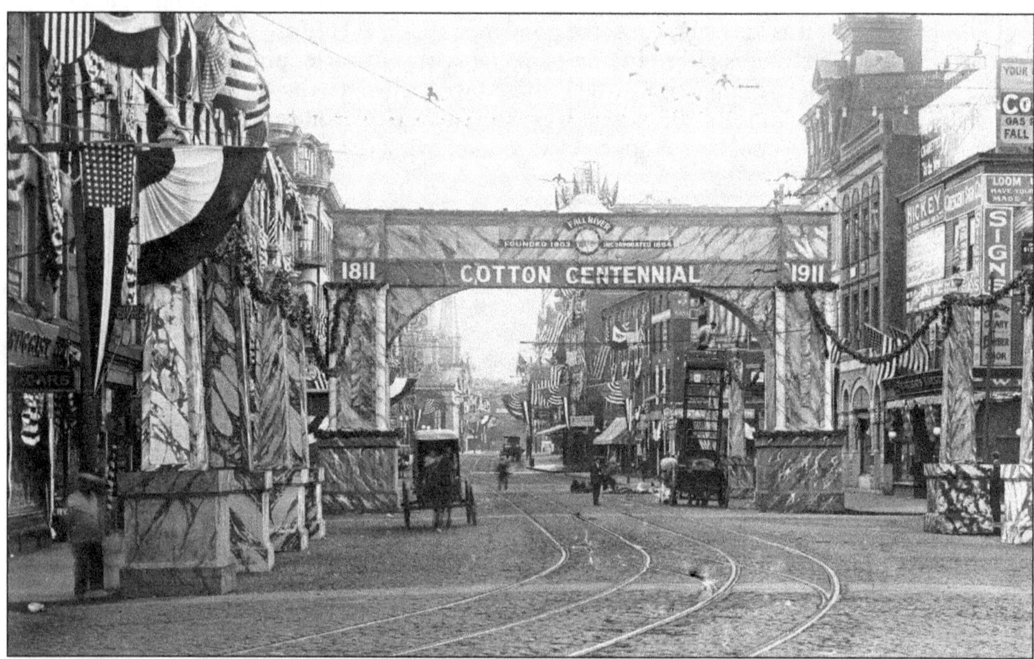

The Cotton Centennial arch was made of wood but painted to look like marble. Each night, visitors were treated to a spectacular sight as the arch was illuminated by strings of electric lights. For a population that still had gas lanterns as streetlamps, this must have been an event to remember. The lights were strung 50 in a row on individual lines so as not to cause a short circuit or fire. (Courtesy of the Fall River Historical Society.)

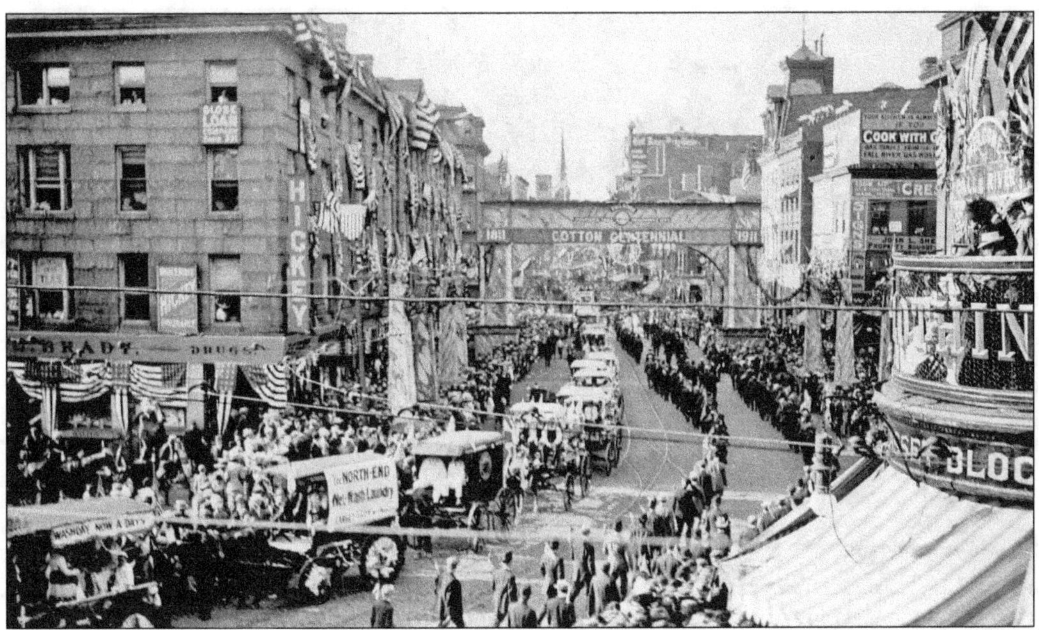

On the evening of the second day of the Centennial Carnival, the city was treated to a concert by the American Band in South Park and a fireworks display in Columbus Park that featured set pieces (standing fireworks displays) of varying beauty and complexity. "Loom-Up Fall River Boys," the theme of the weeklong event, was a song composed by Fall River native George Foley and debuted that night at the concert. It was said that the crowds stayed at South Park until after midnight. The next morning at 10:00 a.m. would be the Ringling Bros. Circus Parade, followed by the Trades Parade at 3:00 p.m. With over 30 percent of the population of the city of Fall River employed by the textile industry, it was said that there was not a soul who did not know someone who worked in a mill. (Both, courtesy of the Fall River Historical Society.)

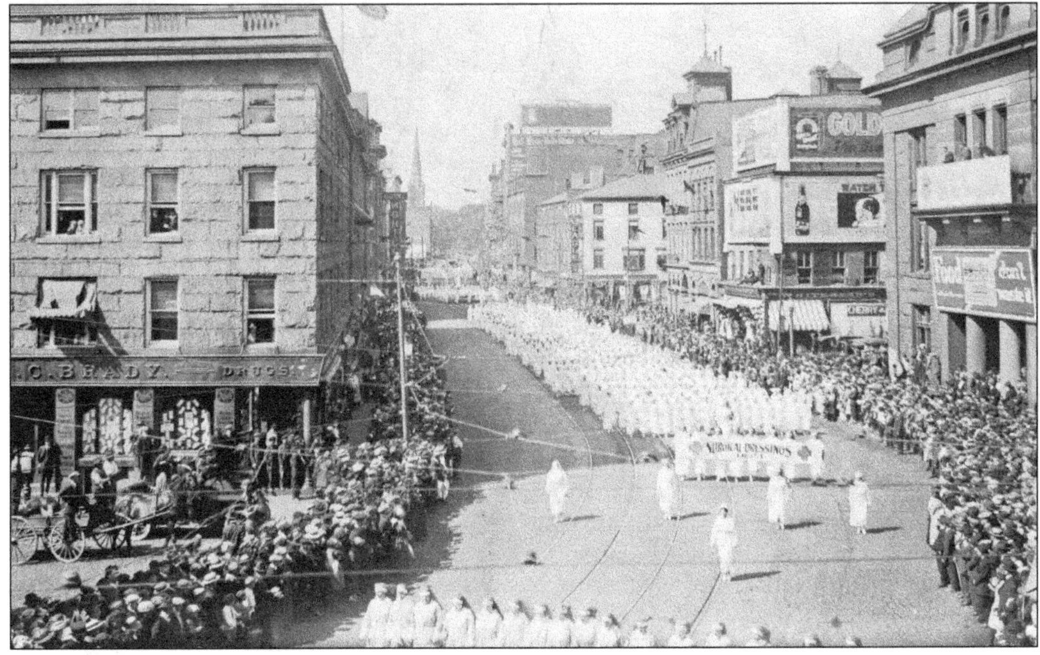

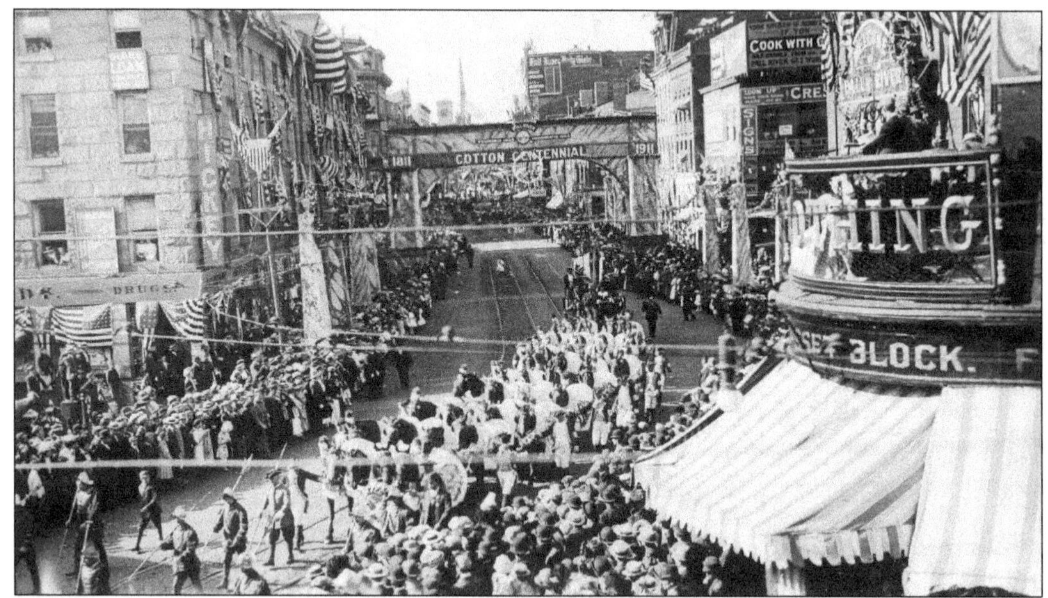

As luck, or careful planning, would have it, on the third day of the Cotton Centennial Carnival, the Ringling Bros. Circus came to Fall River and held its parade at 10:00 a.m. Essentially an advertisement for the circus show, this parade was highly anticipated by the children of the city. This photograph shows a 40-horse hitch, which was quite a feat of prowess as handling that many horses at one time was a big job. (Courtesy of the Fall River Historical Society.)

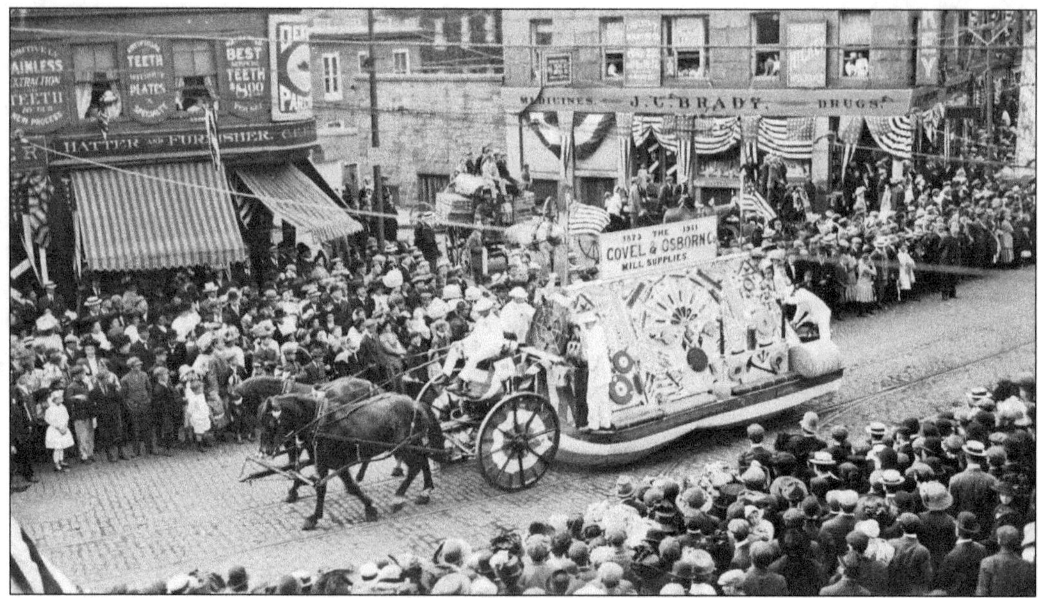

Starting at 3:00 p.m. and lasting almost two hours, the Trades Parade on the third day was quite popular with the crowds. The route began in front of city hall, travelled to South Main at South Park, and then returned to end where it started. Because of this, the parade marchers looked like they had doubled back on themselves and were marching in two directions at once, as one can see in some of these images. (Courtesy of the Fall River Historical Society.)

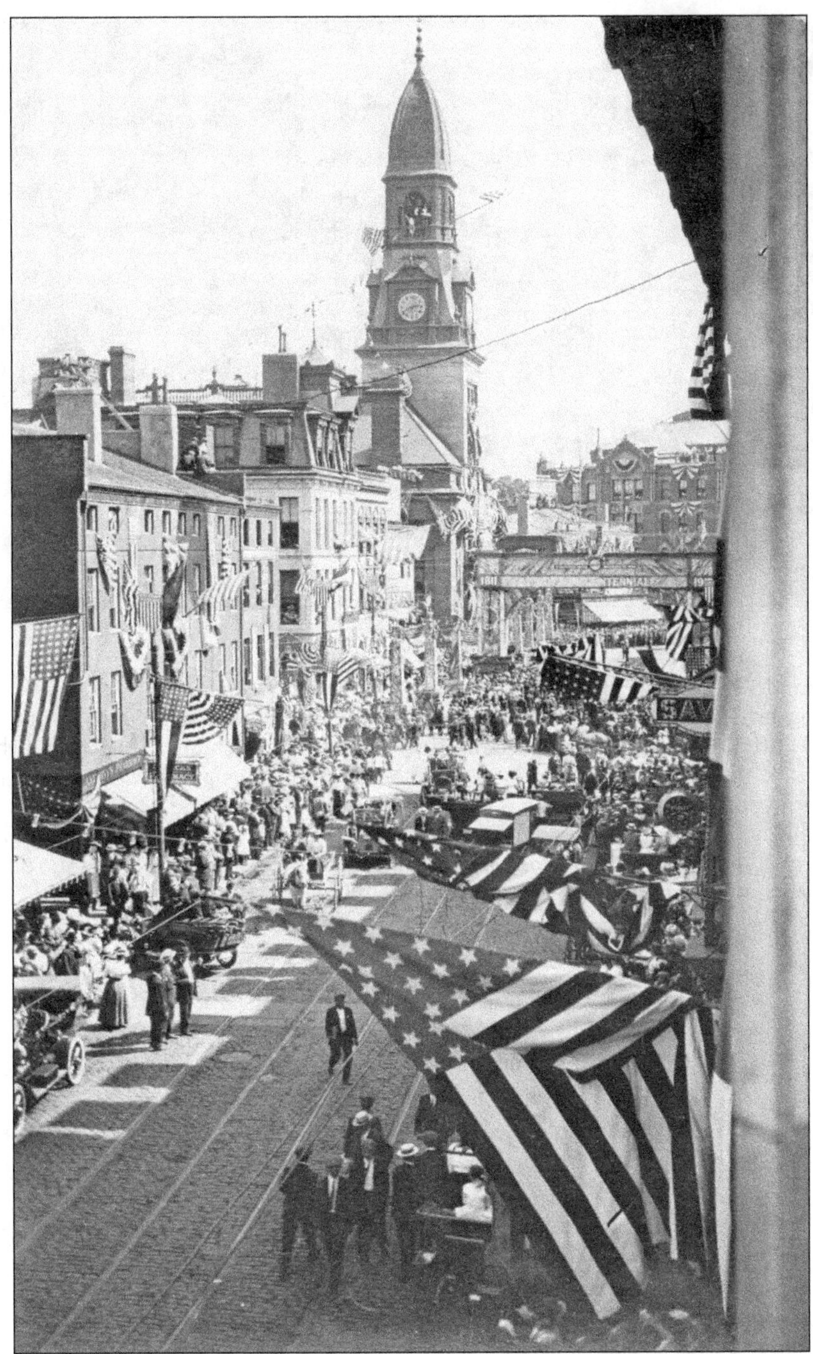

The population of Fall River in 1911 was a little over 120,000. The police estimated that on the third day of the Cotton Centennial Carnival there were well over 150,000 people lining the streets for the two parades of the day—the Ringling Bros. Circus Parade at 10:00 a.m. and the Trades Parade at 3:00 p.m. These crowds were partly due to the fact that the circus had contracted with the railroad to run special excursion trains into Fall River from Taunton and New Bedford, Massachusetts, and Providence, Rhode Island, thereby increasing the attendance at the parade and ticket sales for the big top. (Courtesy of the Fall River Historical Society.)

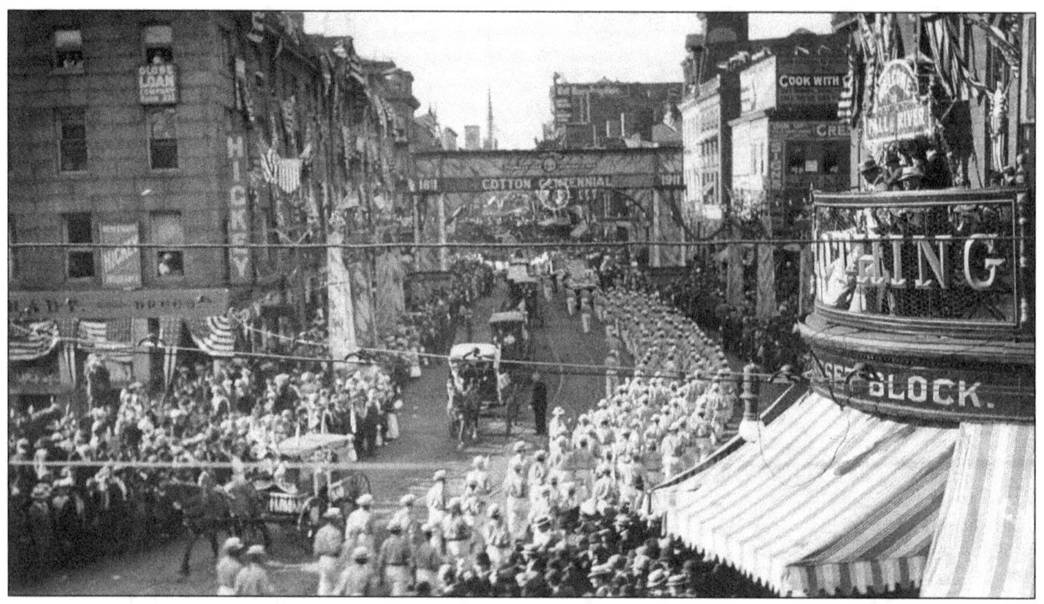

The Trades Parade, held on day three in the afternoon, was an opportunity for the workers and the corporation owners to celebrate the success that the city was enjoying. This vantage point shows the Granite Block opposite, the faux-marble Centennial Arch, and the spire of the First Baptist Church in the distance. It bears notice to comment on the apparel worn by the general populace at the events. Almost everyone is wearing a hat—both men and women. It is obviously past Memorial Day because there are straw hats present, and the early-20th-century gentleman would only wear one of those in the summer. One cannot help but also notice that the dominant dress of the men is a suit and tie. (Both, courtesy of the Fall River Historical Society.)

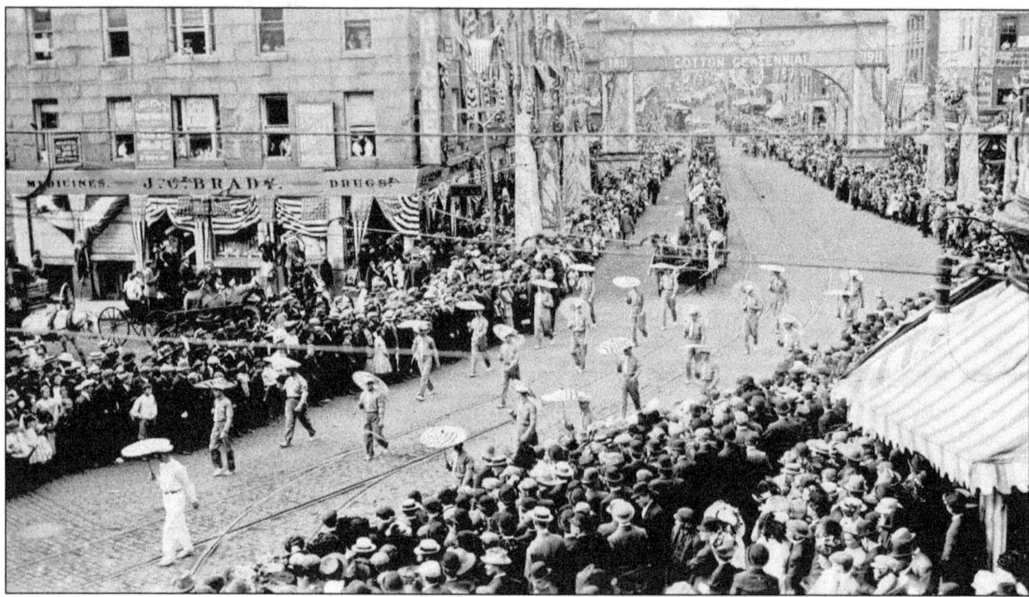

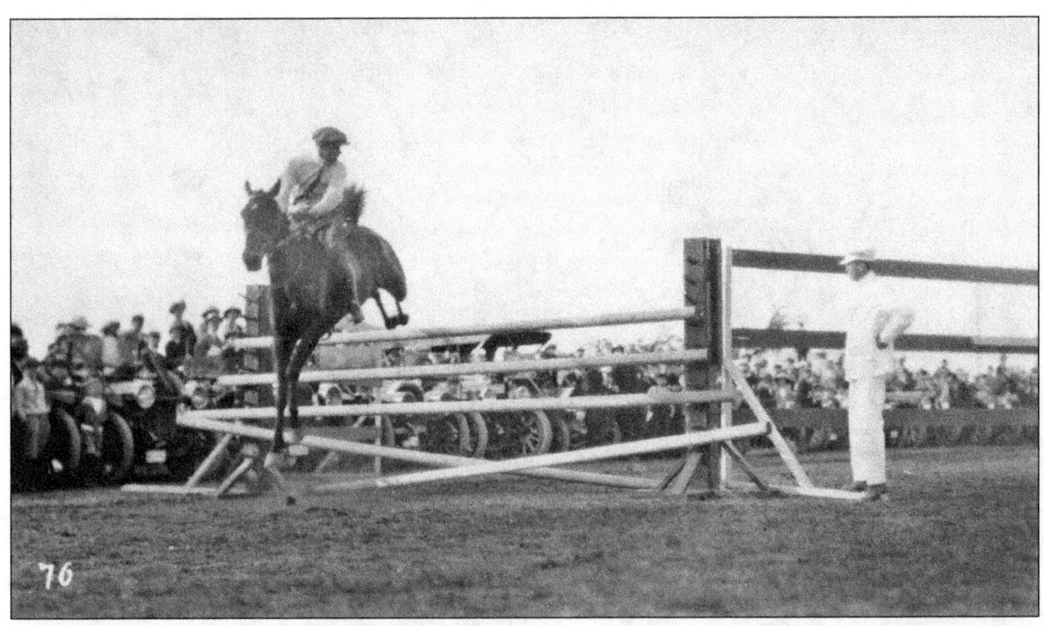

A world-class horse show was held in North Park on the fourth day of the celebration, and Spencer Borden's Arabians were a big crowd-pleaser. Borden, the author of several books and articles on the subject, had stables for his prized equine lineage at his estate on Interlachen, a jut of land that sticks out into the waters of North Watuppa Pond. From extant photographs, one can deduce that riders competed in jumping, dressage, and tandem hitch. Tandem hitch was where, instead of having two horses side by side, they were hitched one in front of the other, and thus tested a driver's skill and control. It is also known that children were somehow involved, as these two youngsters (pictured below) have numbered cards on their backs. In an era when horses, automobiles, and electric trolleys shared the city's streets, a horse show would have been a popular event. (Both, courtesy of the Fall River Historical Society.)

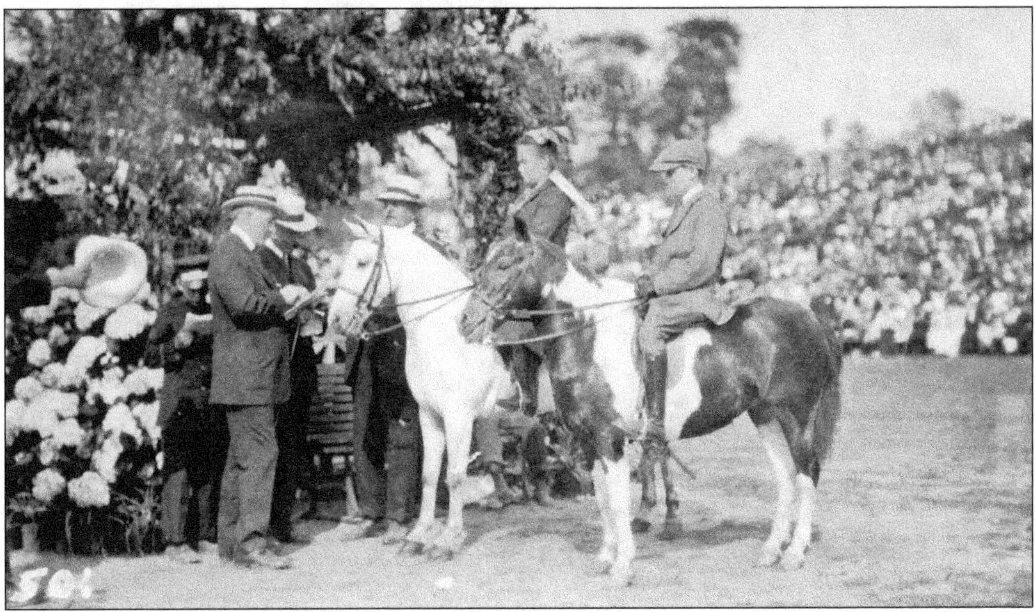

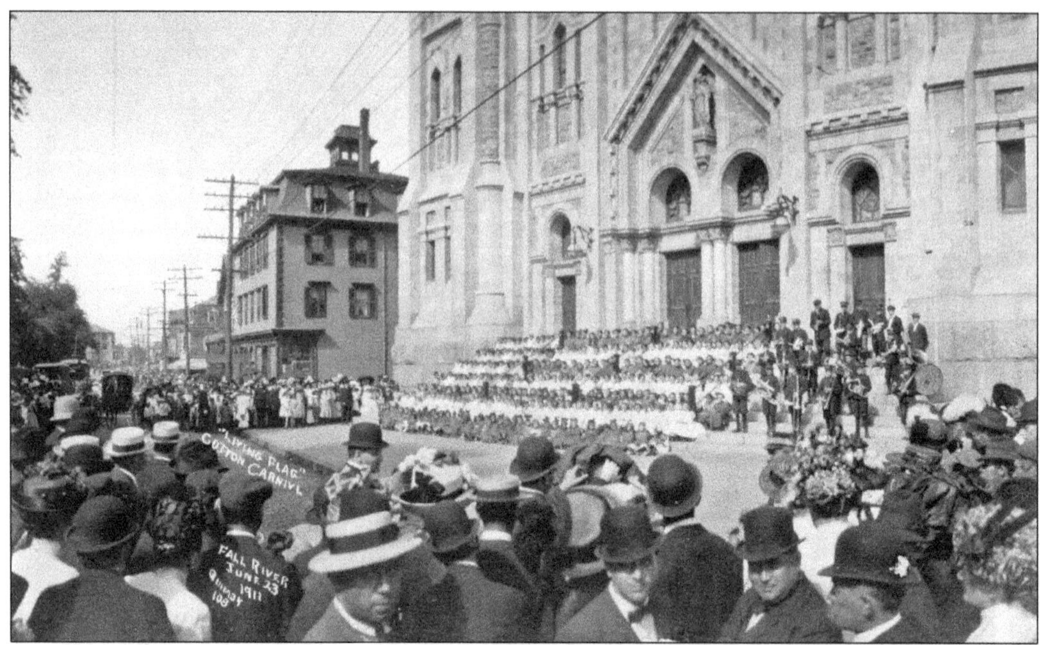

On Friday, June 23, the fifth day of the carnival, the president of the United States, William Howard Taft, attended the celebration. Arriving on board the presidential yacht *Mayflower* and accompanied by the battleship *Connecticut* and two Revenue Marine cutters, the *Acushnet* and the *Gresham*, he landed his transport at the Iron Works dock. Greeted by Fall River mayor Thomas Higgins and Massachusetts governor Eugene Foss, the president was given an extensive tour of the city, with stops along the route. At St. Anne's Church on South Main Street, across from South Park, the president was entertained by 500 French Canadian schoolchildren as they formed a living American flag (above). And the trip would have not been complete without a drive by the old mill on Globe Street (below). (Both, courtesy of the Fall River Historical Society.)

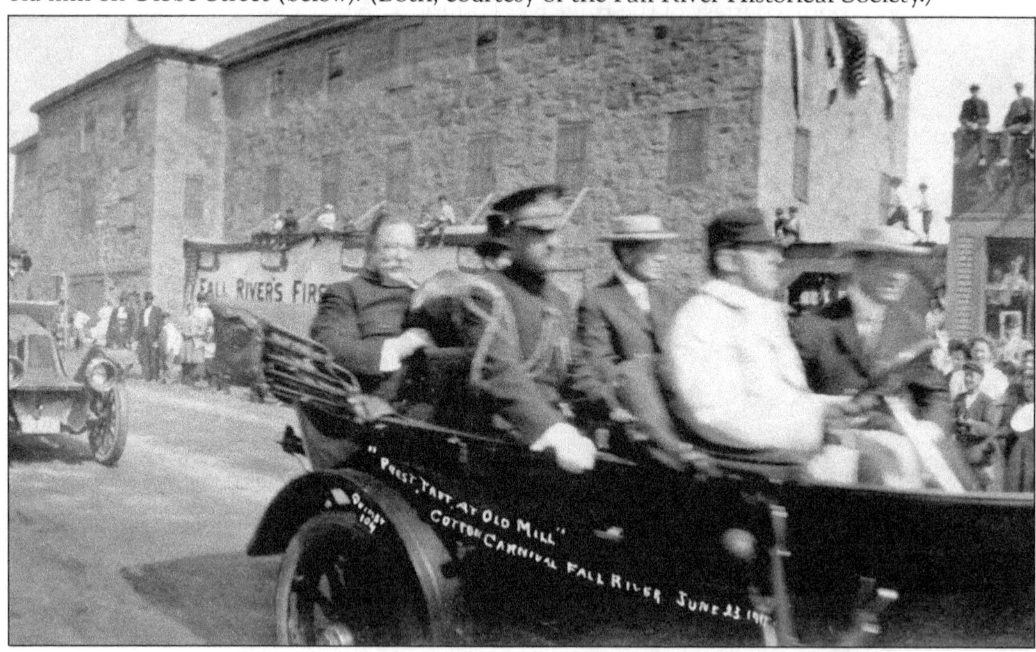

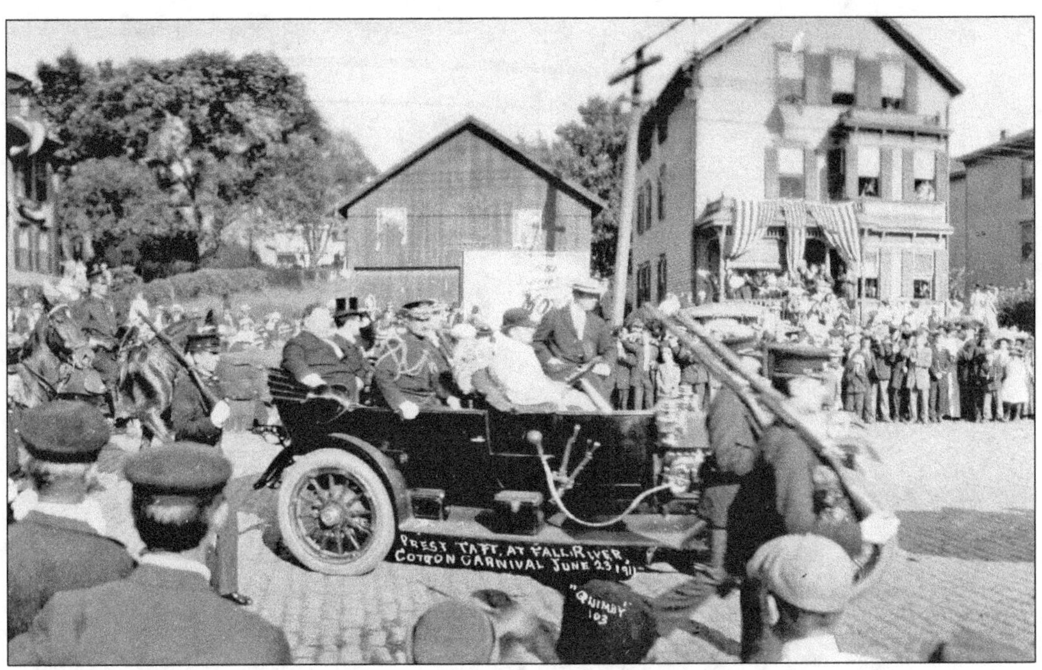

President Taft's whirlwind tour of Fall River included several stops: paying a call on an old friend, Bishop Daniel Feehan, whom he had known from their childhoods together in Millbury, Massachusetts; receiving a bouquet of flowers from the children at St. Joseph's Orphanage in the Flint; touring the machinery exhibit at the armory; and having a guided tour of the Bradford Durfee Textile School across the street. His last stop was to deliver a brief farewell address at South Park, to a crowd estimated by the *New York Times* to be 50,000 strong. Taft wished Fall River "Godspeed in making greater steps forward in the next 100 years" and departed the city shortly after 5:00 p.m. (Both, courtesy of the Fall River Historical Society.)

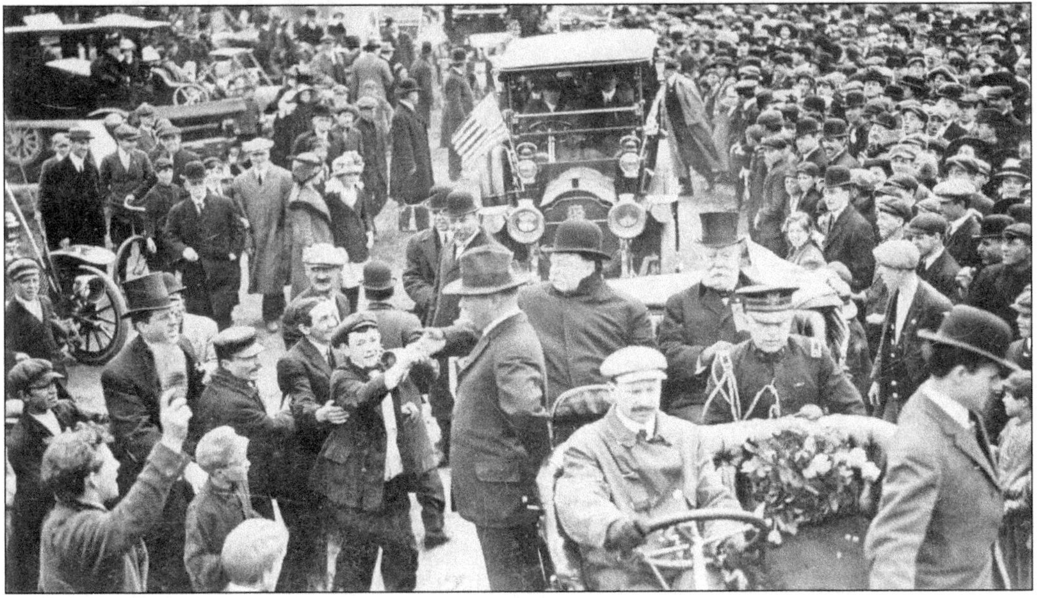

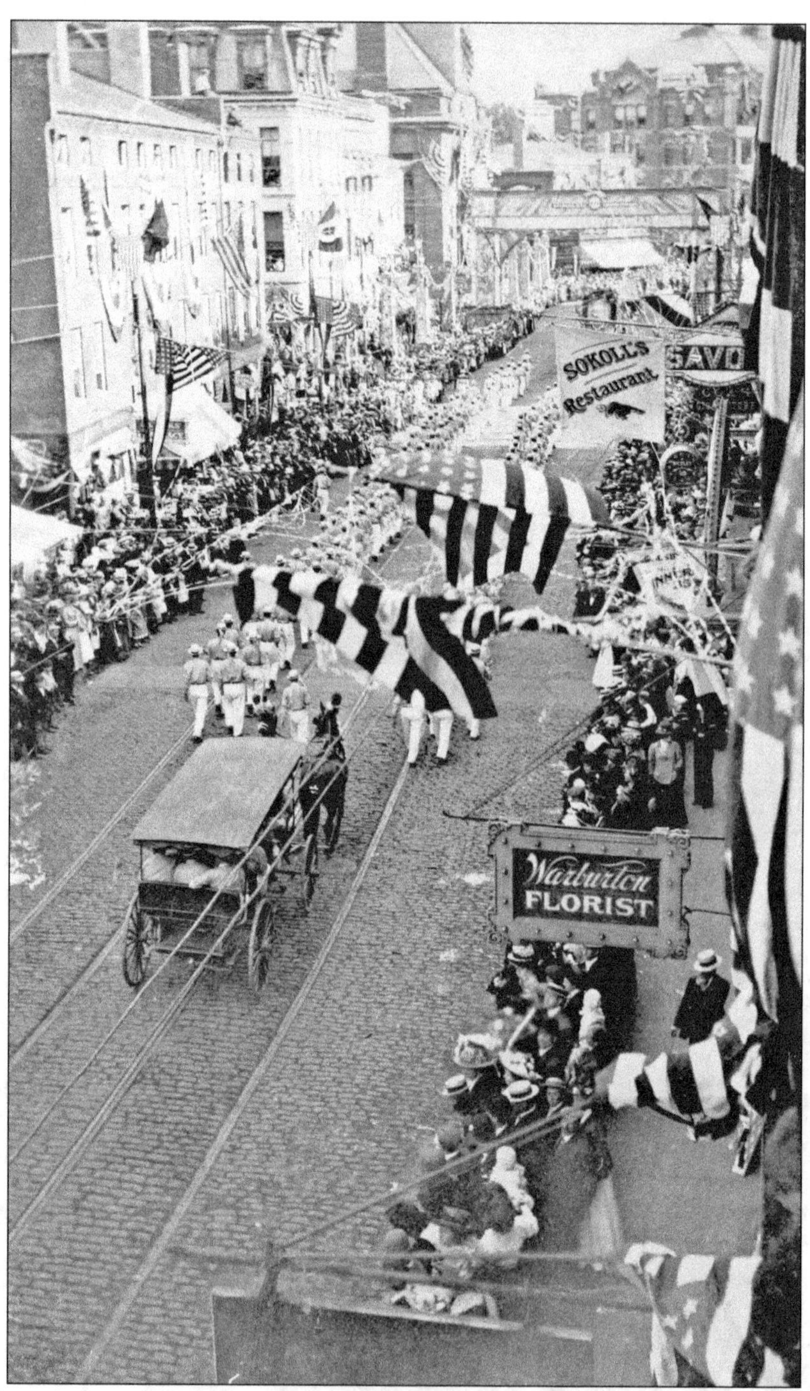

In an article in the *New York Times* on June 18 announcing the festivities, and apparently introducing Fall River to its readership, the city was described in the following terms of its economic impact: "Fall River produces every variety of cloth, from rough linings for shoes to the finest and daintiest fabrics for ladies' dresses. Its factories spin them, bleach them, weave them, and print them—fine goods, coarse goods, twills, jeans, sateens, lawns, fancies, silk dress goods, fine zephyrs, lace curtains, and Marseilles quilts." (Courtesy of the Fall River Historical Society.)

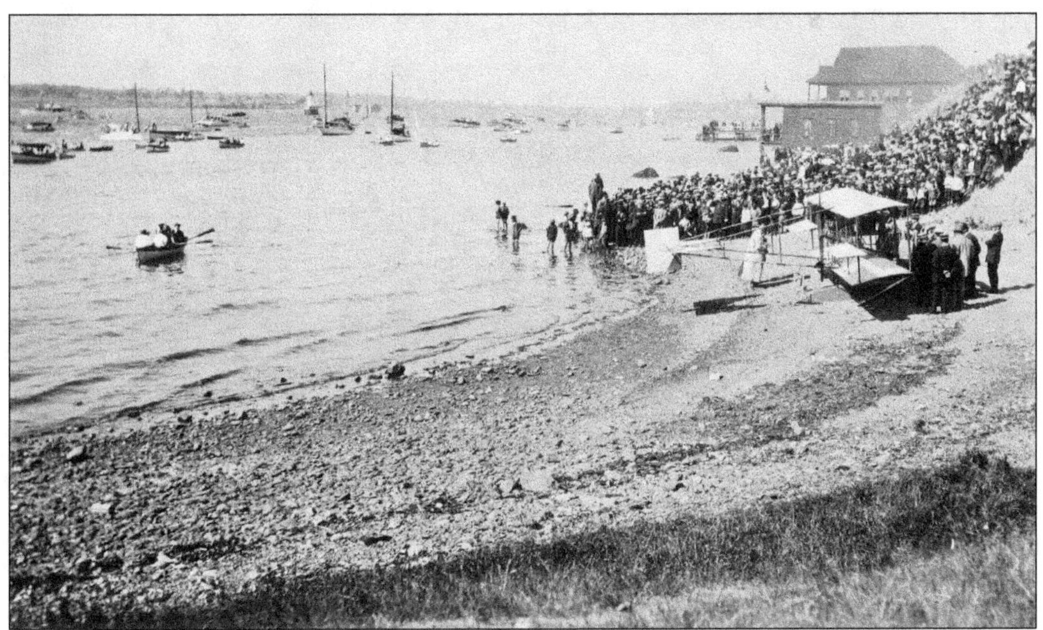

On the final day, June 24, famed aviator Glenn Curtiss gave two demonstrations of his flying prowess in his Curtiss Model D amphibian biplane. Curtiss was a pioneer in American aviation and was one of the fathers of the US aircraft industry. Performing his show at Sandy Beach, Curtiss took off from the water at 50 miles per hour and quickly gained speed to reach his maximum 80 miles per hour. He flew over the beach and the city several times with increasing altitude and then landed amid some rather choppy conditions. After waiting for calmer winds, Curtiss took off again, this time racing a speedboat. The boat, given a head start, was able to reach a speed of 20 miles per hour, but, of course, Curtiss handily beat that figure, to the delight of the crowd. (Both, courtesy of the Fall River Historical Society.)

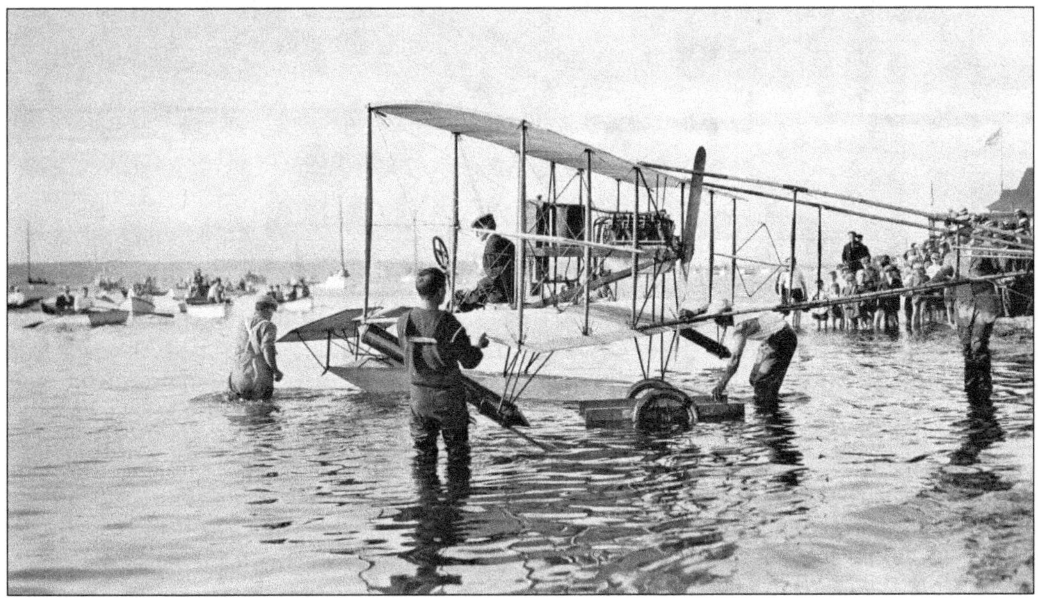

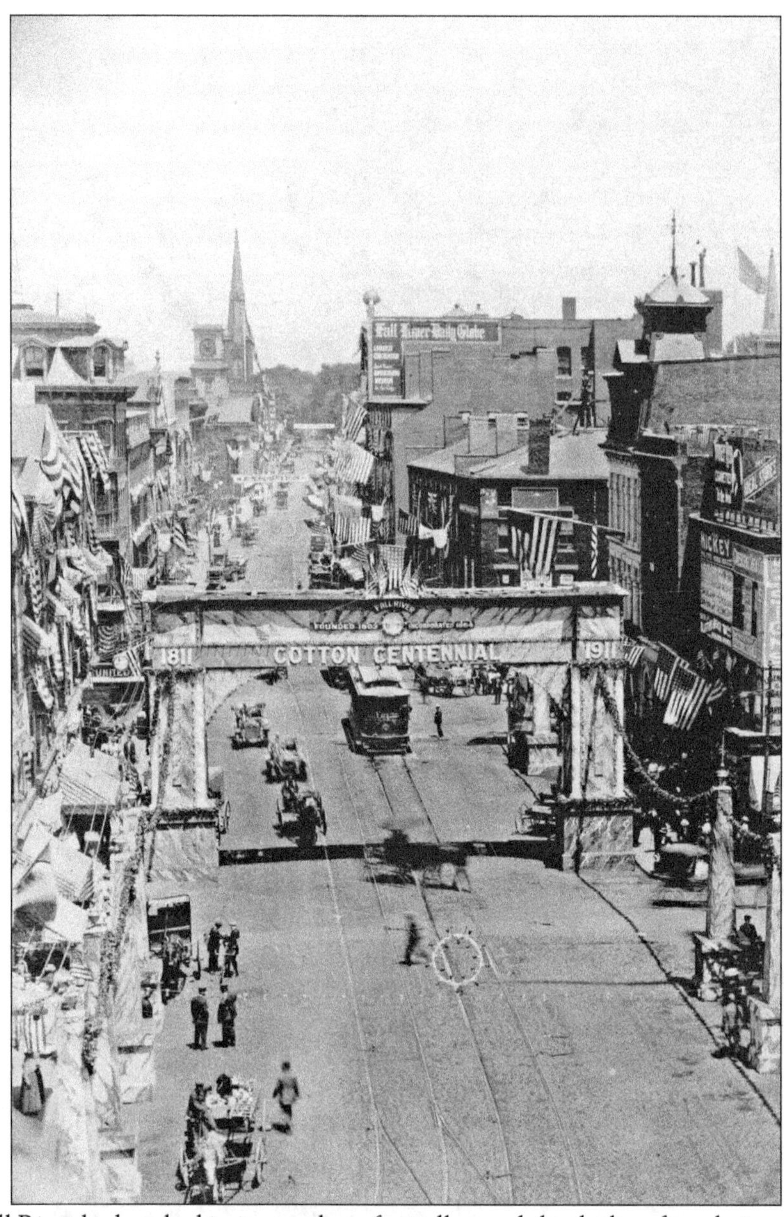

By 1912, Fall River had peaked in its number of spindles, and the decline from being the number one producer of cotton cloth to a struggling city was dramatic. Within a decade, hard times would come to Fall River, well before the stock market crash of 1929. In 1922, there were 30,700 people employed in the mills in the city. By 1924, that figure took a nosedive to 20,000 and never recovered. The South, which produced the raw material that then had to be transported to the North for processing into cloth, had invested in building its own mills and fitted them with the latest technology that could produce finished pieces at a faster rate. Fall River's mill owners had not reinvested their profits in updating their machinery. In addition, without unions, the labor to create the textiles was cheaper in the South. Fall River had to fall back onto the needle trades as an industry, and when those jobs went overseas—again, for cheaper wages—what was once a thriving and prosperous city was, by the 1960s, an old mill town that had seen its best days. (Courtesy of the Fall River Historical Society.)

Four

Recreational Pastimes and Entertainments

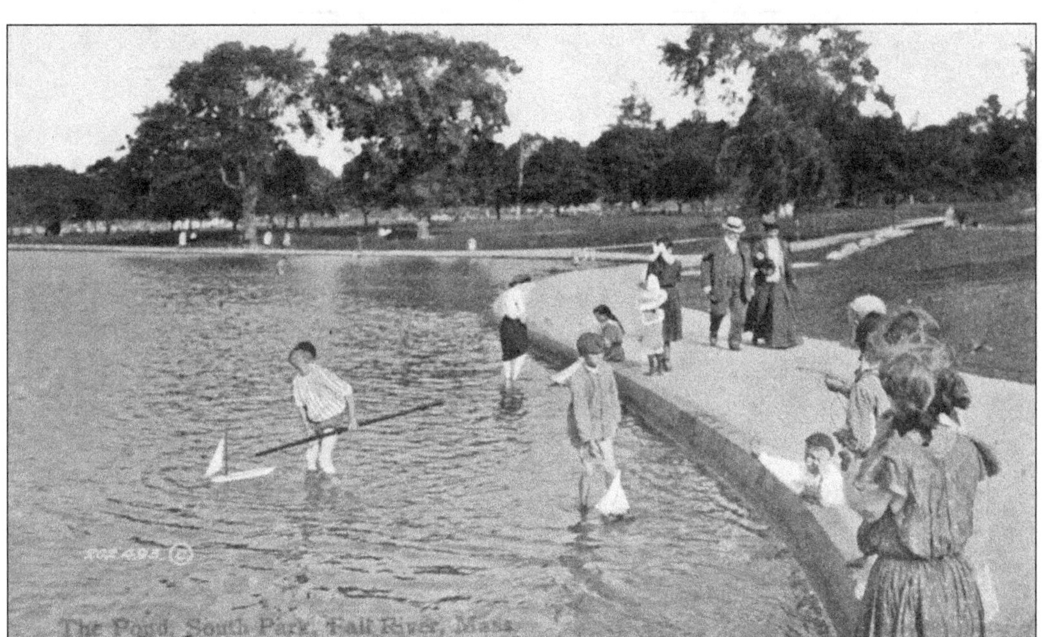

On page 158 of his *Centennial History of Fall River, Mass.*, Henry Earl writes: "The brains that planned and the capital and enterprise that have promoted the growth of Fall River have happily entertained a more generous and humanitarian view of their trust. Appreciating the gregarious nature of a community of working people, the first thought was to provide an easily accessible ground for their assemblage and enjoyment out of labor hours." (Courtesy of Michael Brimbau.)

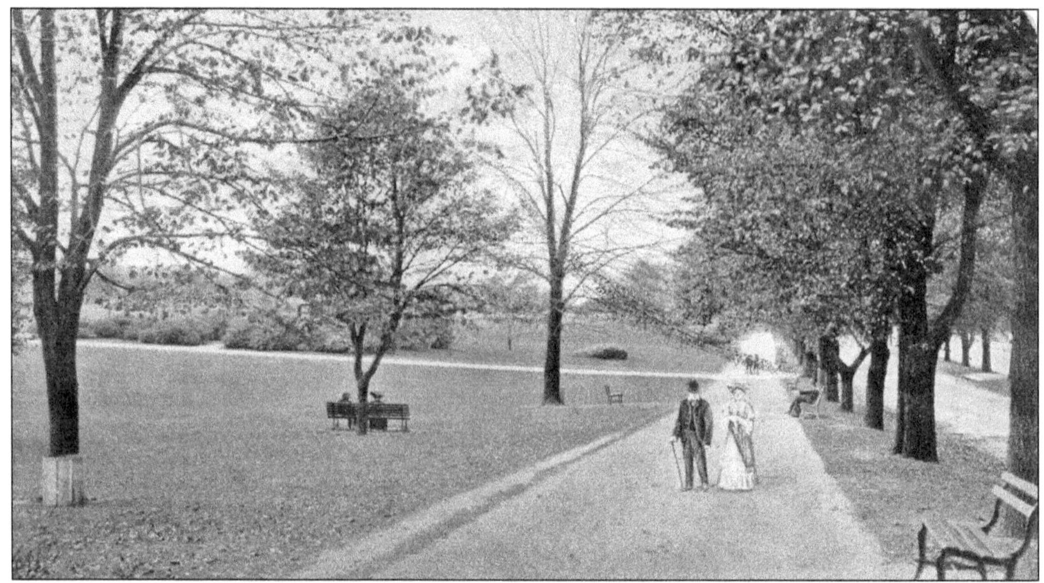

One of three Frederick Law Olmsted parks in Fall River, South Park (now called Kennedy Park) is 57 acres in size, running east and west from South Main Street to Mount Hope Bay. The original plans for the park in 1871 included a parade ground and ball field (known as "the Green"), meandering and looping carriage ways, a stable yard and paddock, a pavilion with terrace, and meadow, all outlined with landscaping and the use of trees as natural boundaries. (Courtesy of Michael Brimbau.)

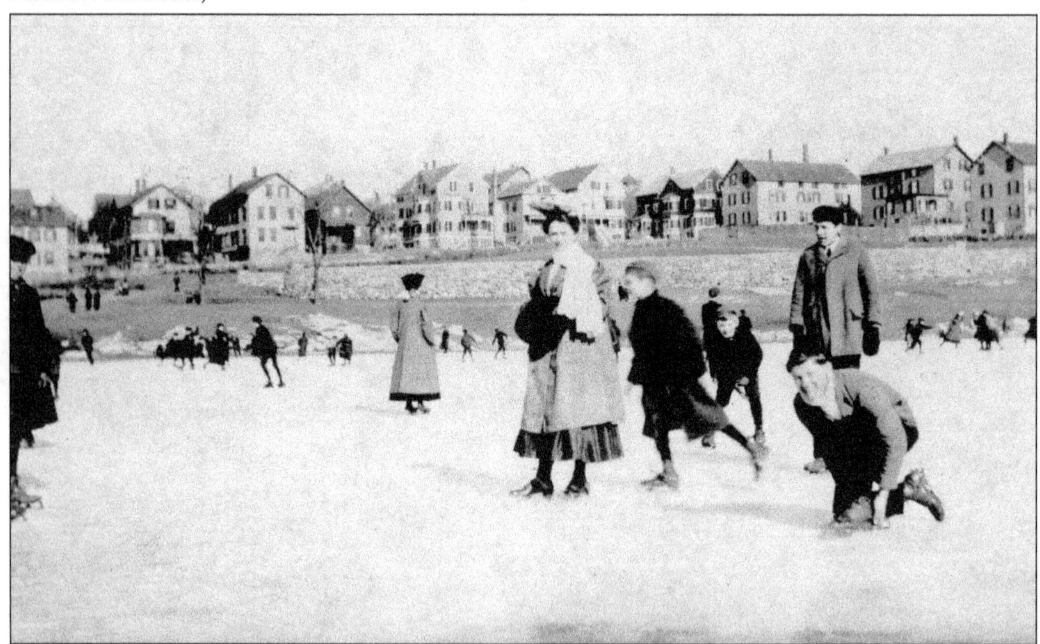

In 1868, the city secured two areas of unimproved land for the purposes of creating a park. The northeast parcel, comprising 15 acres, was known as Ruggles's Grove, and with its natural growth of trees, according to Earl, it "required little if any additional outlay to render it a charming and salubrious resort." This image shows a happy scene of ice-skating on the pond in Ruggles Park in 1916. (Courtesy of Michael Brimbau.)

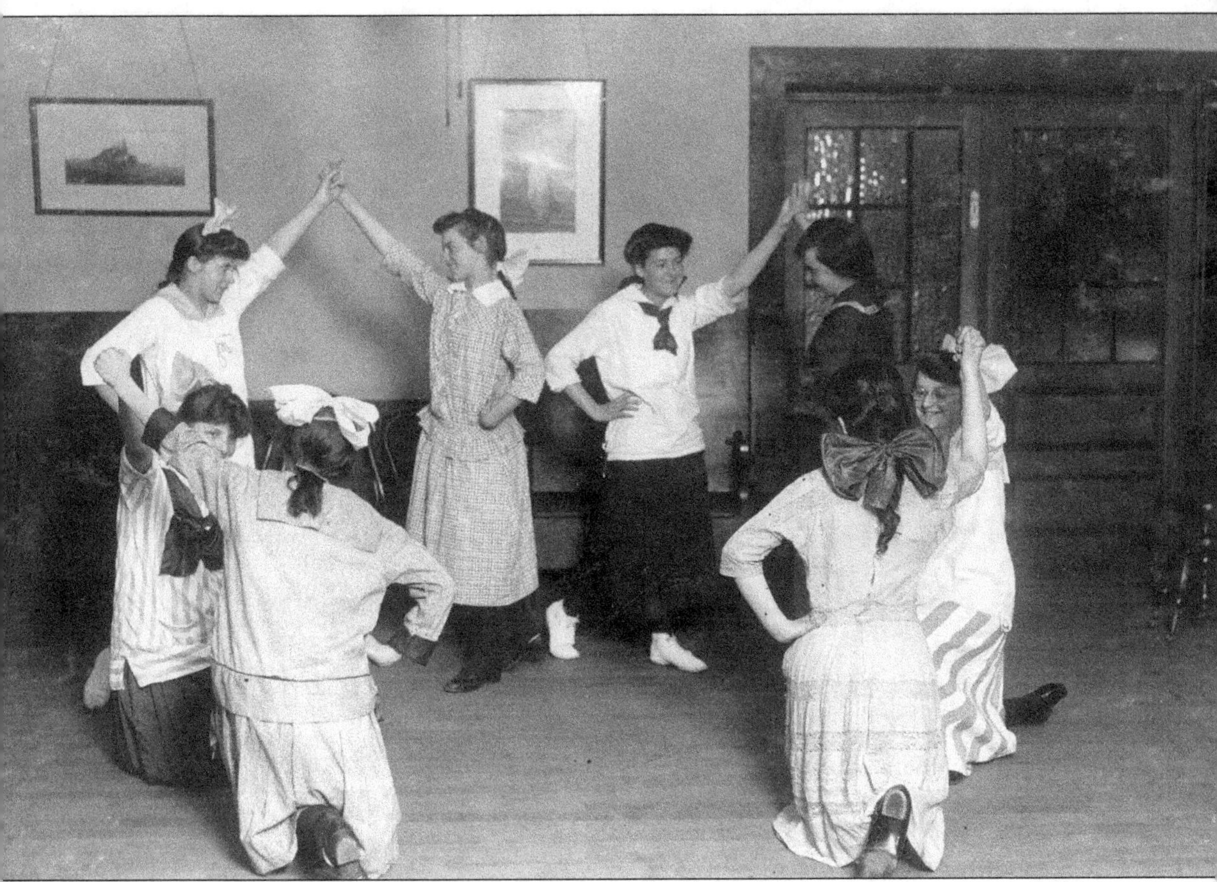

Organized in 1873, the Fall River Women's Union provided the women and girls of the city an opportunity for self-improvement and recreation. A sewing school was added in 1879, and in 1883, it offered classes in millinery, dressmaking, cooking, and gymnastics. By 1909, the union had secured a building for the organization and divided its work into three departments: the House Department, with the aim of furnishing comfortable housing at a moderate cost for the supporting women; the Social Work Department, the center of recreational and educational activities for the women and girls of Fall River; and the Industrial Exchange Department, where women could sell articles of their own making. The Women's Union was organized "to promote the welfare of women and girls, especially those who are dependent upon their own exertions for their support, by providing them at a moderate cost with lodgings, a reading room with good literature, a gymnasium, instruction in sewing, cooking, and other industrial arts, helpful music and social entertainment, and otherwise to aid them and better their condition." (Lewis Hine photograph, courtesy of the Library of Congress.)

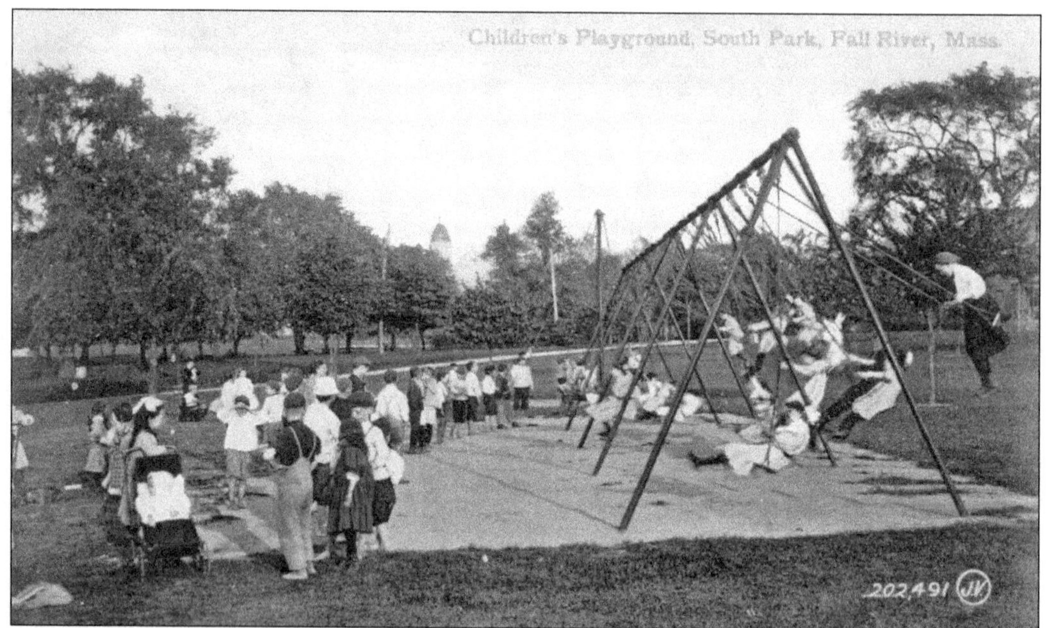

The urban landscape of Fall River is dotted with lovely parks, playgrounds, and walking paths for the enjoyment of its citizens. Forward-thinking city fathers insured that future generations would have a place to recreate that was within a 10-minute walk from any home in the community. The parks of Fall River are vital to the positive well being of its residents and, to that end, are protected, maintained, and, when funds allow, improved. (Courtesy of Michael Brimbau.)

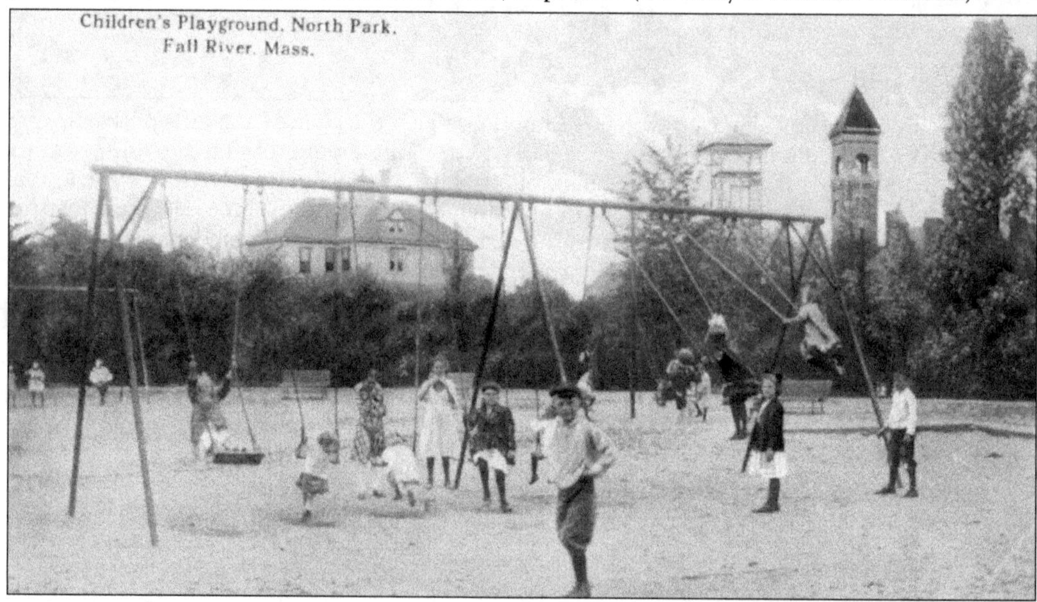

Frederick Law Olmsted was born in Hartford, Connecticut, in 1822. He inherited his love of scenery from his father, John, a successful dry goods merchant, who took the young Frederick on "tours in search of the picturesque" throughout New England after the death of his mother, Charlotte. His career as a landscape architect and conservationist included more than 500 commissions, including 100 public parks and recreational grounds (New York's Central Park is his most famous design). Fall River is proud of its three Olmsted parks. (Courtesy of Michael Brimbau.)

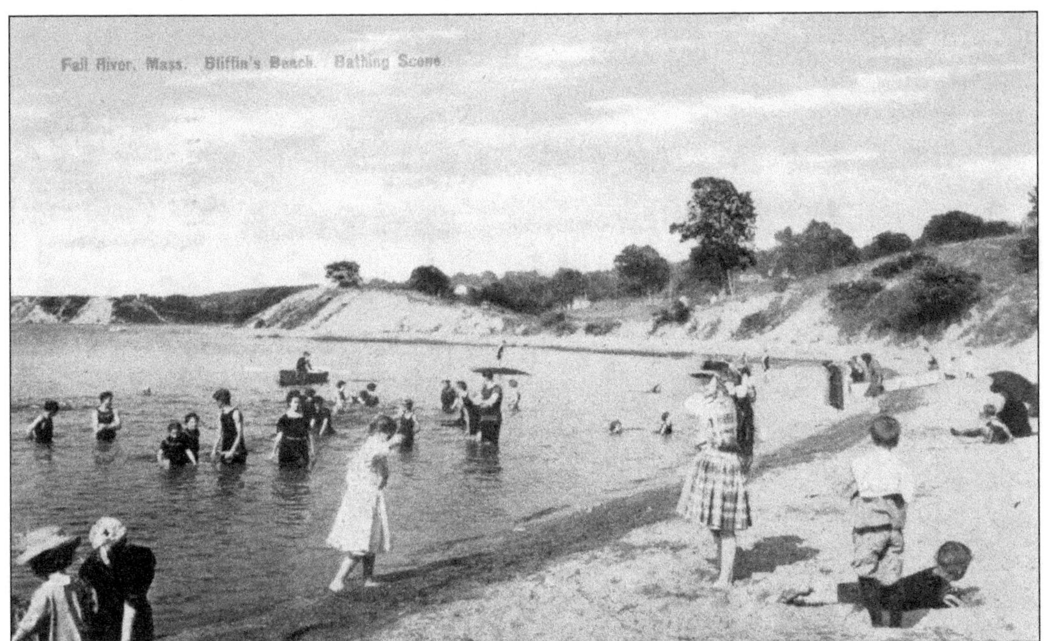

Bliffin's Beach was located in the Steep Brook section of Fall River, in the North End. While it is no longer in existence, the residents who remember it do so fondly. Many a happy hour was spent swimming in the Taunton River. Mary Ann Wordell remembers the following: "There was a diving board, diving platform, three rafts, a handball court, pavilion, concession, and, of course, the jukebox. I sold hot dogs and hamburgers at the concession with my aunt. The beach was closed due to pollution. Bliffin's Beach was an integral part of my childhood as it was for many youngsters growing up in the 1940s and early 1950s." At one time, there were two beaches in this area—Bessie's Beach and Bliffin's Beach (formerly known as Lannigan's Beach, after the name of the owner). (Both, courtesy of Michael Brimbau.)

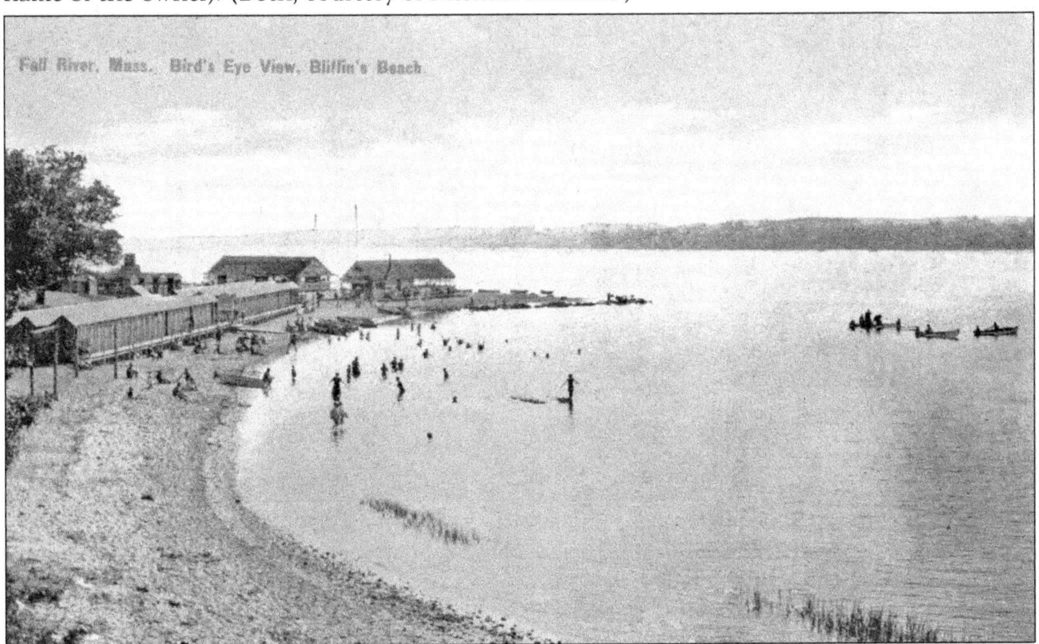

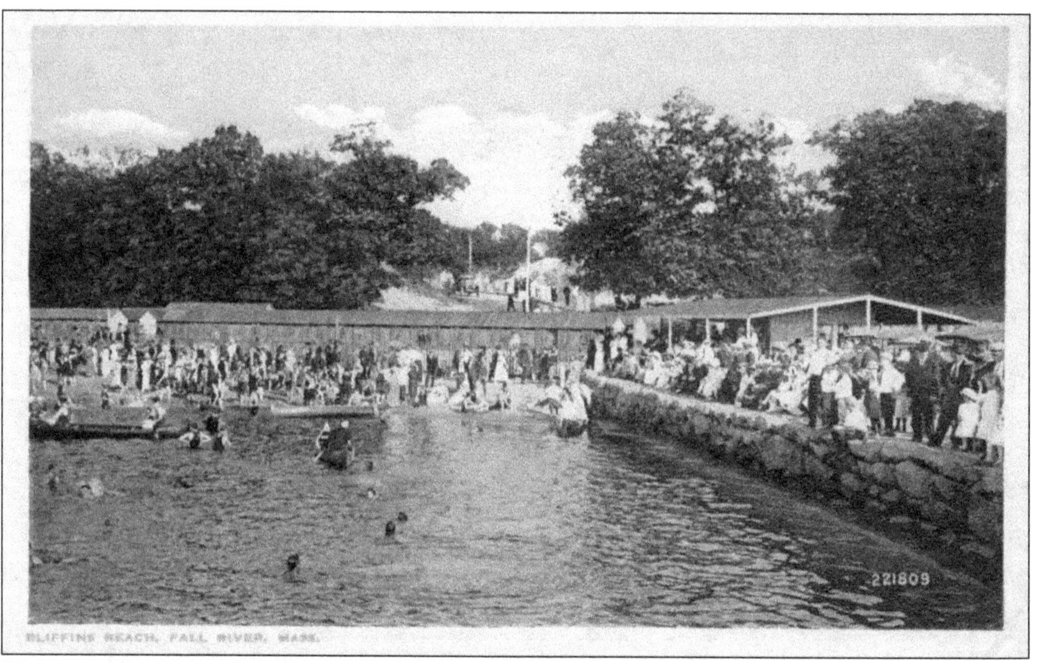

Due to ever-increasing amounts of pollution in the Taunton River, caused by runoff from the mills and poor filtration of sewage, Bliffin's Beach was closed, never to reopen. This postcard is from 1916. (Courtesy of Michael Brimbau.)

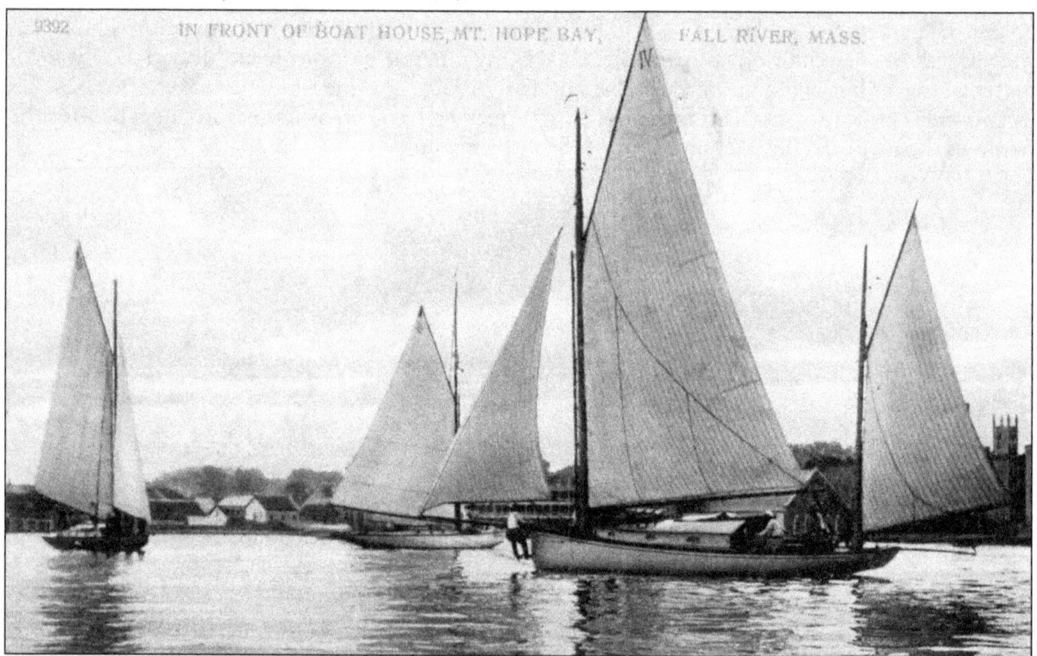

Fall River encompasses some 38 square miles, with 31 square miles of land and 7 of water. The main watershed is North Watuppa Pond, the second-largest natural body of water in Massachusetts. Along with the South Watuppa Pond, it forms the source of the Quequechan River, which runs, now underground for a great deal of its length, to the tidewater at Mount Hope Bay. (Courtesy of Michael Brimbau.)

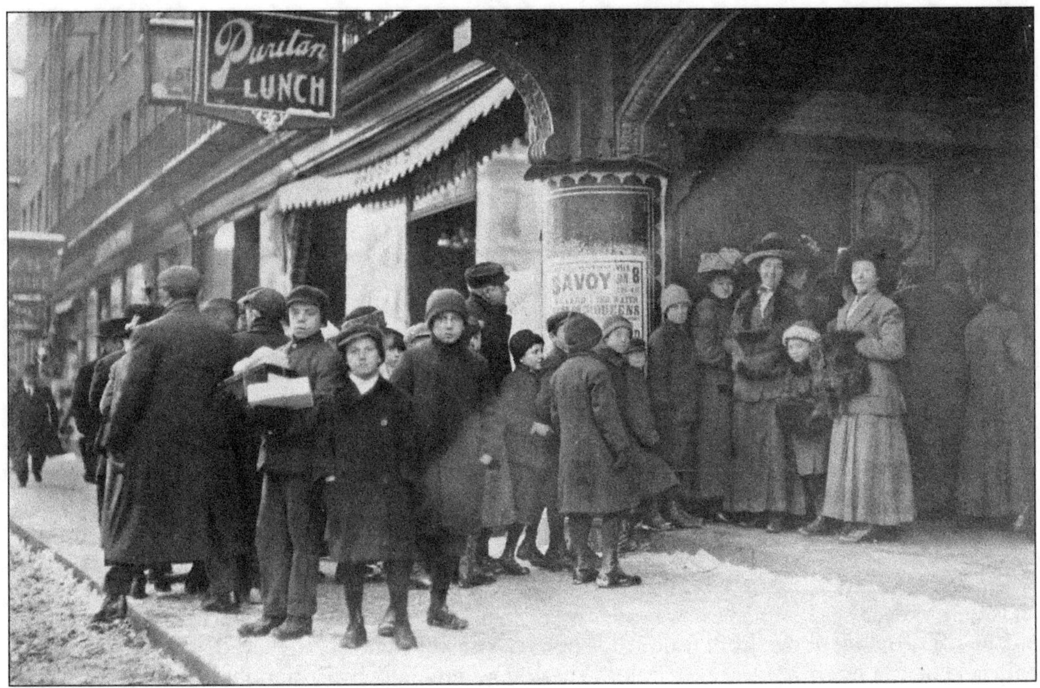

At one time, Fall River was a stop on the theater circuit, and some of the best-known entertainers and actors played at the Durfee Theatre on North Main (across from the Eagle Restaurant). It was demolished in 1973 to make way for a Bank of America. Here is a long line at a vaudeville show at an unidentified theater in 1912. (Lewis Hine photograph, courtesy of the Library of Congress.)

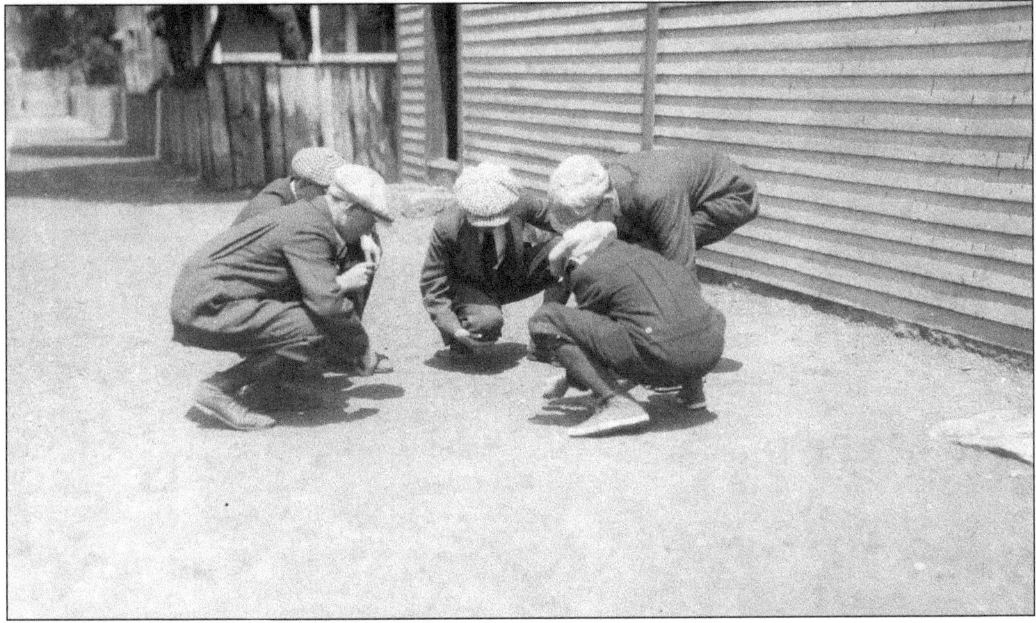

These 14-to-16-year-old mill boys are shooting craps on a Sunday near the King Philip Mill on Tuttle Street in 1916. A one-piece suit of clothes with a checkered cap seems to be some sort of mill uniform, as this garment repeatedly appears in images by Lewis Hine that are annotated as "mill boys." (Lewis Hine photograph, courtesy of the Library of Congress.)

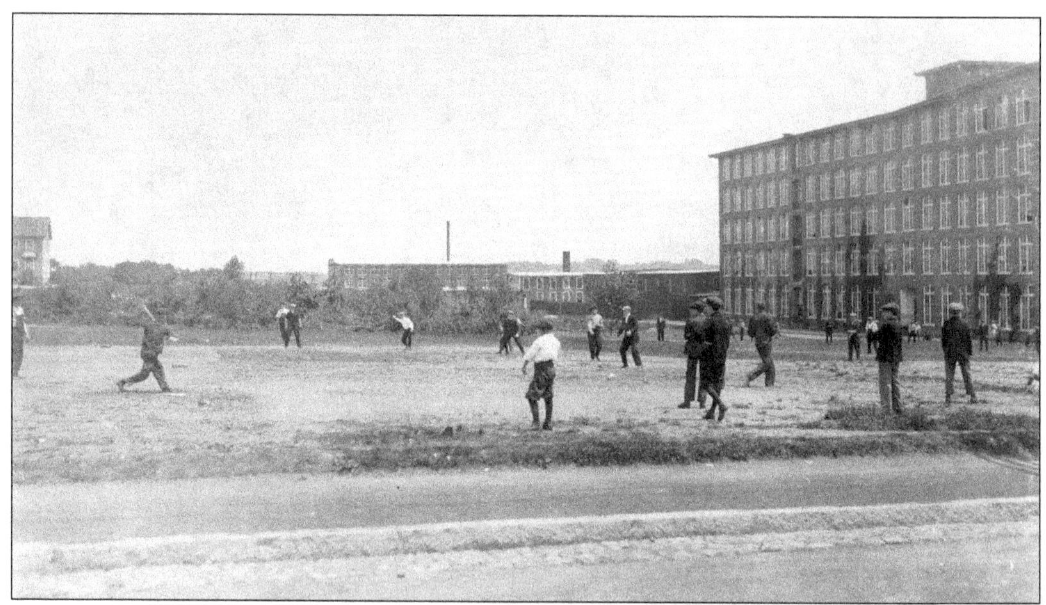

Kids will forever be inventing ways to blow off steam and create play in between more serious pursuits. The image above from June 1916 shows a baseball game being played at the Kerr Thread ball field at the noon hour break. Below, these boys are enjoying a handball game. According to the photographer, they are "probably not working boys." While not depicted here, "peggy" ball was a street game that was wildly popular in Fall River. All that was needed to play were a wooden ball and a stick. The ball was placed on a small seesaw, popped into the air by stomping on the elevated side, and then hit as far as possible. The object was to be the one to hit the ball the farthest. (Both, Lewis Hine photographs, courtesy of the Library of Congress.)

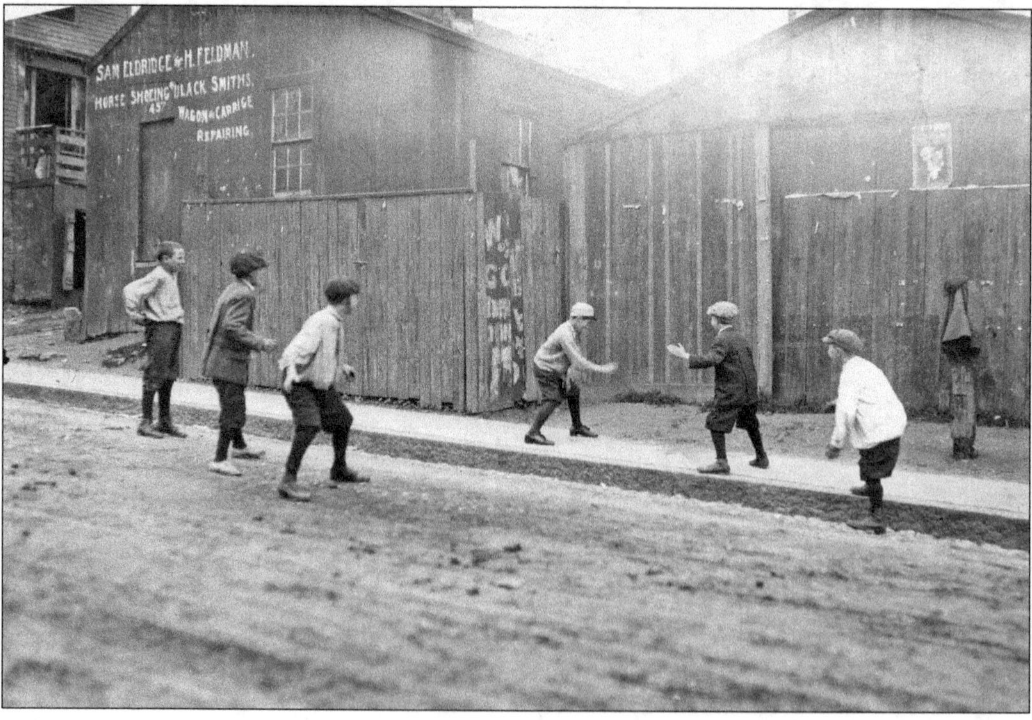

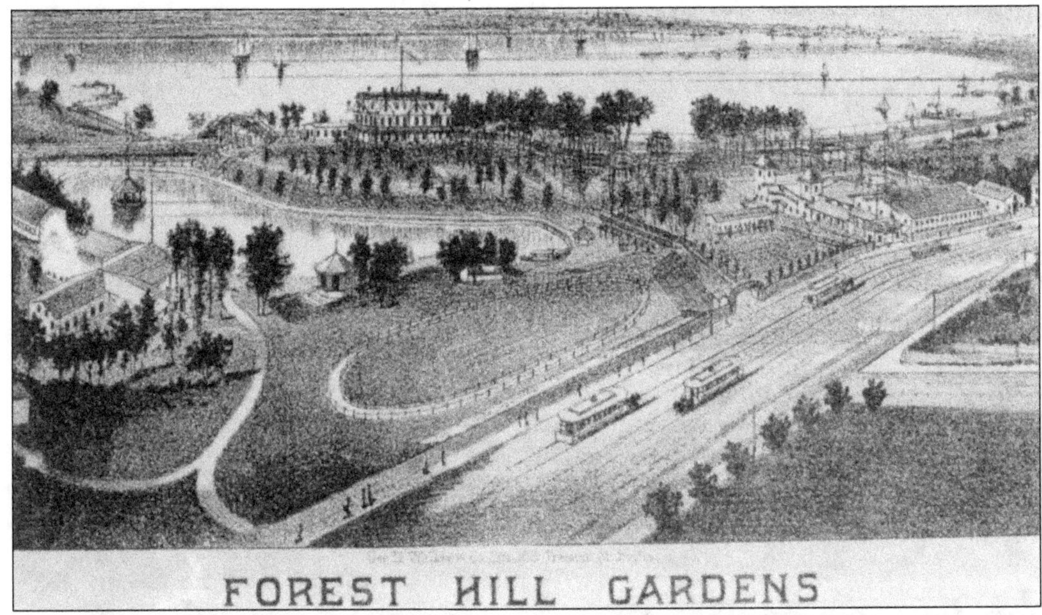

Forest Hill Gardens was the brainchild of George F. Mellen, its president and general manager. Located in the Steep Brook section of Fall River, on the former Ashley's Grove, it was well equipped for recreational tourists, with a hotel, skating rink, dance hall, amusement hall, restaurant, clam house, and a pond filled with saltwater drawn from the Taunton River. Mellen ran Forest Hill Gardens at a loss in 1881 and sold it at auction. The original stockholders took over and operated it in 1882 and 1883, also without a profit. They sold the land and buildings to Bishop Hendricken, who converted the hotel in 1885 into St. Vincent's Home, an orphanage run by the Sisters of Mercy for the "English-speaking Catholics of Fall River." (Both, courtesy of Bill Goncalo.)

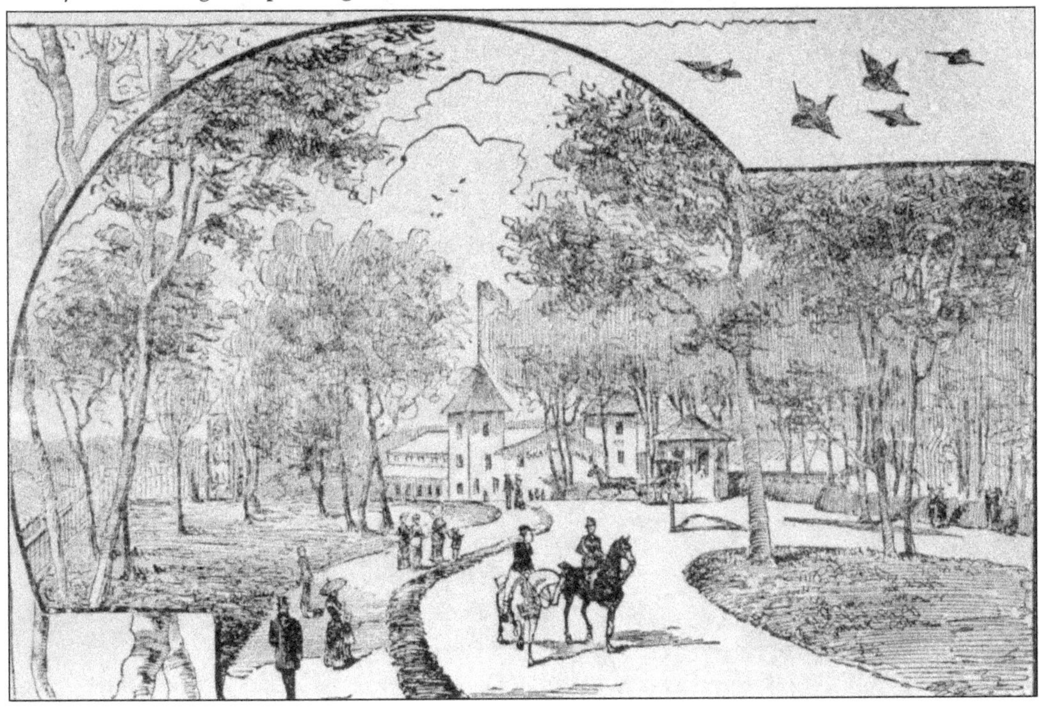

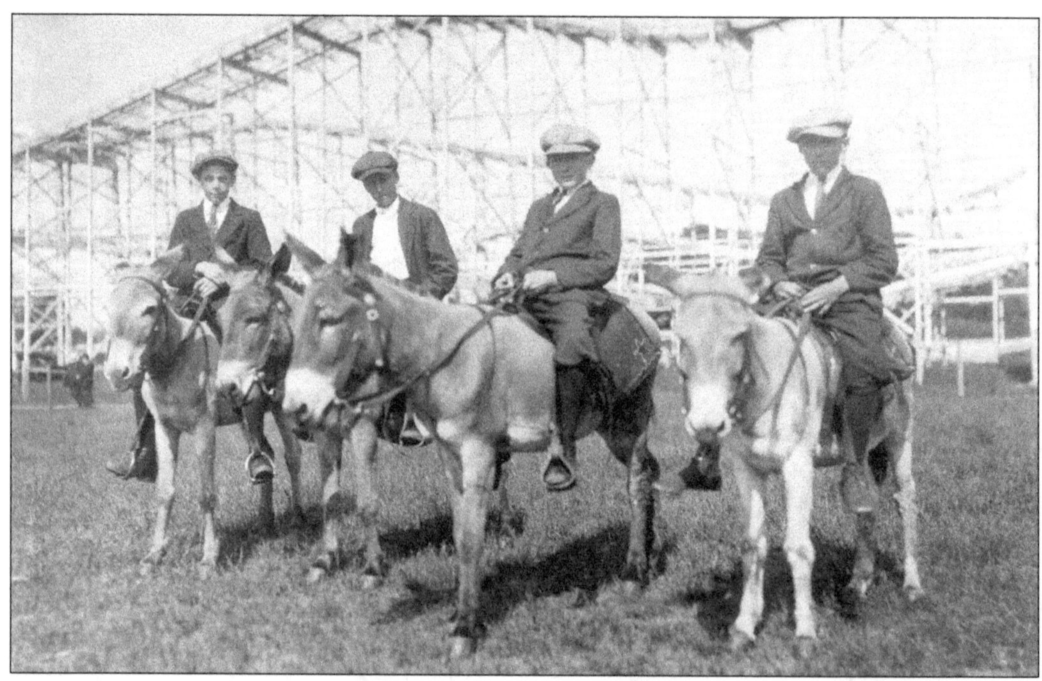

Sandy Beach provided the residents of the area with a wonderful place to relax and enjoy the shoreline of Mount Hope Bay. In addition to the beach, there was a swimming area and an amusement park that included a roller coaster. These images from 1916 show a little bit of what it must have been like to enjoy a Sunday at Sandy Beach. A popular destination, Sandy Beach could be reached by trolley from practically anywhere in the city. (Both, Lewis Hine photographs, courtesy of the Library of Congress.)

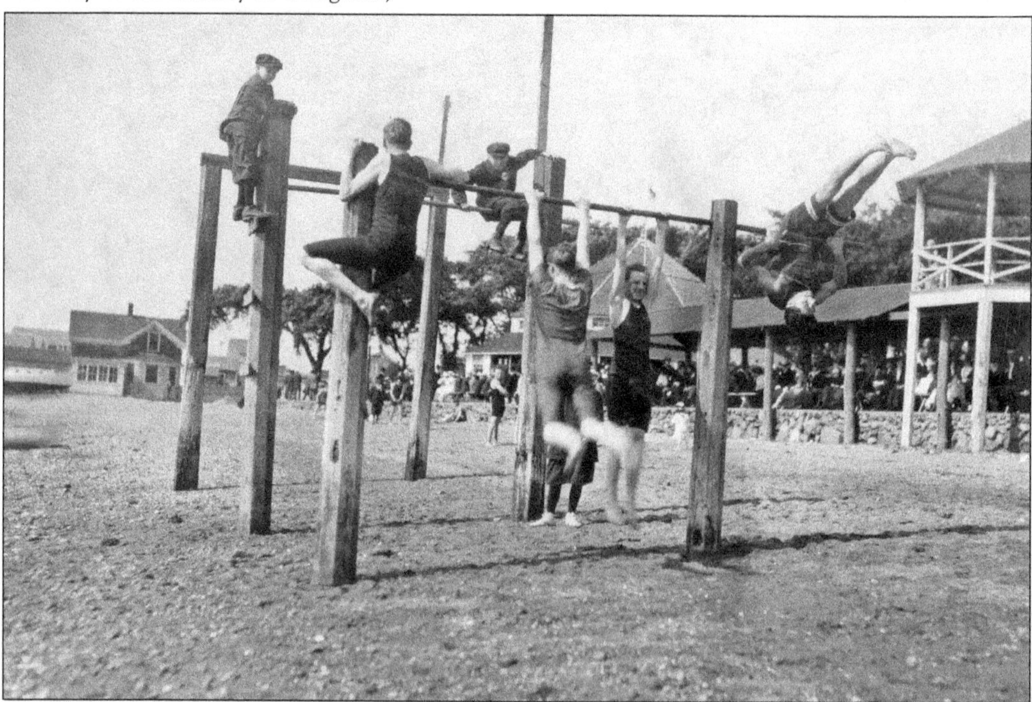

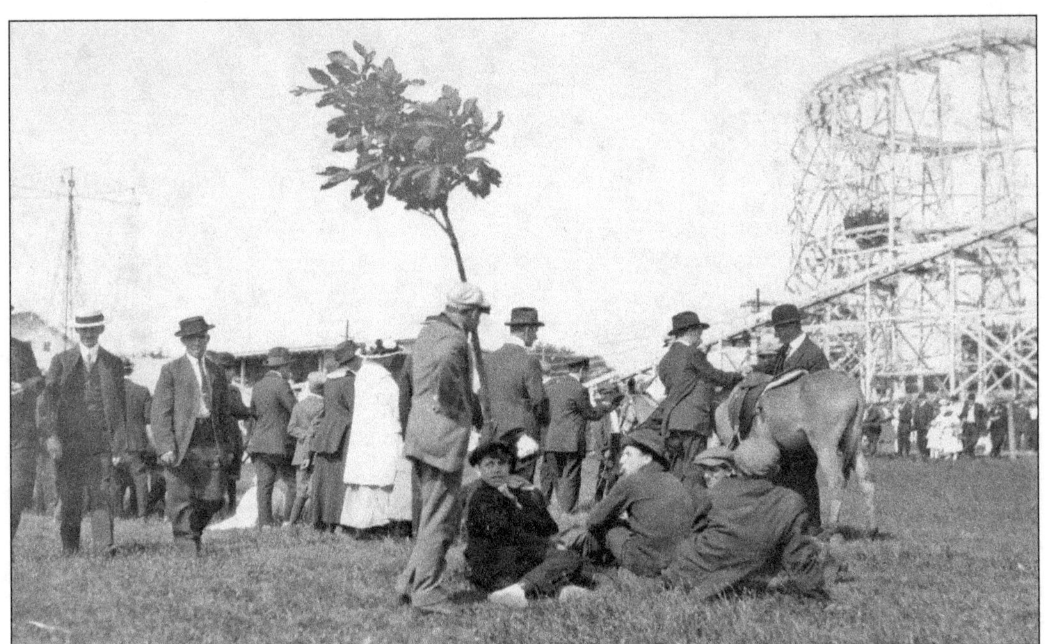

Sandy Beach was located in the South End of Fall River, where the sewerage disposal and treatment plant sits in 2012. It provided all-around amusement, including a large dance hall, located west of and alongside the railroad tracks. On May 10, 1930, the dance hall caught fire, completely destroying it as well as the bathhouse and hotel. Alleging that the fire started from a spark from a passing locomotive, the owners, Alvaro Dubois and his family, sued the New Haven Railroad. The courts eventually found that the dance hall was indeed set ablaze by a spark. It had been a hot day, and the shingles on the building were very dry from being heated by the sun. The fire began on the roof, according to a neighbor who testified that she had seen the fire start after a locomotive had gone by. (Both, Lewis Hine photographs, courtesy of the Library of Congress.)

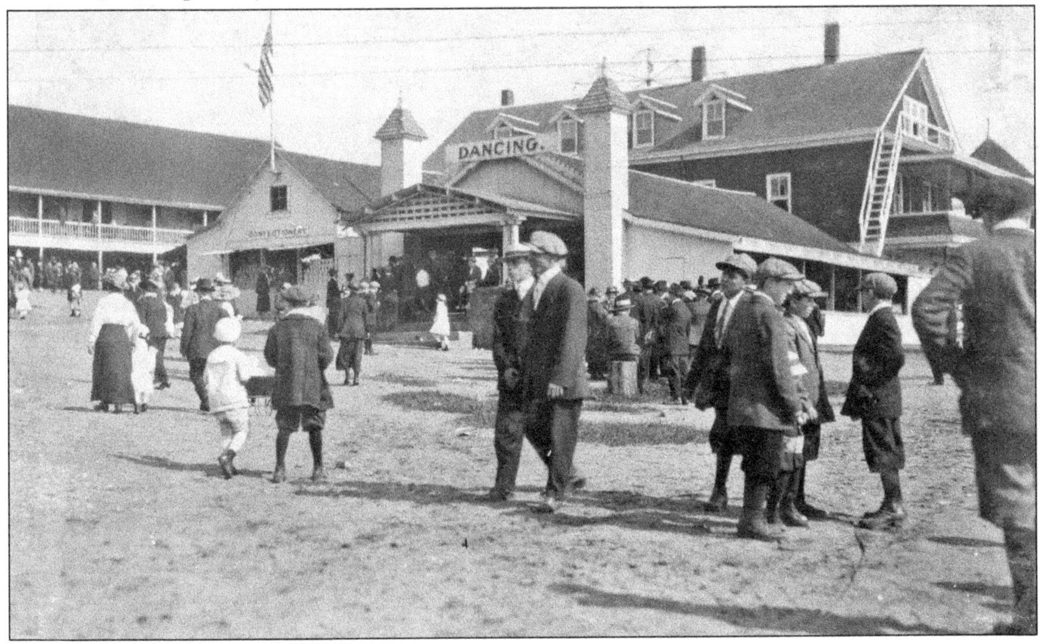

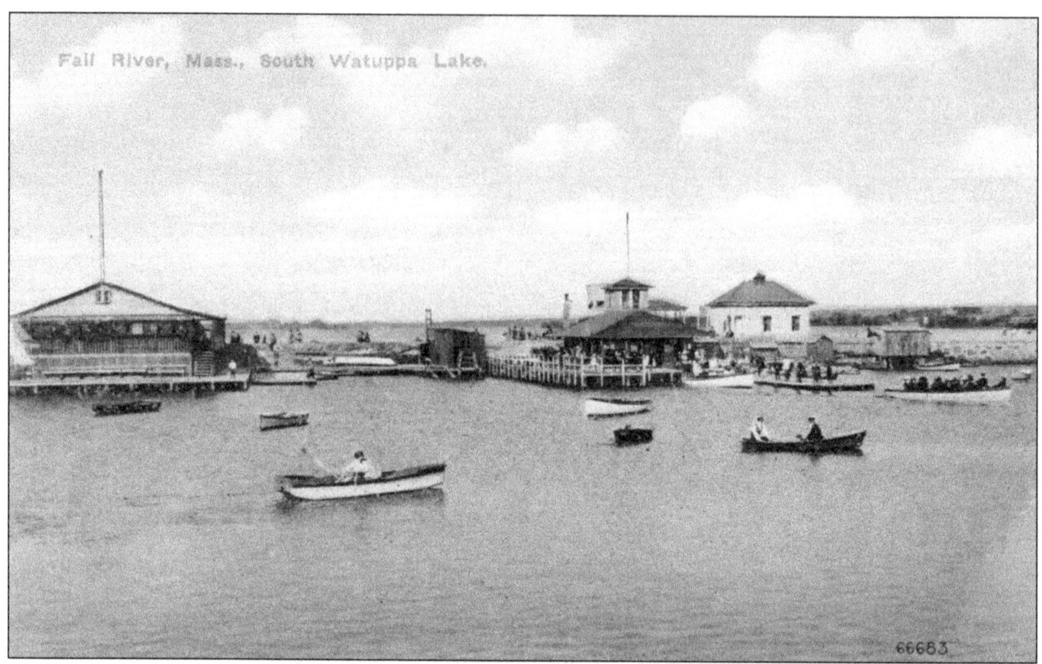

These rowboats are located in an area that was called Middle Pond, a body of water that was situated between the railroad bridge and the causeway (Pleasant Street) leading to Westport, Massachusetts. During the winter months, when the water was frozen, Middle Pond was a popular ice-skating location. (Courtesy of Michael Brimbau.)

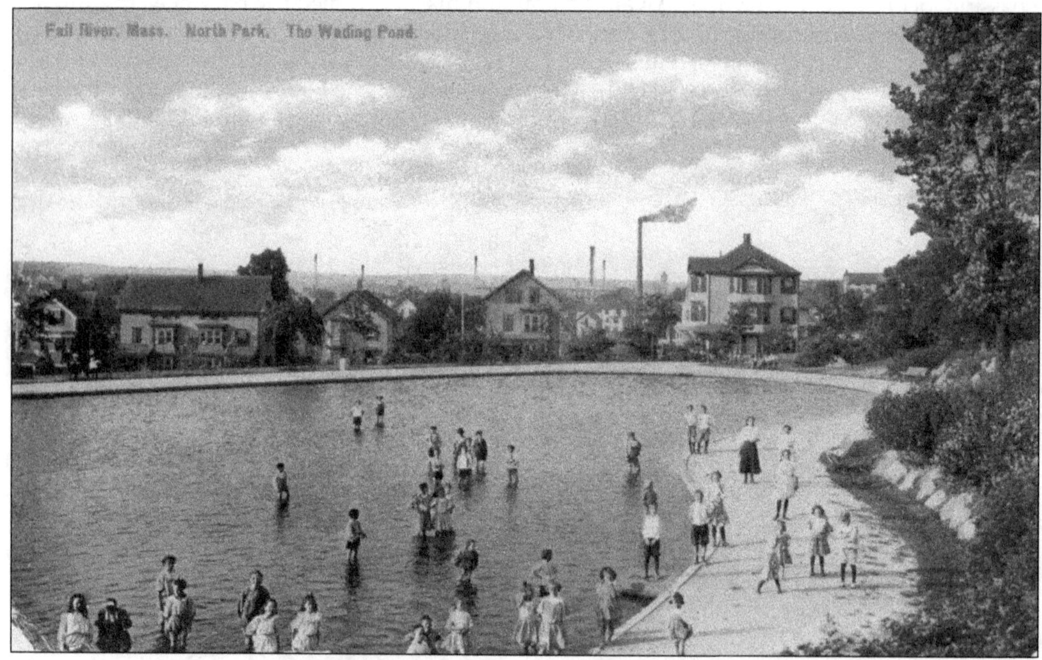

The wading pools that were located in both North and South Park were an opportunity for folks to cool down on a hot day. In the winter months, the pools would become ice-skating rinks, and many a hockey game was played on their surfaces. Neither pool is in operation any longer, and the space is now mostly used by skateboarders. (Courtesy of Michael Brimbau.)

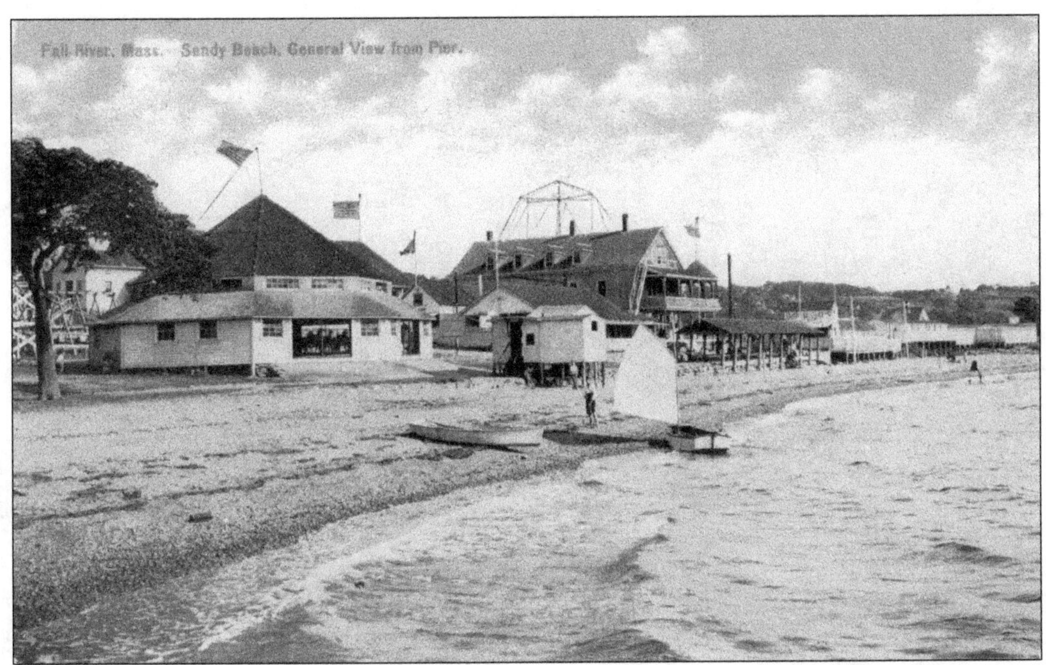

Sunday was the most popular day to visit Sandy Beach in the summertime, and it was known as a great place for picnics, getting a tan, swimming in Mount Hope Bay, dancing, and hanging out with friends. The hurricane of 1938 ruined what was left of the park and beach after the fire of 1930 had destroyed the buildings. The storm caused serious erosion of the shoreline all along its path. Just like so many other former beach areas in Fall River, Sandy Beach lives only in the childhood memories of some. (Both, courtesy of Michael Brimbau.)

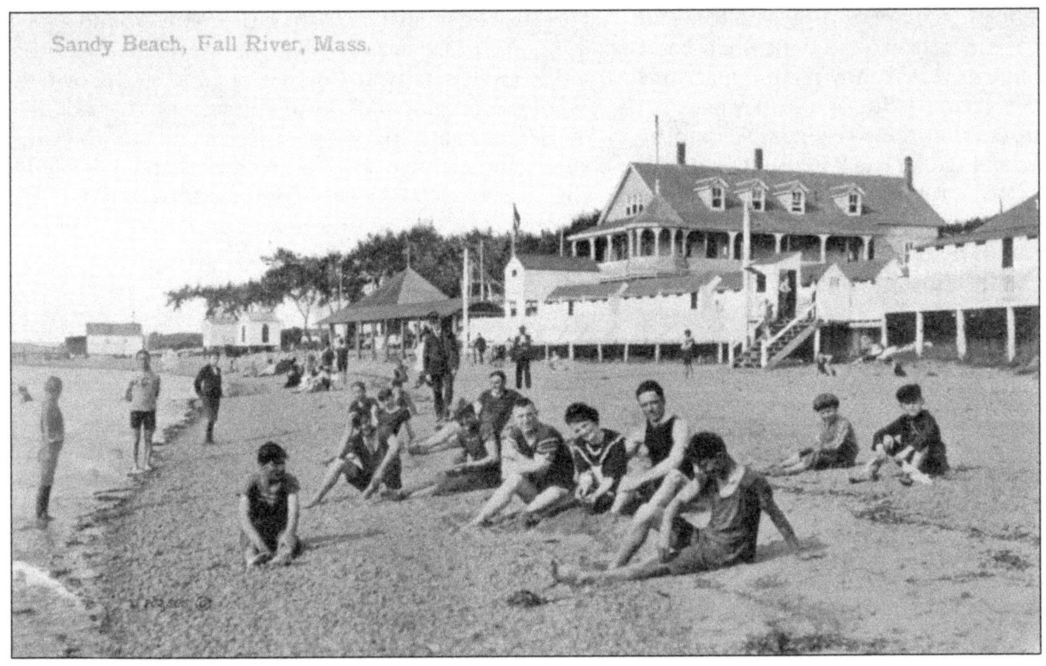

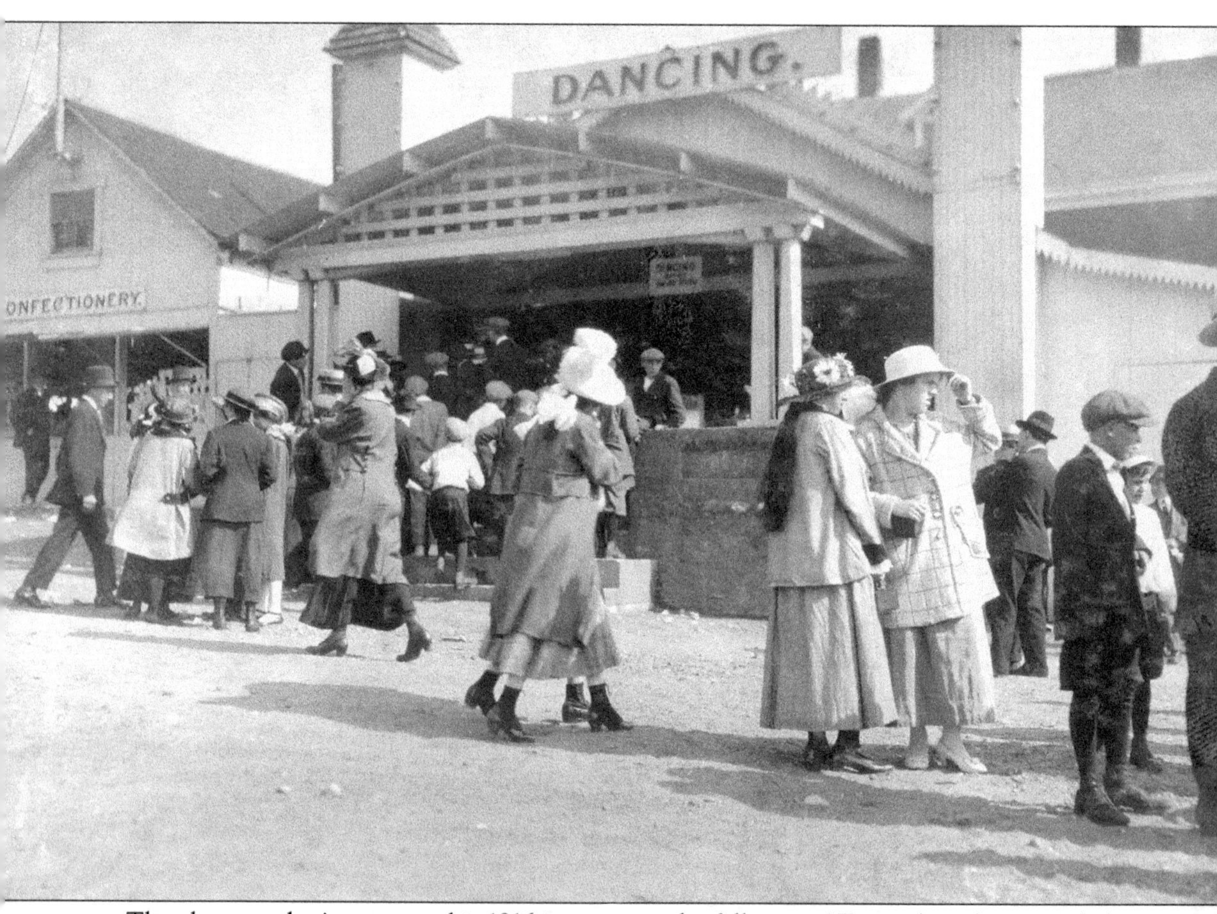

The photographer's notes on this 1916 image state the following: "Two girls in foreground about 15. Mr. Tebbutt says dance hall bad conditions. Saturday evening dancing would be about the same as this. Penny picture machine attracting crowds." Sandy Beach was built by the owners of the trolley line as a trolley park at the end of the line in an effort to entice people to ride the trolleys on the weekends. According to amusement park historians, these small trolley parks accounted for the large number of roller coasters and amusement rides in cities at the turn of the 20th century. Sandy Beach had a figure-eight roller coaster, the most common type found in the trolley parks, but instead of a train of connected cars, this coaster used four-person individual cars. The only remaining figure eight-roller coaster from this era is in Altoona, Pennsylvania. (Lewis Hine photograph, courtesy of the Library of Congress.)

Five

To and Fro (Trolleys, Trains, Ships, and Cars)

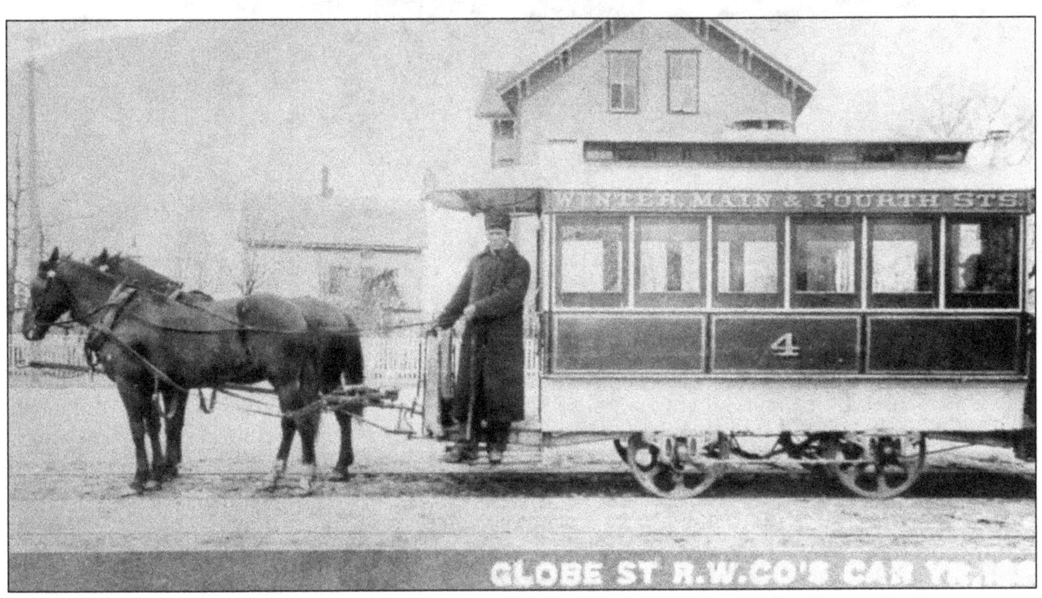

In 1891, the Board of Aldermen voted to grant permission to the Globe Street Railway to use the streets of the city to erect poles and wires for the "moving of cars by electric power. The right to use additional streets for the extension of tracks was also granted." By 1894, the Globe Street Railway had 25.29 miles of line, 88 cars, 92 motors, and 8 horses, carried 4,475,720 passengers, and had gross earnings of $222,294. (Courtesy of Michael Brimbau.)

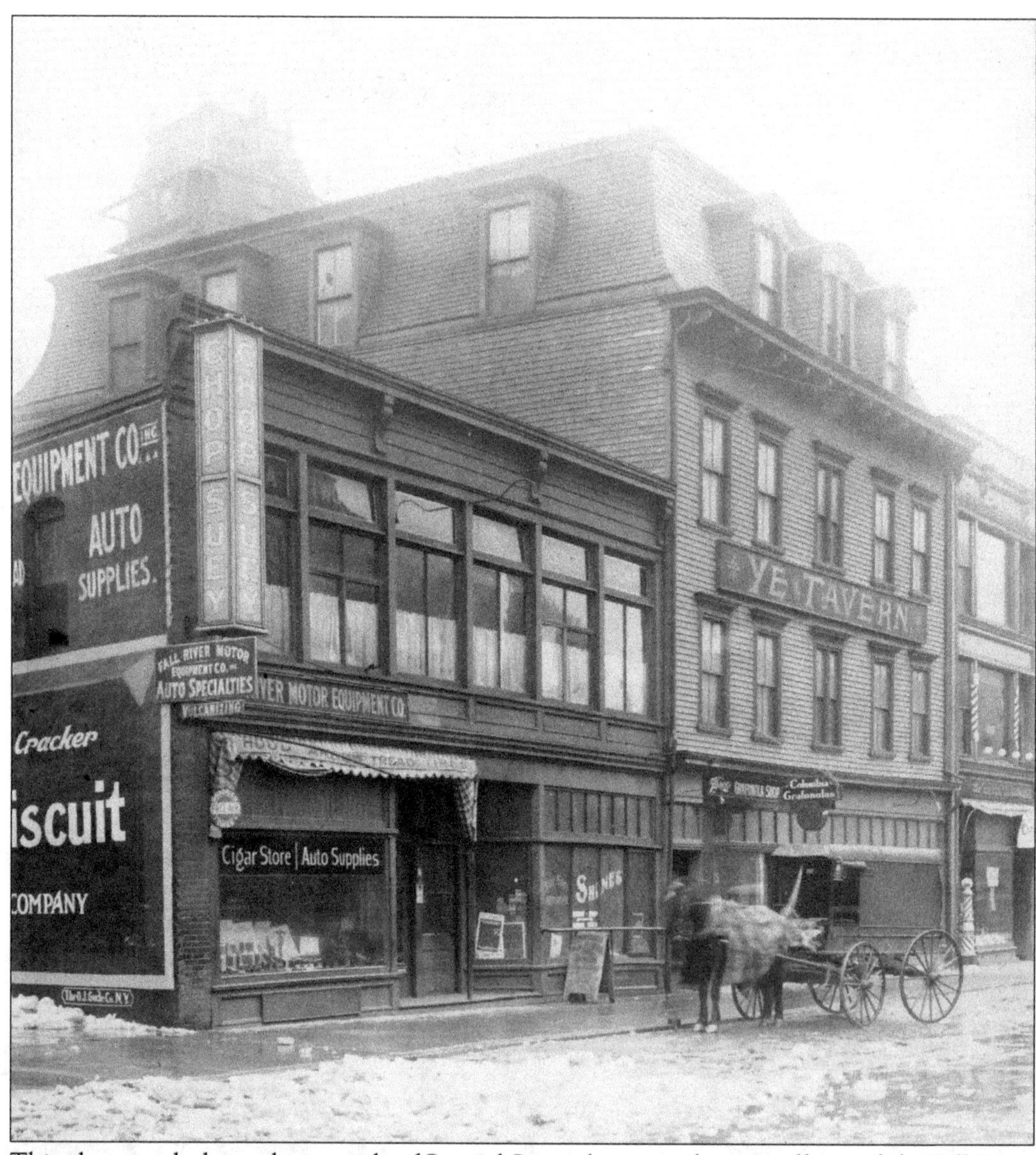

This photograph shows the east side of Second Street, between the post office and the Fall River Fire Station, in the winter. Note the first storefront, the Fall River Motor Equipment Company, which advertises that it carries auto supplies and cigars (an interesting combination of goods). And yet, outside of this establishment is parked a horse-drawn wagon. Well into the 20th century, horses shared the roads with automobiles in Fall River as that mode of transportation was more economically viable for the delivery and conveyance of goods. And since many residents still stabled their own horses on their property, it would be quite some time before the horse, as a mode of transportation, would become obsolete. (Courtesy of the Fall River Historical Society.)

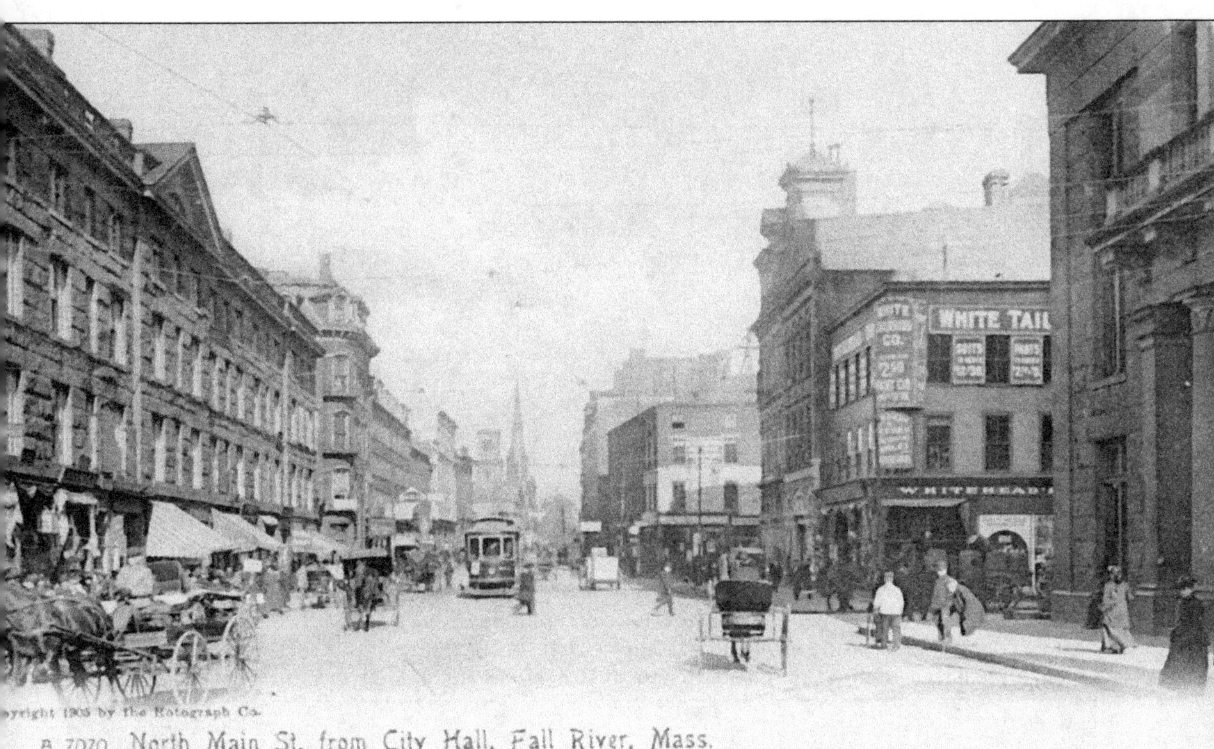

This c. 1904 view of Main Street perfectly depicts the juxtaposition of the old and the new as it relates to transportation. Here, in front of the old city hall and Granite Block, one can find electric trolleys, used for mass transportation, and the individual horse-drawn conveyance, used for business and pleasure. In addition, pedestrians are seen going about their business, offering a glimpse into a time that fell between two eras. This would last well into the 1920s, as an economic downturn starting in the early part of that decade made it impossible for many to own their own automobiles. (Courtesy of Michael Brimbau.)

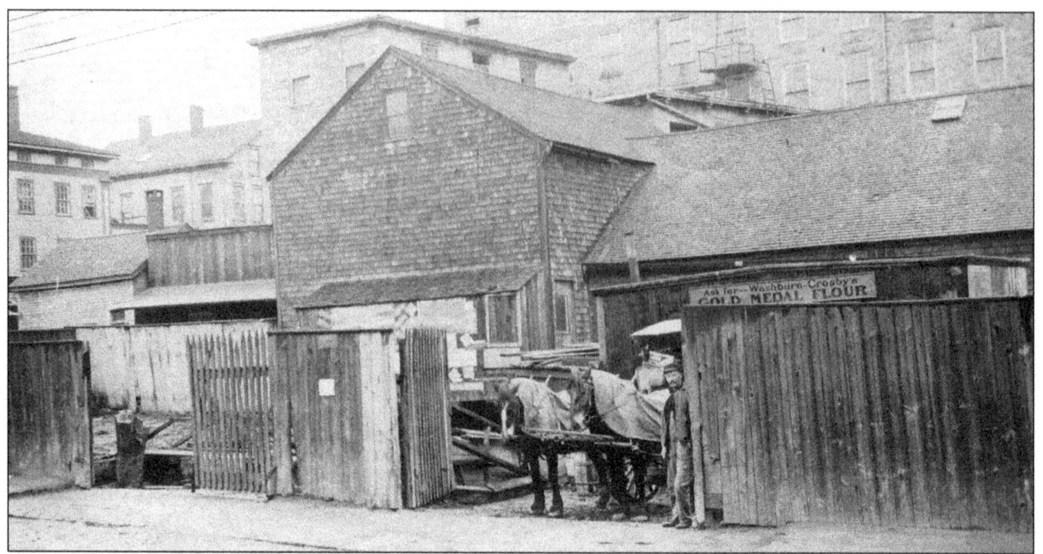

Prior to inhabiting a new building in 1906 is the former Allen, Slade & Co. on the east side of Third Street. As a purveyor of wholesale groceries, the company used horse-drawn wagons for pickup and delivery of goods and services. To facilitate their bottom line, businesses would often have a stable on site to feed and house their teams. (Courtesy of the Fall River Historical Society.)

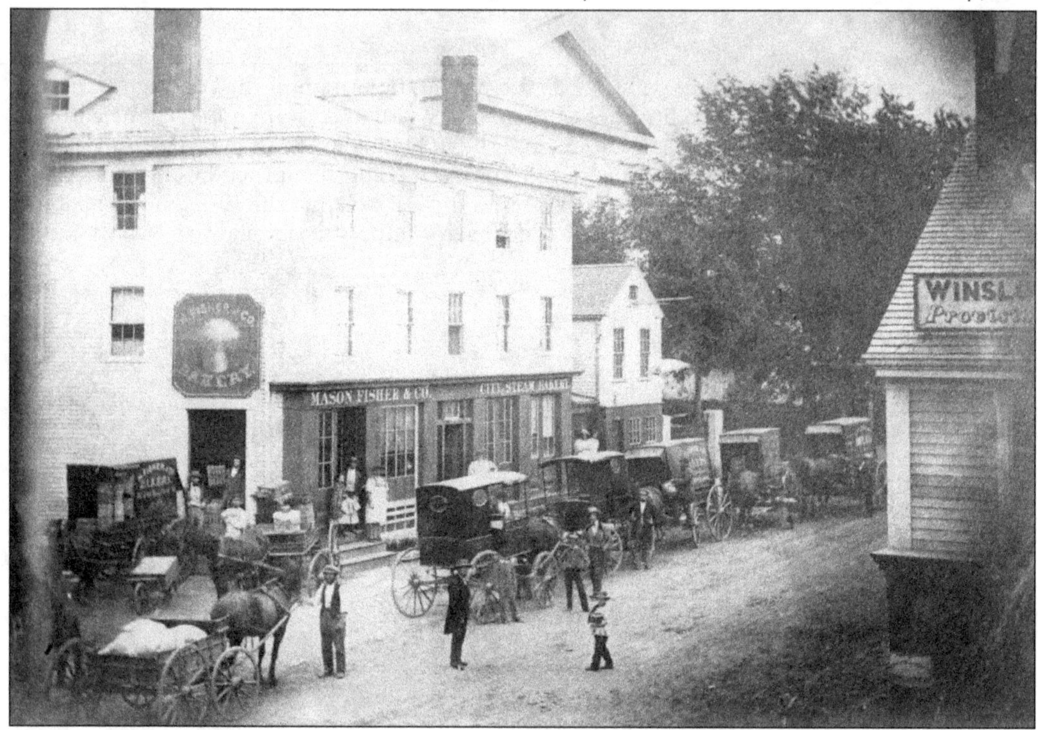

This very early shot of the northeast corner of Bedford and Purchase Streets shows the Mason Fisher & Company Bakery and the Central Congregational Church beyond. It is early morning, and the wagons line up for their day's transport. Bread and other such baked goods were delivered to the home in days before the supermarket, as were milk, butter, and ice. (Courtesy of the Fall River Historical Society.)

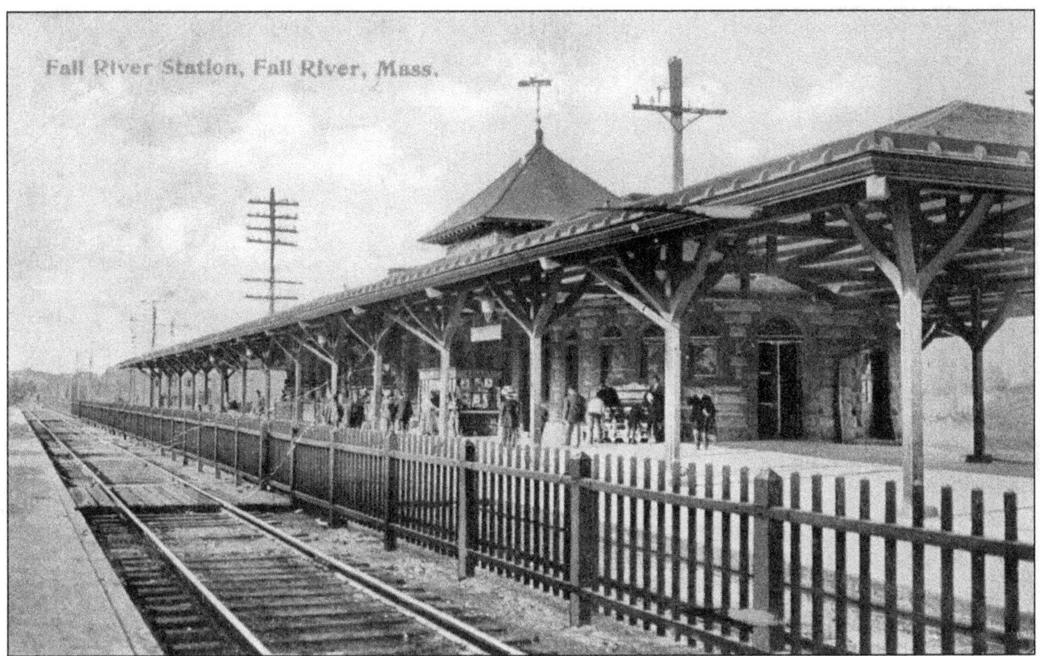

The postcard above depicts the rear, or train side, of the main train station in Fall River, located on North Main Street, across from Lincoln Avenue. The station was torn down in the late 1950s to make way for an A&P supermarket, and the site is now home to an AutoZone. The postcard below is the front of the same station. The first railroad servicing Fall River was the Fall River Branch Railroad in 1845. Author Harold Clarkin states that the station was located south of Central Street "at a point under the south end of the present viaduct" and ran to Myricks, in Berkley, Massachusetts. It was begun with capital from the Fall River Iron Works and local citizens. (Both, courtesy of Michael Brimbau.)

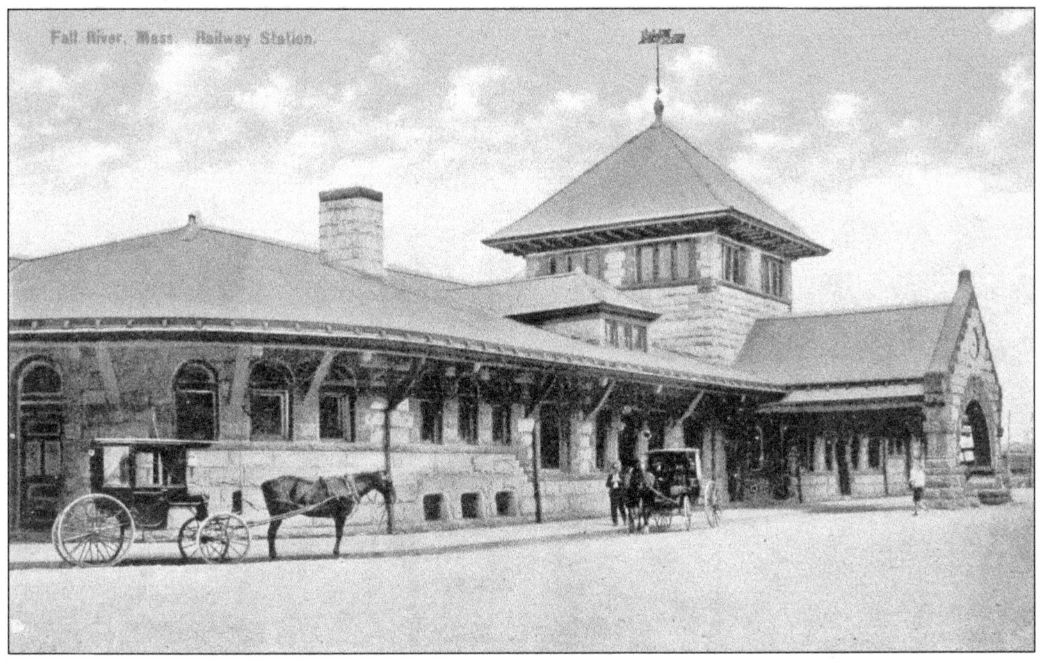

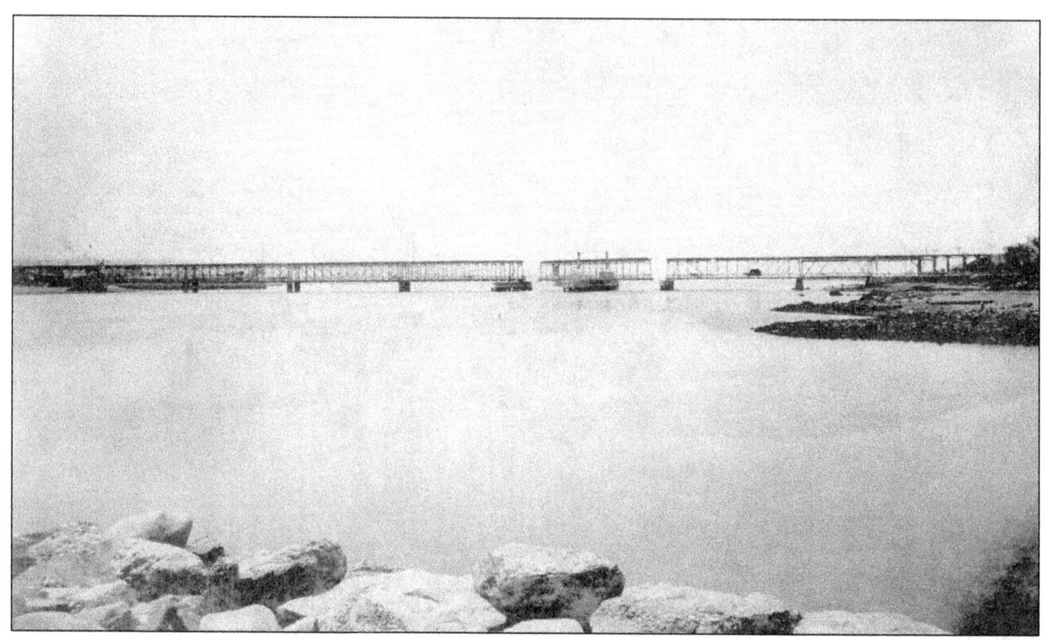

Slade's Ferry Bridge opened to the public on January 4, 1876. At 955 feet long and 20 feet wide, it cost $305,000 and was paid for by the Old Colony Railroad Company. The first train crossed it on December 6, 1875. Prior to the bridge's completion, a ferry maintained by the Slade family was used to transport people, goods, and supplies across the Taunton River to Somerset. The transport evolved from rowboat, to sailboat, and then a boat propelled by horses in 1826. Still later, before the bridge was built, a steamer was used to traverse the river. (Both, courtesy of Michael Brimbau.)

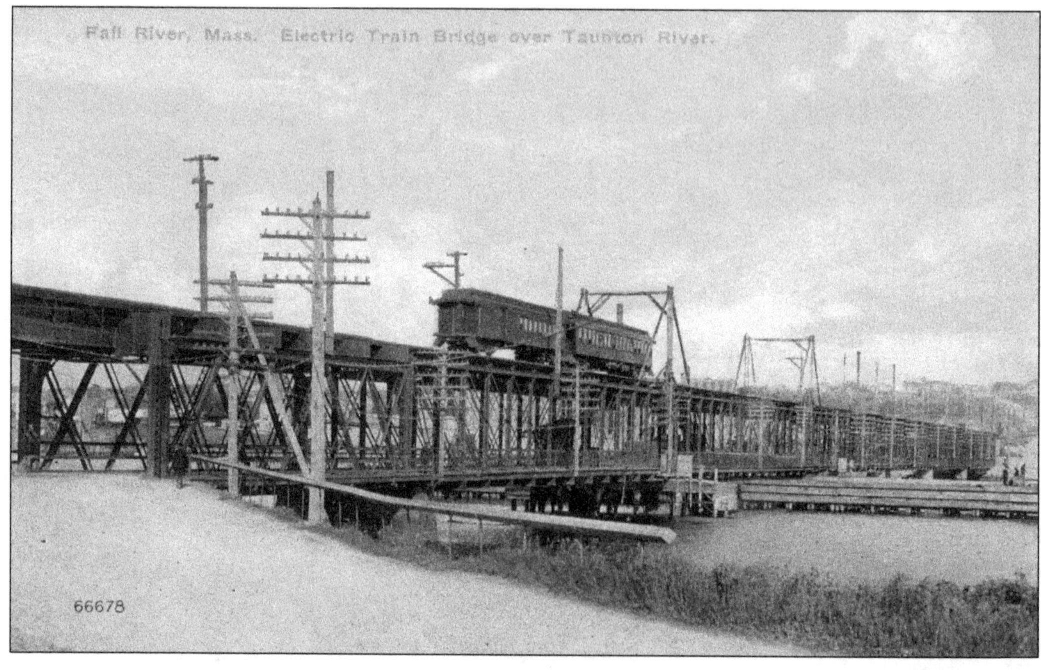

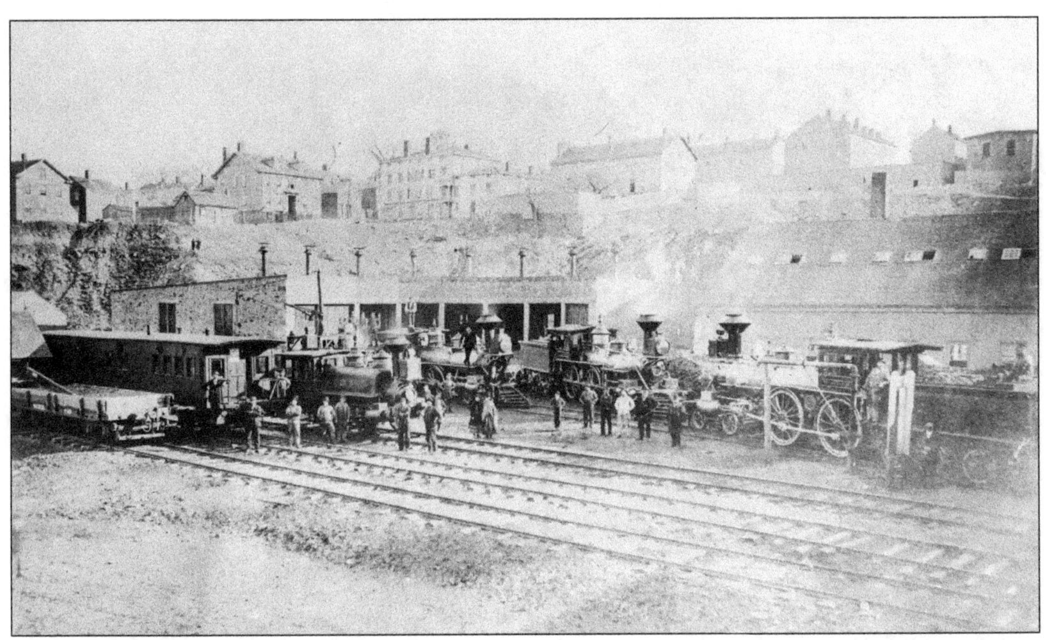

The first railroad station built in Fall River was located, according to Harold Clarkin, "south of Central Street at a point under the south end of the present viaduct." First used in September 1845, it was 180 feet in length, 75 feet wide, and two stories high. This early photograph (above) is of the original roundhouse (where the engines were stored and turned around), located northeast of the station on the south side of Central Street and east of the viaduct. It was used until 1870 and was replaced by the structure seen below (next to the Metacomet Mill), a larger roundhouse that was erected at the bottom of Division Street on Diamond Street. It was torn down in 1926. (Both, courtesy of the Fall River Historical Society.)

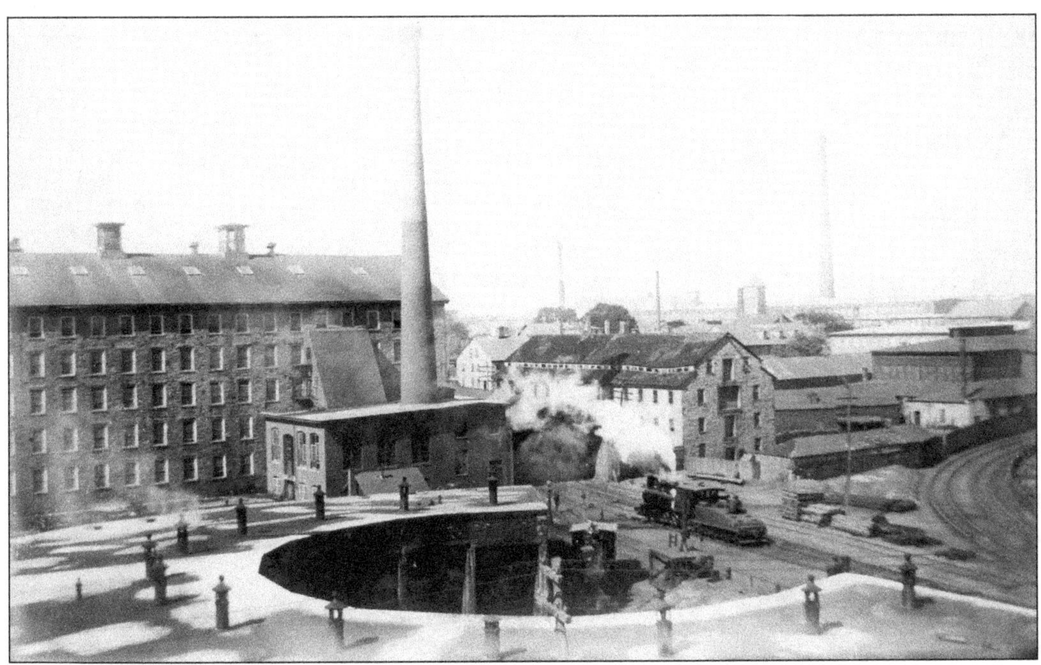

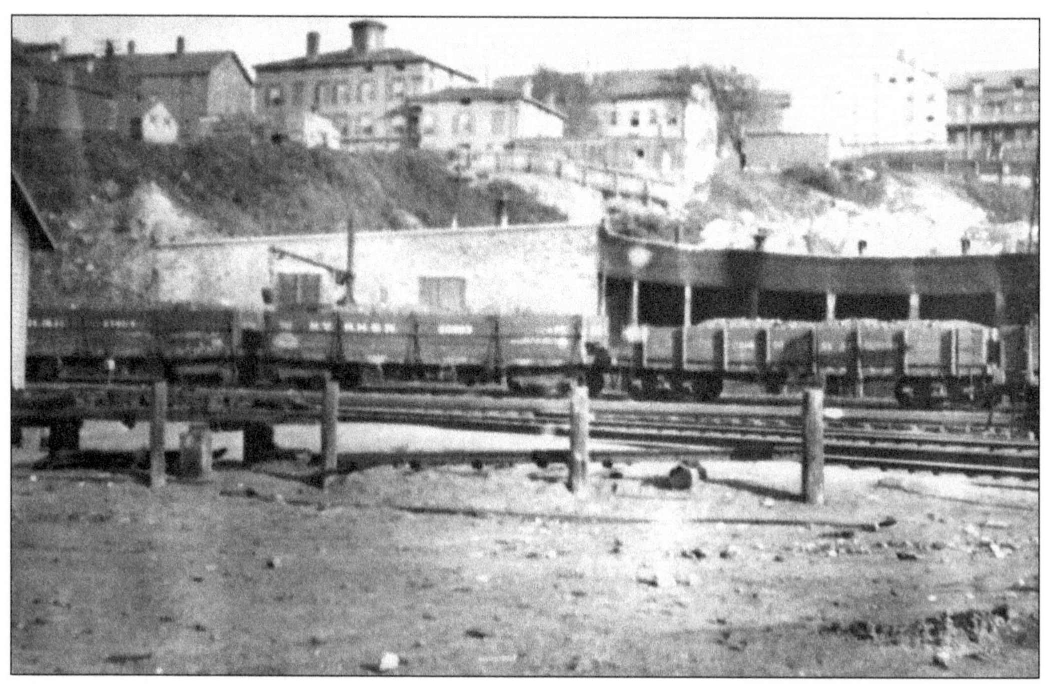

Above is another view, looking easterly across tracks, of the original roundhouse, just south of the tunnel. The coal in these cars was used to power the boilers in the mills. In 1911 alone, the mills in Fall River consumed over 850,000 tons of coal, and each piece had to be transported to the city, as Fall River does not have its own natural supply. The below image is the same general area but the view is looking northeast at a point south of the tunnel. The original roundhouse is seen halfway up the image on the far right, behind the coal cars. The tunnel that ran under Central Street was 225 feet long, 16 feet wide, and 15 feet high. (Both, courtesy of the Fall River Historical Society.)

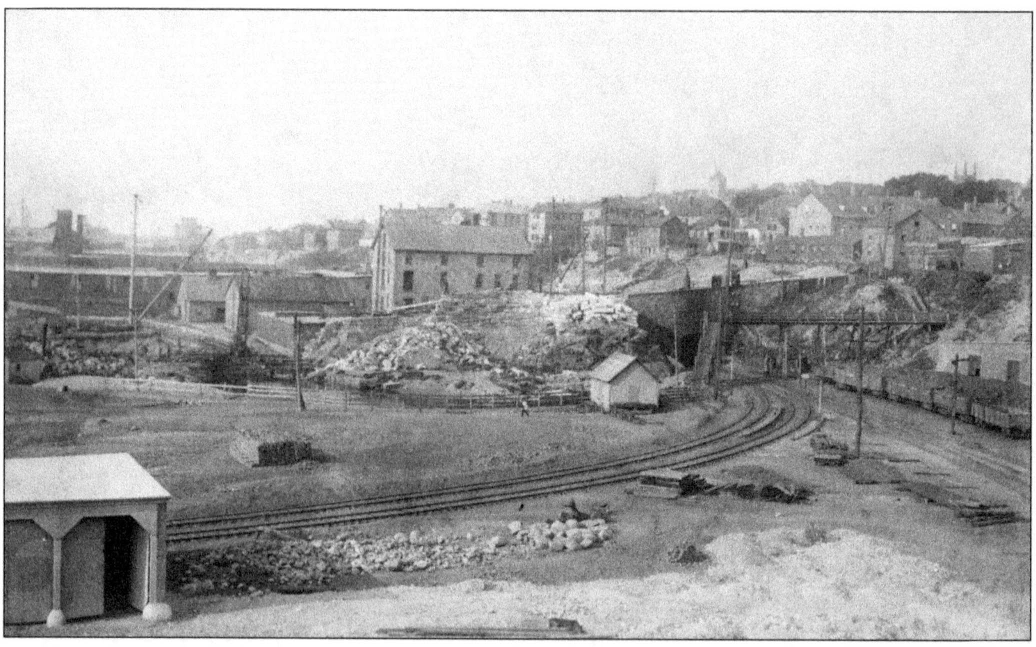

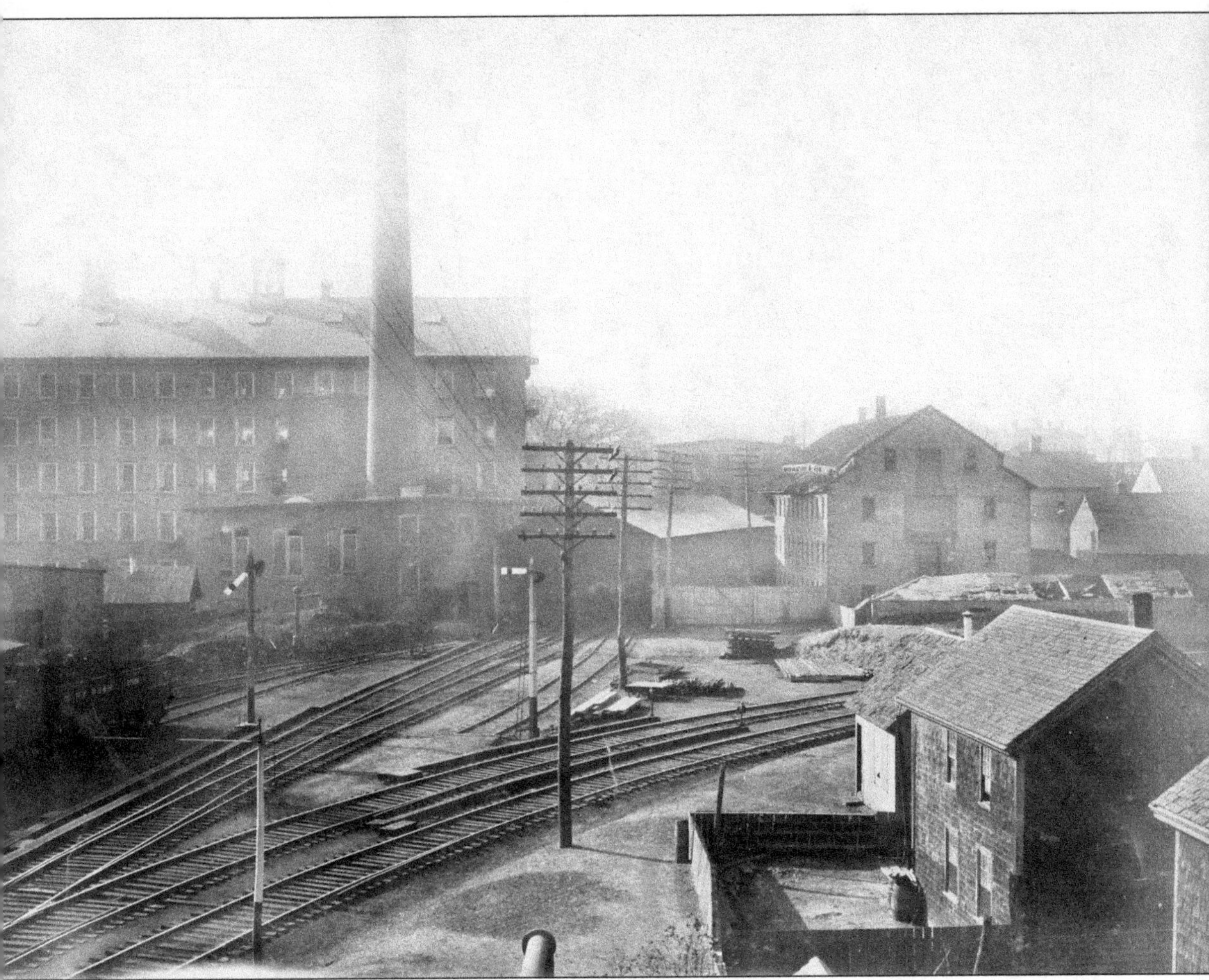

This bleak scene shows the rear of the Metacomet Mill and the brick arch (in the distance if one follows the tracks to the left). The mills in Fall River created a great deal of air pollution, as the fly ash (containing the poisonous heavy metal pollutants arsenic, cadmium, mercury, selenium, and beryllium), released by the hundreds of smokestacks that filled the city, rained down upon the homes, gardens, schools, playgrounds, and drying laundry of its residents. Houses were generally painted dark brown to avoid having to be repainted as frequently. The US Bureau of Labor Statistics reported that, between the years 1908 and 1912, "mill operatives were twice as likely to die from tuberculosis than non-mill workers and that the risk of death from other causes was 20-percent higher for mill workers than for any other member of the population. Tuberculosis accounted for 45-percent of all deaths of mill operatives aged 15 to 44 during the study period." (Courtesy of the Fall River Historical Society.)

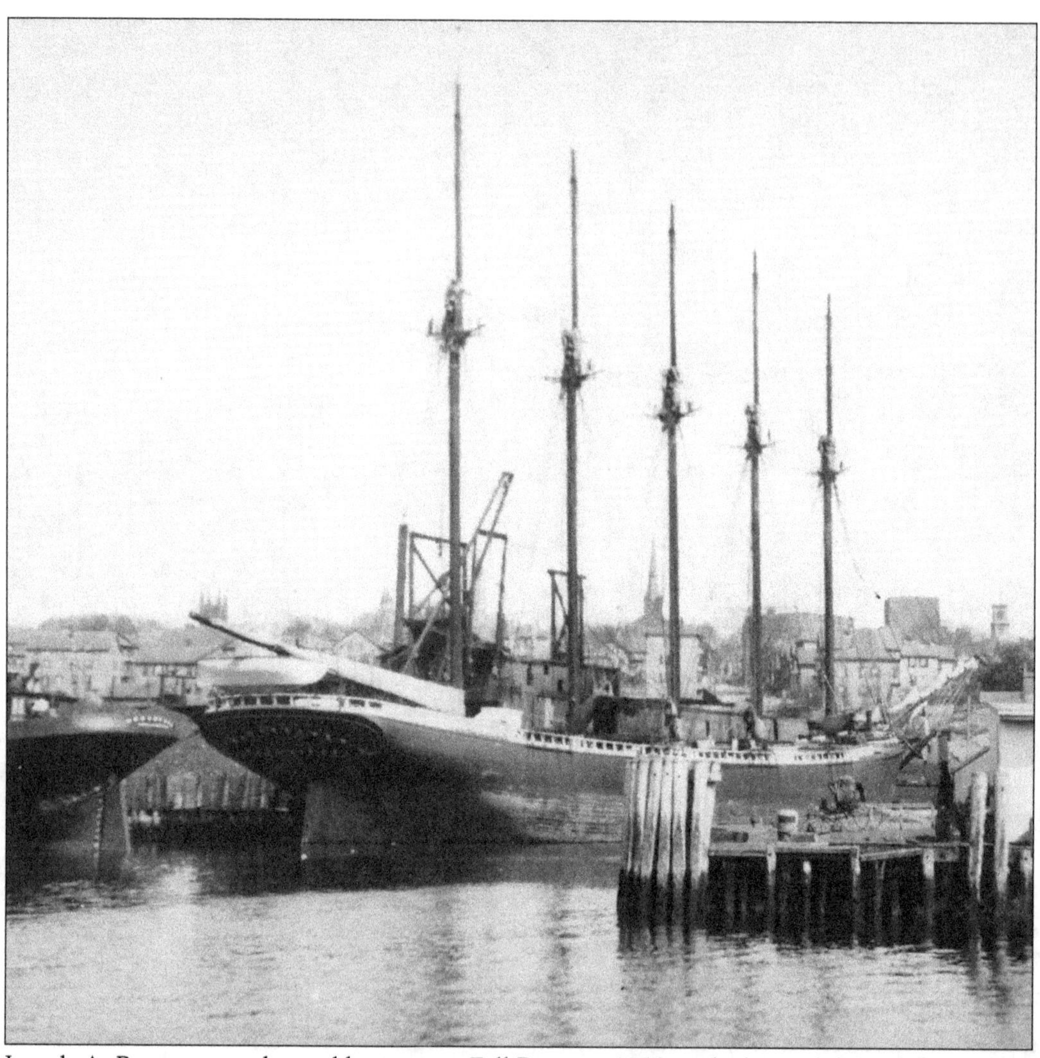

Joseph A. Bowen started a coal business in Fall River in 1856, with the coal delivered to him at Morgan's Wharf. In the beginning, Bowen did all the work himself—unloading the coal, soliciting the orders, loading the delivery carts, and delivering the coal. Sarah V. Bowen, his sister, kept the books and weighed the coal. In 1869, Bowen purchased Slade's Wharf, and he and his new partner Charles P. Stickney formed J.A. Bowen Company. In order to meet demand for coal, Bowen had become interested in coast-wide transportation. To that end, he had an ownership interest in four schooners. One of them, the *Mary W. Bowen*, a five-master, was launched in 1900. She had a capacity of 3,500 tons, which made her the largest schooner afloat. She was used until 1917 and then sold to the US government to transport war materials. On July 8, 1917, a torpedo fired by a German U-boat sank her while en route from New York to Le Havre, carrying machine oil. There were no casualties. This photograph is of the schooner *Mary W. Bowen*, just unloaded, in Fall River. (Courtesy of the Fall River Historical Society.)

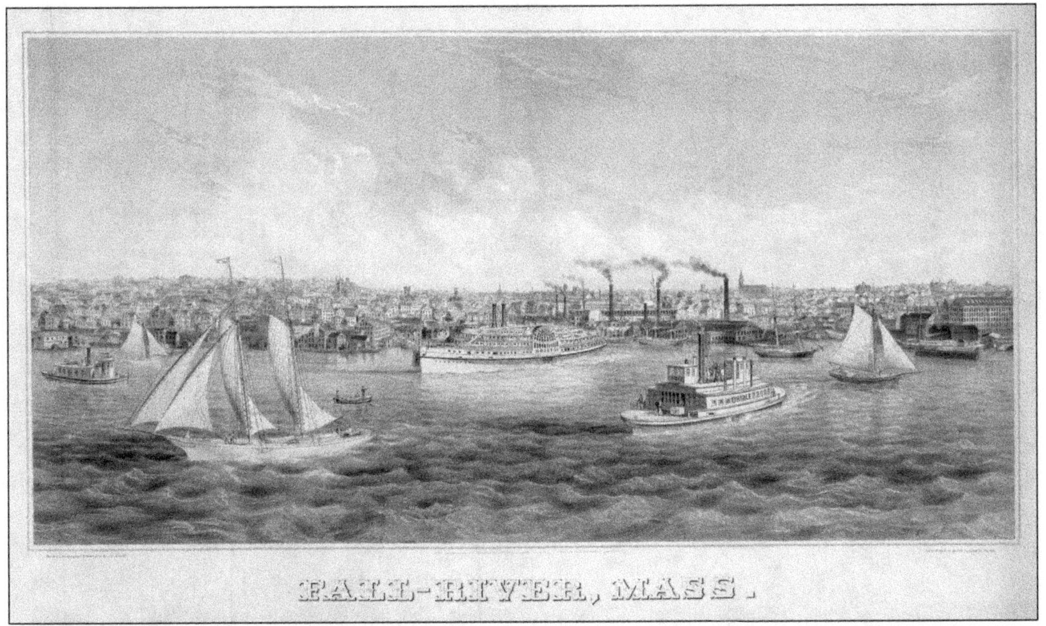

These two whimsical lithographs, depicting activity in Mount Hope Bay and in the harbor at the Taunton River in 1870 (above) and 1873 (below), are not that far removed from the truth. Fall River's water ports were quite active during the early days of mill expansion as heavy schooners, like the *Mary W. Bowen* (depicted to the left), frequented the waterway to deliver their loads of coal. Pleasure sailing has always been a part of any city that sits on a body of water that reaches to the sea, and Fall River not only enjoyed that sport but also had the good fortune to be connected to all points south by way of the Fall River Line. Schooners, steamers, paddle wheelers, sailboats, and yachts all have been present in abundance on the shores of Fall River. (Both, courtesy of Michael Brimbau.)

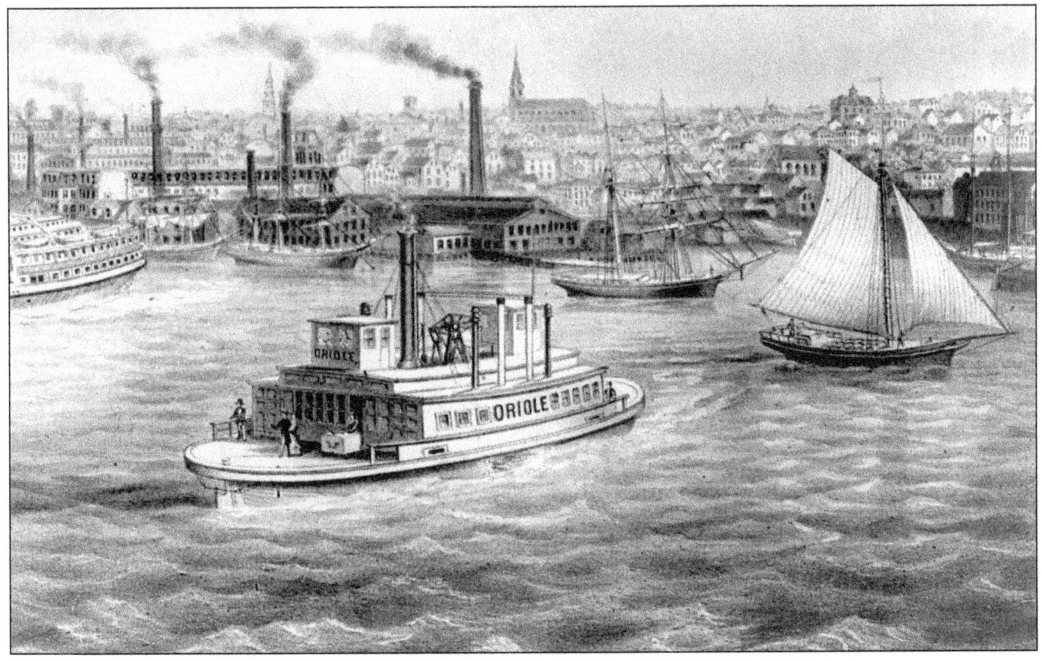

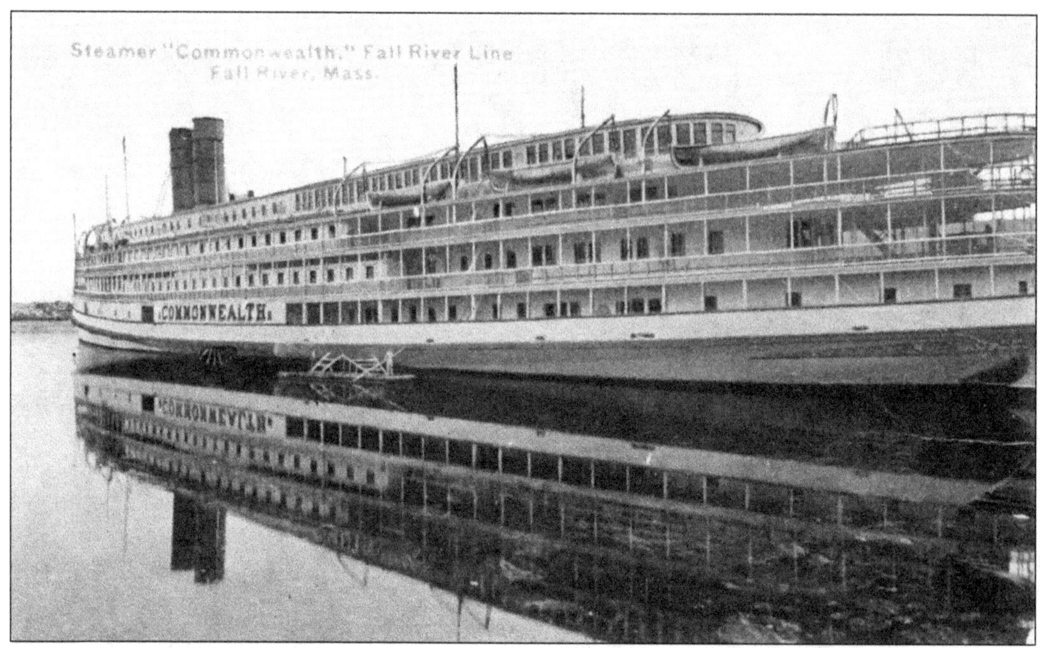

The Fall River Line operated between 1847 and 1937. It was a combination steamboat and railroad travel package between Boston and New York City, a route of 228 miles. Passengers boarded the boat train in Boston at 6:00 a.m. and arrived in Fall River at 7:26 p.m. The ship portion of the journey departed Fall River at 7:30 p.m., took on passengers in Newport, and then departed Newport at 8:30 p.m., arriving in New York City at 7:00 a.m. New York passengers on their way to Boston boarded the steamer at 5:00 p.m., stopped in Newport at 3:00 a.m., and arrived in Fall River at 5:00 a.m. They then boarded the boat train in Fall River at 5:20 a.m. and arrived in Boston at 6:50 p.m. (Both, courtesy of Michael Brimbau.)

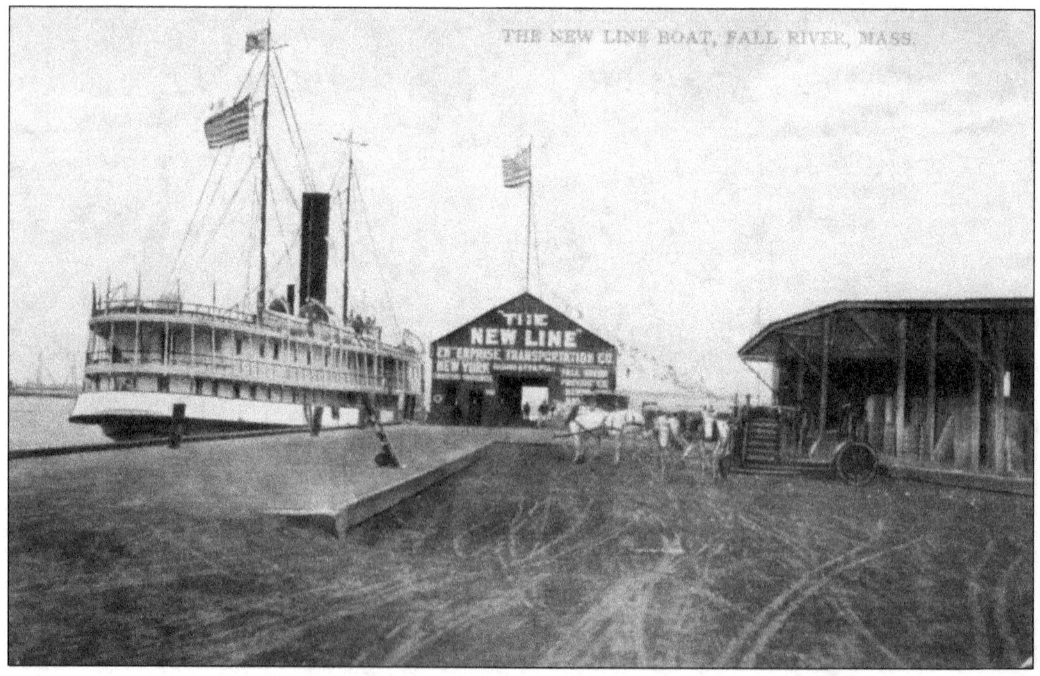

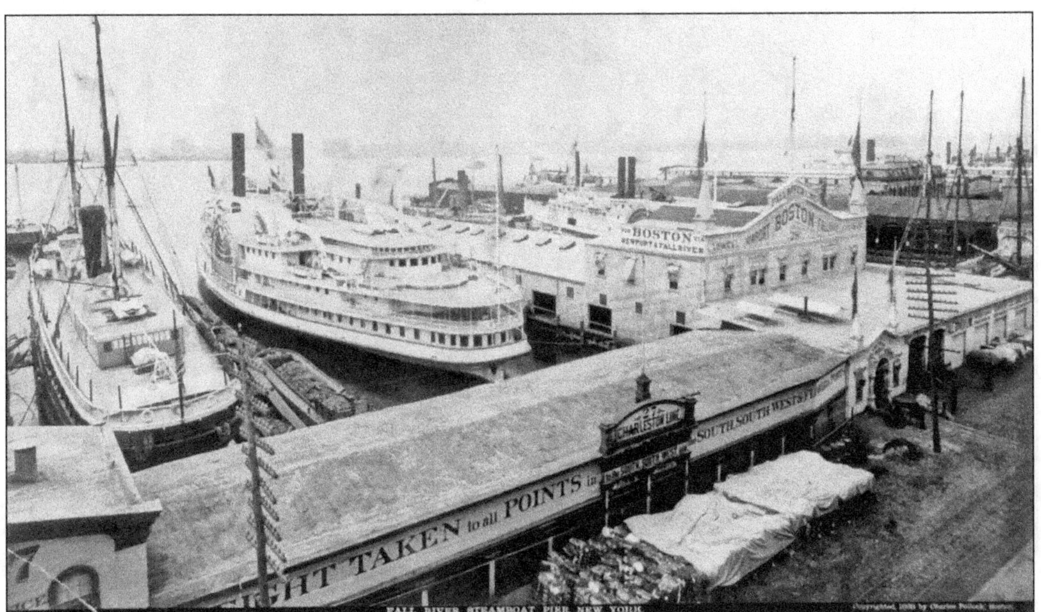

Established as the Bay State Steamboat Company, the Fall River Line was first owned by Col. Richard Borden and his brother Jefferson Borden, who, in 1845, completed the rail line between Fall River and Taunton, New Bedford, Providence, and Boston. They added regular steamboat service between Fall River and New York two years later in 1847. The brothers sold their company to the Narragansett Steamship Company, owned by Jim Fisk and Jay Gould. In 1867, Fisk moved the terminus to Newport, only to return it to Fall River in 1869. In 1874, the Fall River Line was sold to the Old Colony Railroad, which became the Old Colony Steamboat Company. Between the years 1874 and 1937, over 19 million passengers were carried on the Fall River Line. The below photograph shows the shore from Joseph A. Bowen's coal wharf. (Above, courtesy of private collection; below, courtesy of the Fall River Historical Society.)

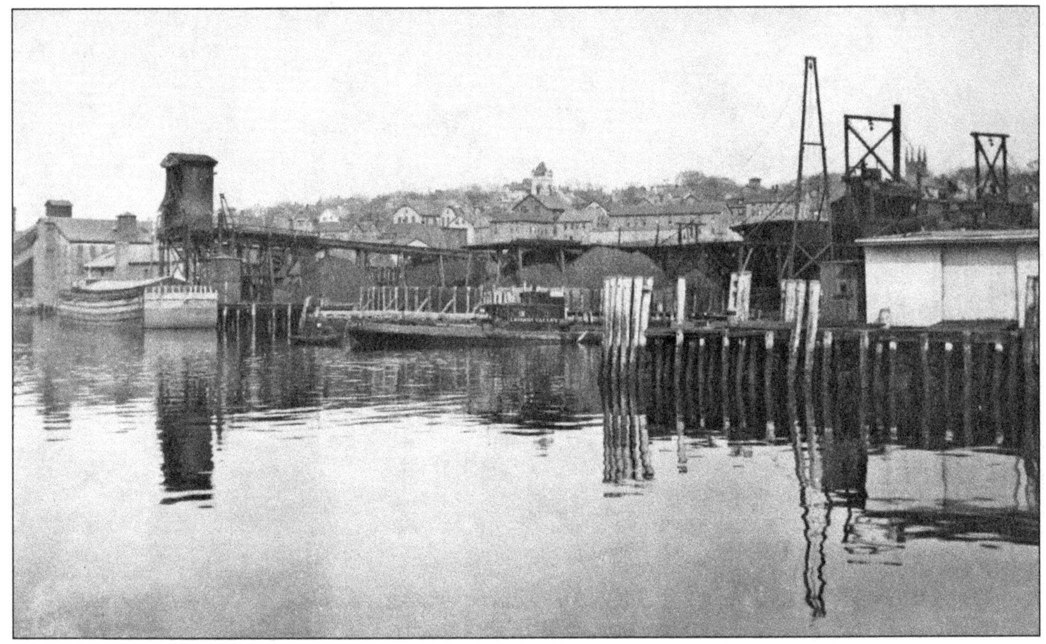

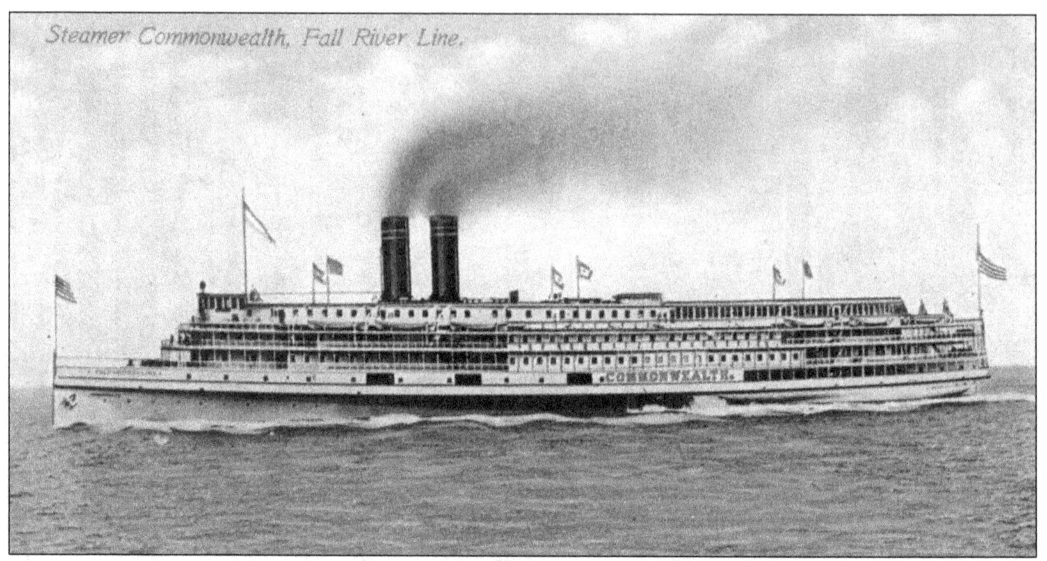

The *Commonwealth* (1908), the "Queen of the Sound," could carry 2,000 passengers and was a six-story floating hotel that was wider than the *Lusitania* and could carry almost as many passengers as that ocean liner, and as much freight. The *Pilgrim* (1883) was constructed of iron and was the first American vessel to have a double hull with watertight compartments to improve its flotation. It was designed to be unsinkable, and in fact, the ship hit an uncharted rock, which created a 100-foot gash in its hull, in 1884. The *Pilgrim* steamed quite safely to port. The postcard below states that "the *Iron Monarch of Long Island Sound* is considered Fire Proof, Unsinkable, and secure amid all perils." At 370 feet long with a capacity of 1,200 passengers, the *Pilgrim* made the trip between Fall River and New York City in 8.5 hours. Of note is that this ship was equipped with Thomas Edison's new invention, electric lights. (Both, courtesy of Michael Brimbau.)

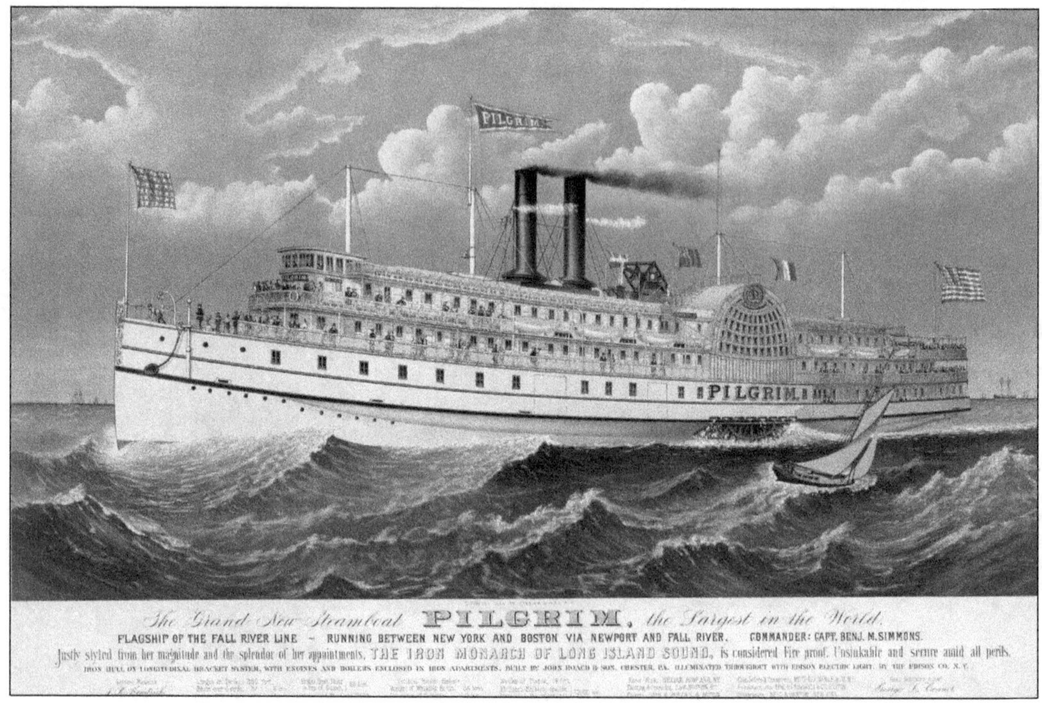

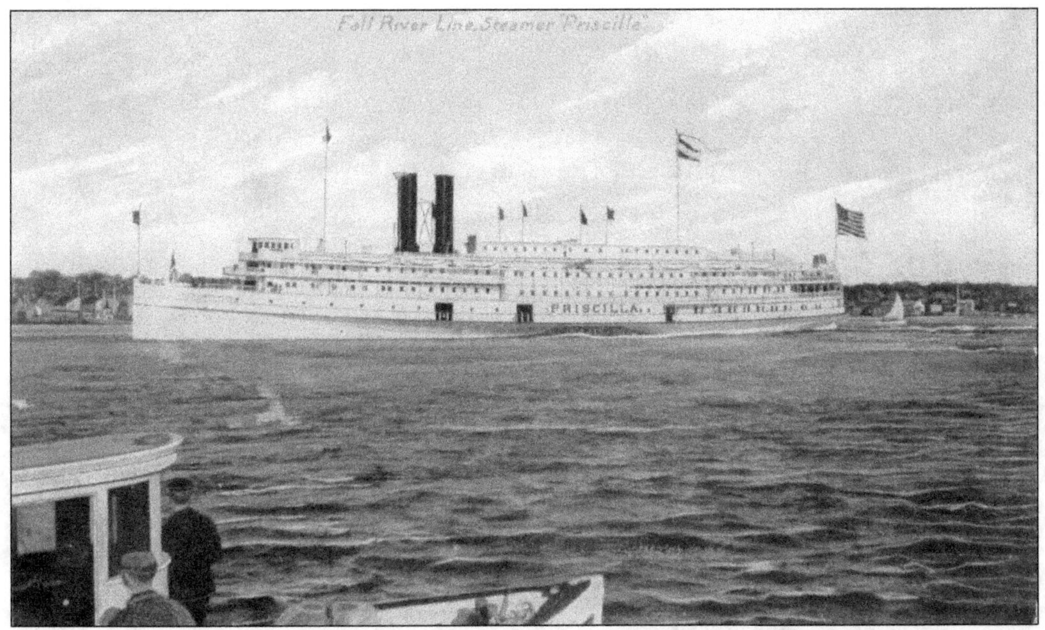

The *Priscilla* (1894), in its day, was the world's largest side-wheeler at 440 feet. The *Puritan* (1889) was over 420 feet in length, 52 feet in breadth, weighed 4,500 tons, and was designed as an elegant steamship with Italian Renaissance styling, including gold inlaid detailing in the cabins. It was made of steel and iron and, according to the postcard below, "built on the double hull bracket plate longitudinal system with watertight compartments and bulkheads. It is unsinkable and practically indestructible." (Both, courtesy of Michael Brimbau.)

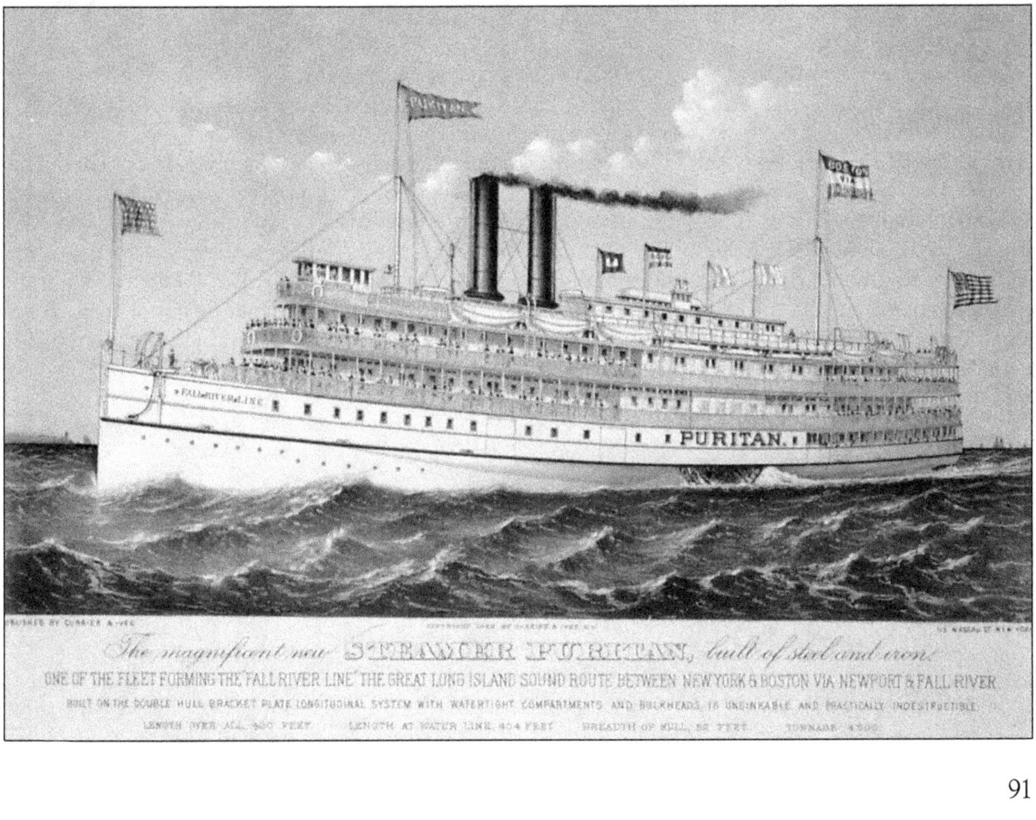

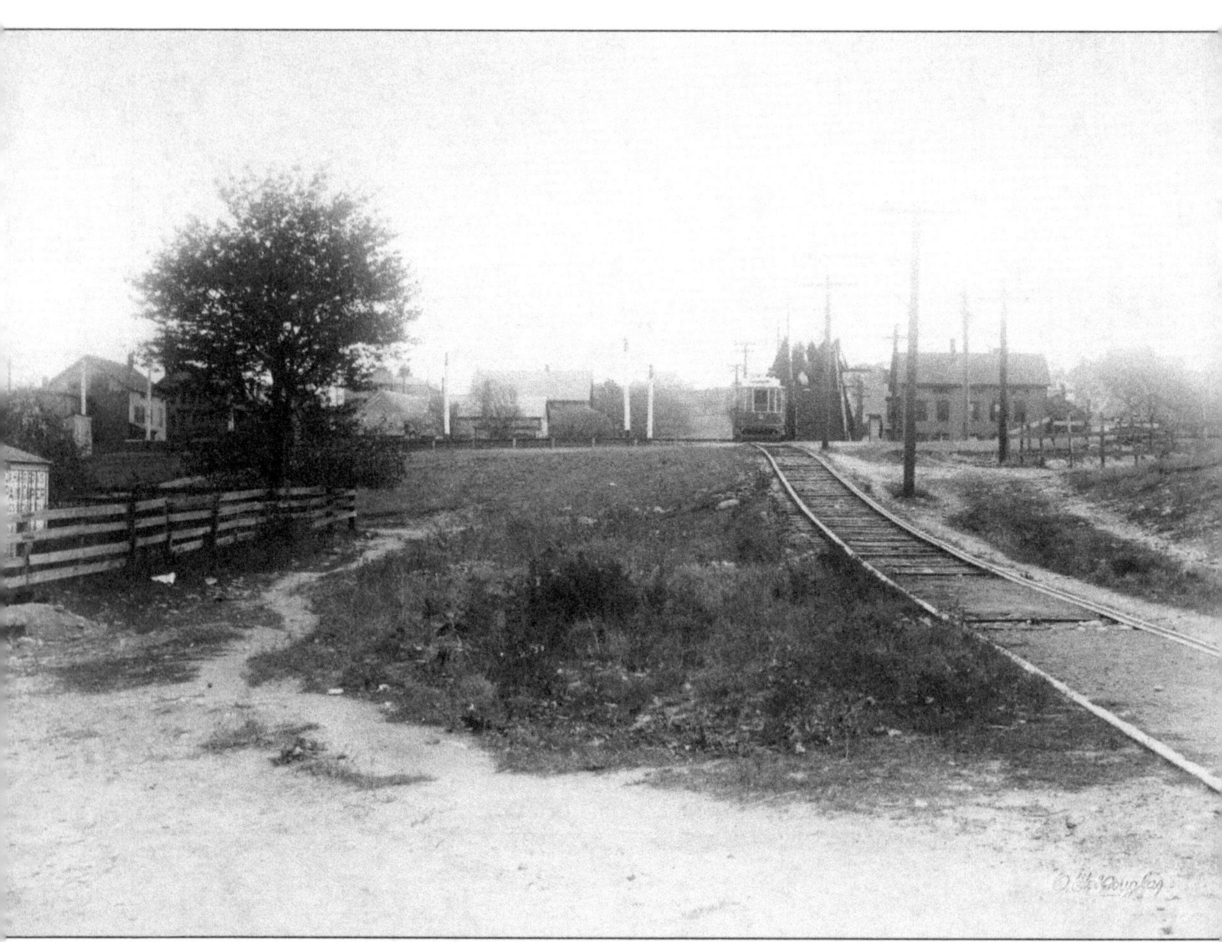

This photograph is of the lower end of President Avenue, the area west of a railroad bridge that is there in 2012. Today, Al Mac's Diner would be somewhere in the lower right-hand corner. The picture dates to about 1897–1903, because that is the period when the trolley cars began traveling across the Taunton River. The railroad company refused permission for trolley cars to cross its tracks. To the right of the trolley car, one can see a flight of stairs built by the trolley company for passengers to disembark (passengers called it "the Mountain") and climb up and over the railroad tracks to the other side to board a trolley waiting to take them into the city or to continue their journey to Swansea, Somerset, Taunton, and so on. This was all made unnecessary when the City of Fall River required the railroad to elevate all of its grade crossings in the city. This was accomplished around 1904. (Courtesy of Bill Goncalo.)

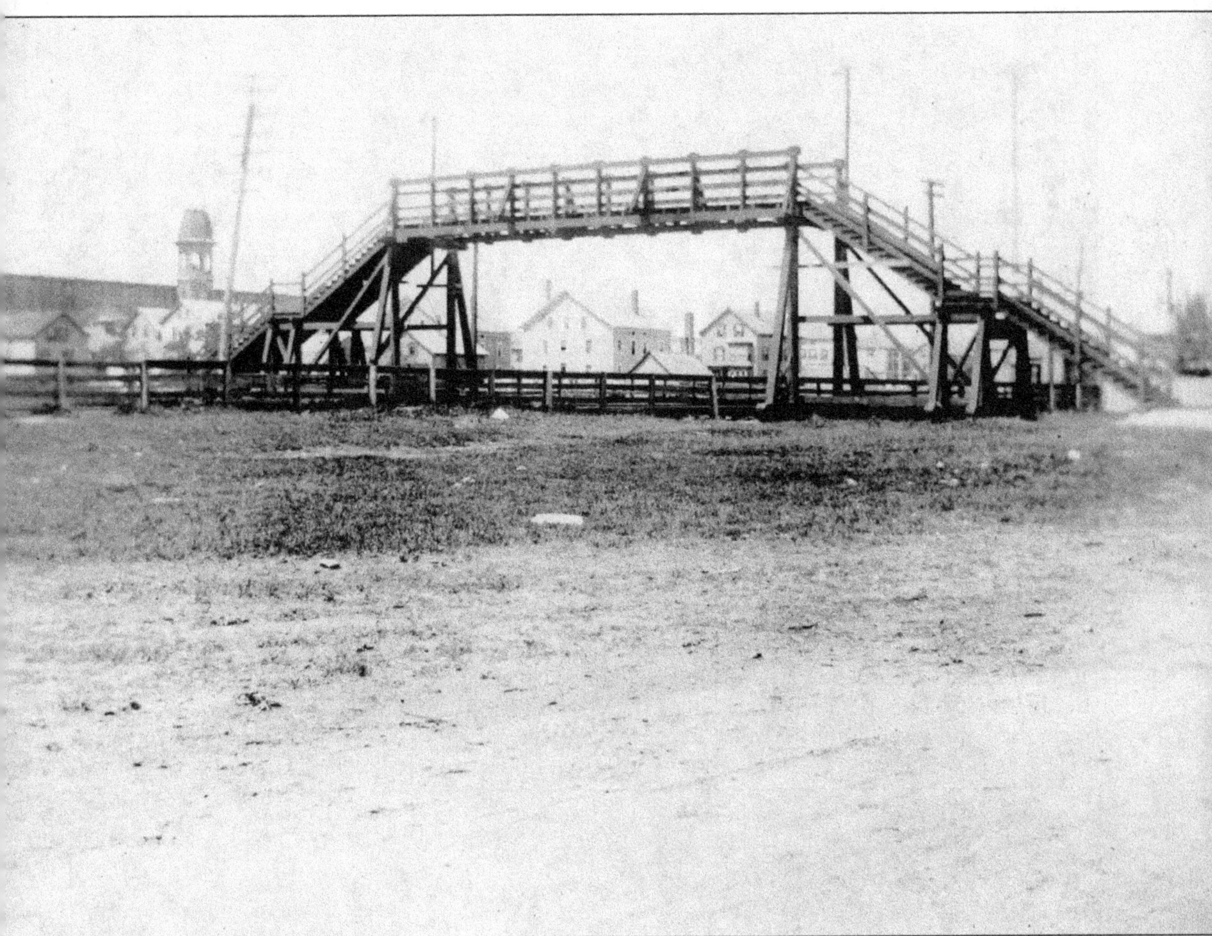

This is a photograph of the Mountain on President Avenue as described to the left. Mechanics Mill is in the background. Today, the tower has been modified with the top cap of the octagonal stair tower removed, and the arcades redesigned. According to trolley expert George Petrin, to get to the Slade's Ferry Bridge, the trolley would have continued westerly on President Avenue, turn northerly on Davol Street for one block, arriving at the junction of Davol Street, Brownell Street (on the trolley's right), and Remington Avenue (on the trolley's left). The trolley would have turned left onto Remington Avenue and followed it directly to the Slade's Ferry Bridge. Remington Avenue and Brownell Street were directly across from each other and separated by Davol Street, much like Rock Street ends at Bedford Street but the street directly across from it is Third Street. (Courtesy of the Fall River Historical Society.)

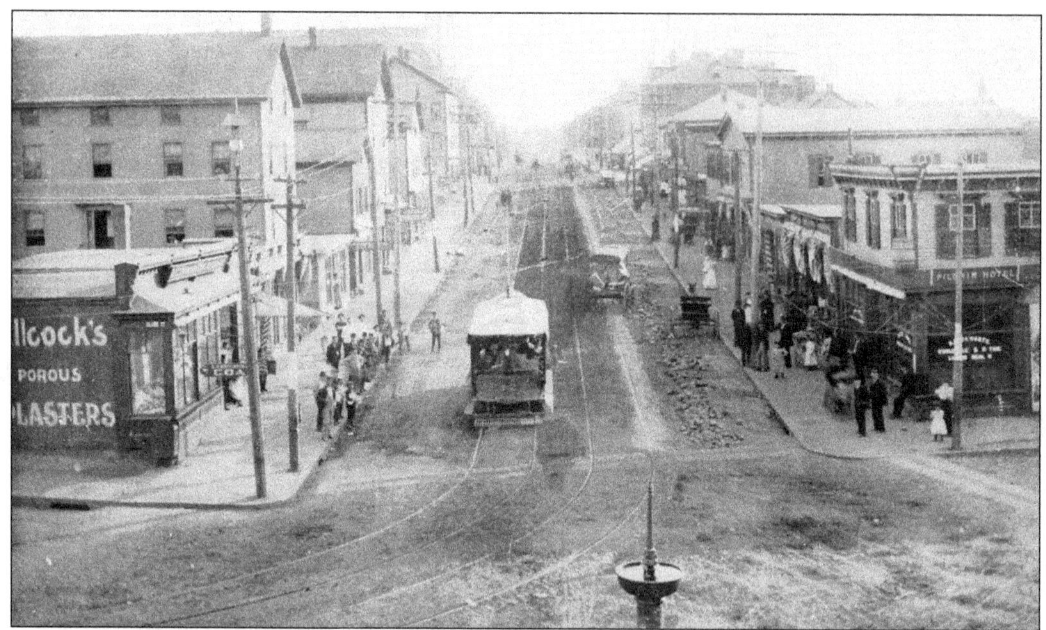

This view of Globe Four Corners shows a trolley from the Globe Stage Line, the Pilgrim Hotel, and business activity around St. Patrick's Church. The fountain in the foreground was for horses, should they be thirsty. This area was named after the Globe Yarn Mills, founded in 1881. Constructed of brick, these mills were built in the fourth style of mill architecture—increased width for efficiency, no towers, low-pitched roofs, and only two to three floors. (Courtesy of private collection.)

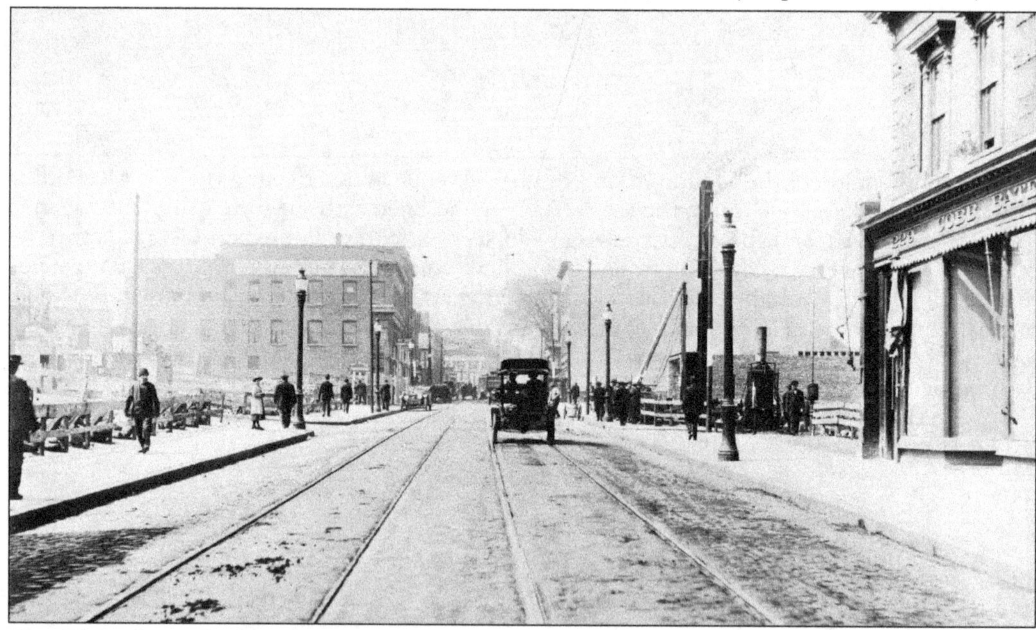

The Globe Street Railway began operation in April 1880. Tracks laid on Main Street connected the center of the city with the Bowenville Station. The horse-drawn cars were replaced by electric trolley cars in September 1892. Trolley cars were replaced by motor buses in September 1936. This photograph depicts the trolley tracks on South Main Street from No. 229 to Morgan Street. (Courtesy of the Fall River Historical Society.)

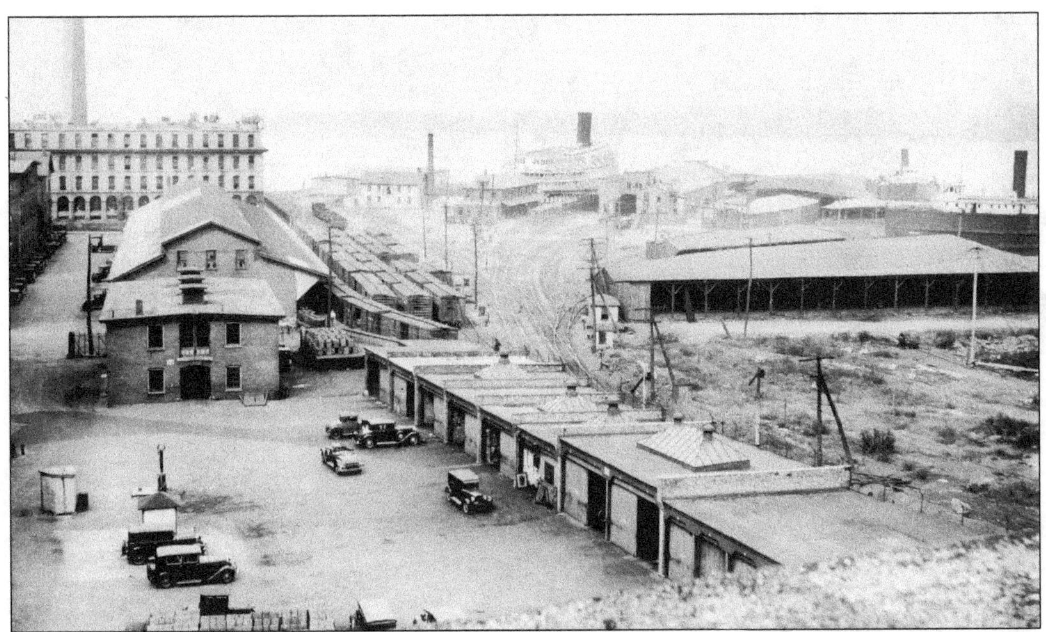

This 1929 photograph, looking westward, was taken from the top of the Metacomet Mill and shows the Fall River Line pier. From here, one would take the boat train to Boston after sailing the night boat from New York City. Or, for the opposite route, one would disembark from the boat train and take this unidentified steamship to New York City, arriving by 7:00 a.m. (Courtesy of the Fall River Historical Society.)

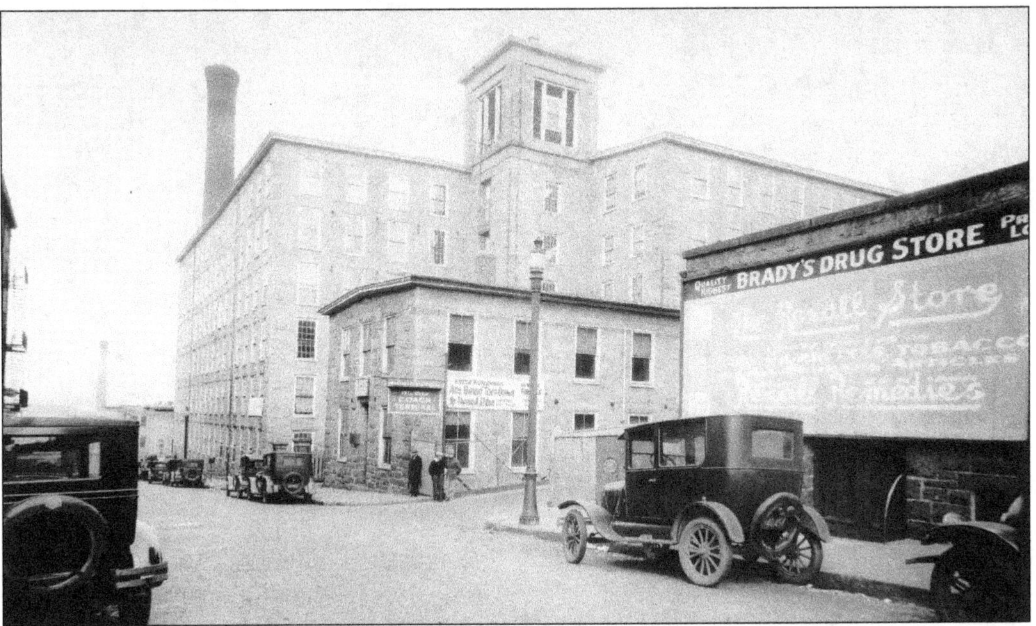

This is probably one of the last few images of the Pocasset Mill, as seen on Pocasset Street from Main Street. On February 2, 1928, a fire was started in the abandoned Mill No. 2, probably by some demolition workers who were trying to keep warm, and destroyed a big portion of Fall River's downtown, including the Pocasset Mill, the Granite Block, the Durfee Block, several theaters, and a synagogue. (Courtesy of the Fall River Historical Society.)

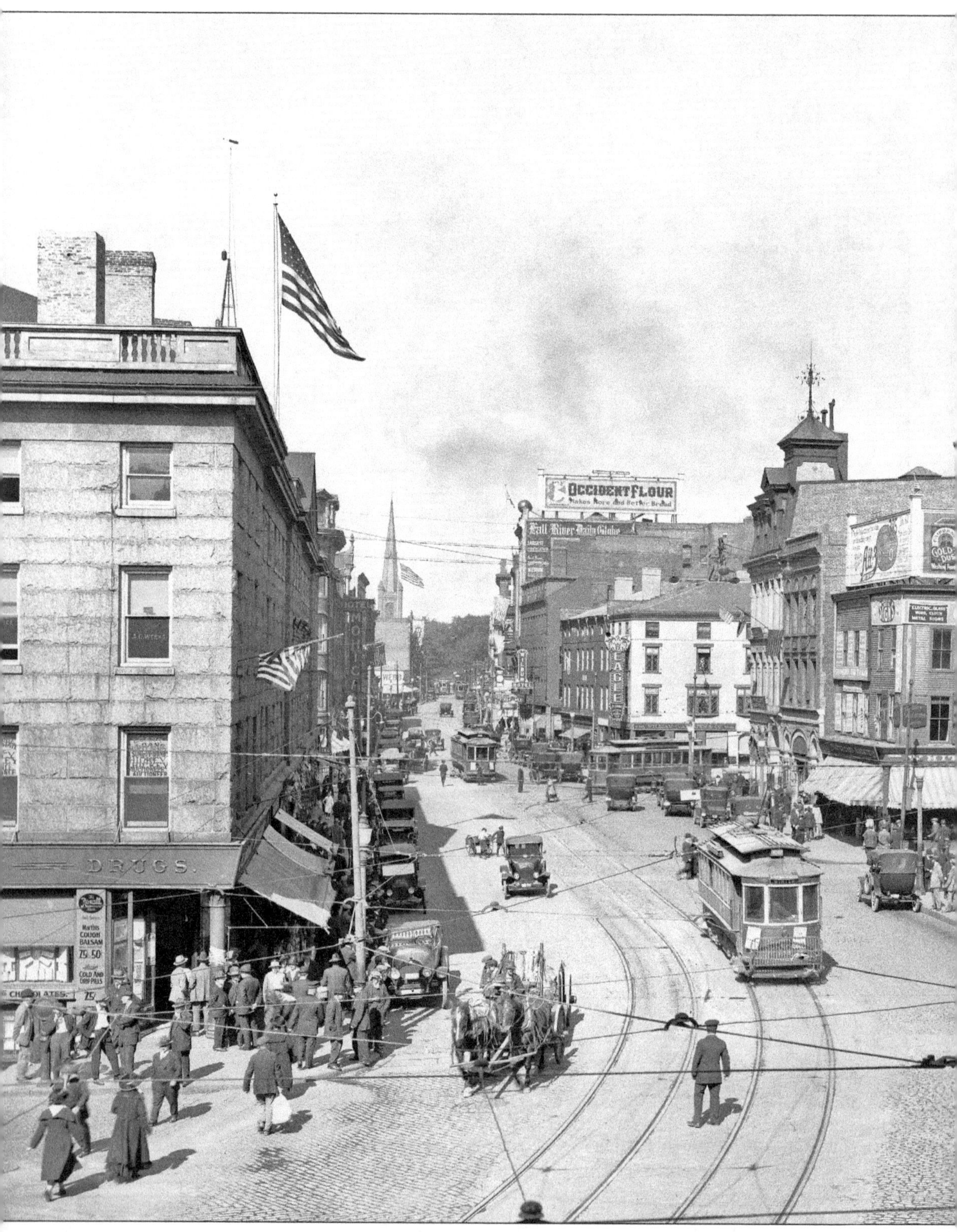
OCCIDENT FLOUR
Makes More and Better Bread
Fall River Daily Globe
DRUGS.
COUGH BALSAM

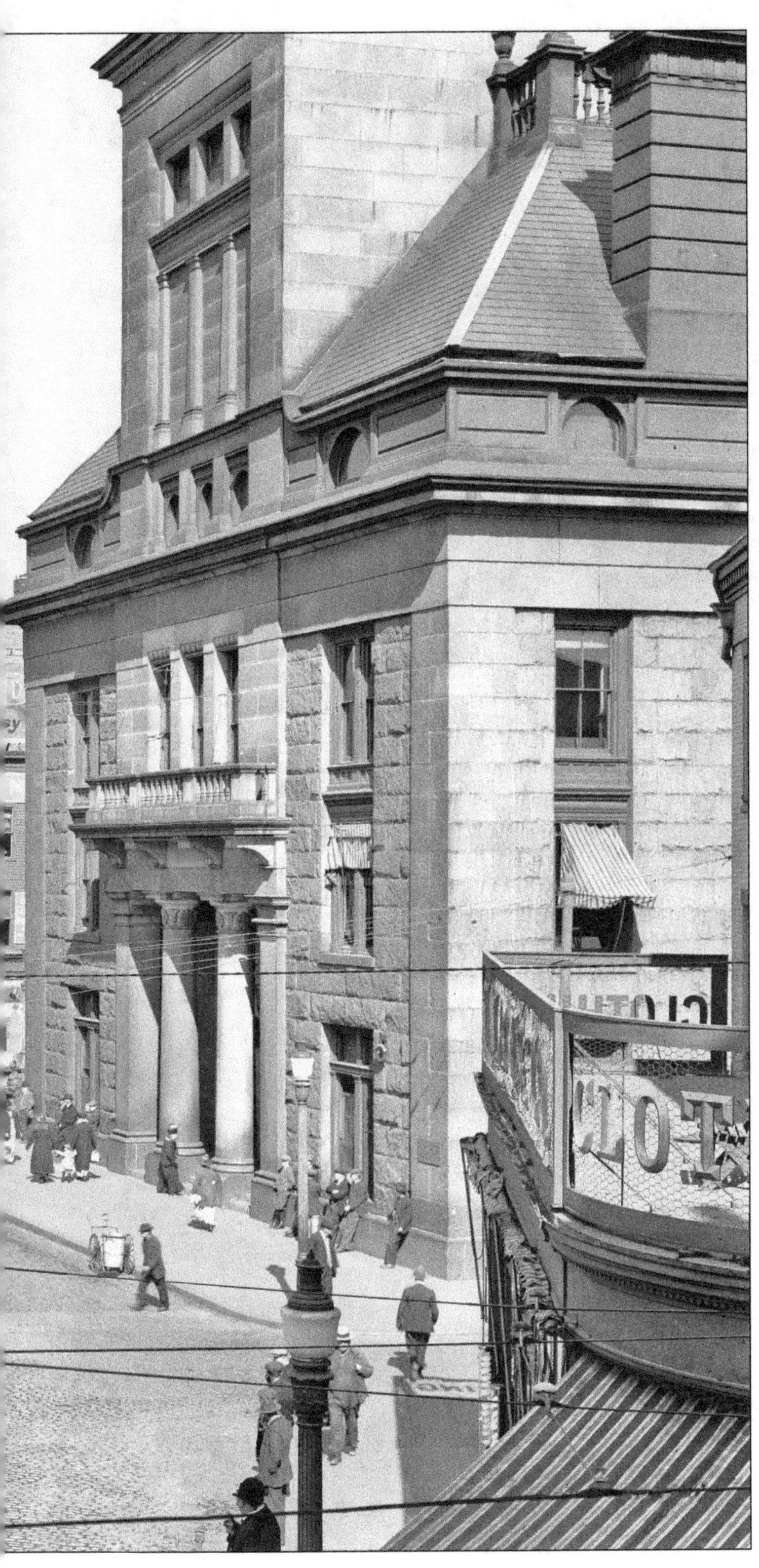

One can safely say that at one time Fall River had automobiles, trolleys, trains crossing streets at grade level, and horse-drawn carriages/vehicles all sharing the roads, while the Fall River Line was in operation at the pier down by the American Print Works. This magnificent scene of North Main Street, as it passes by the old city hall, clearly shows the normal, everyday hustle and bustle of an urban community. Everyone is well dressed, wearing hats, and oblivious to the massive changes that are to befall the city in a few short years when another conflagration is going to forever change the landscape of the downtown. (Courtesy of private collection.)

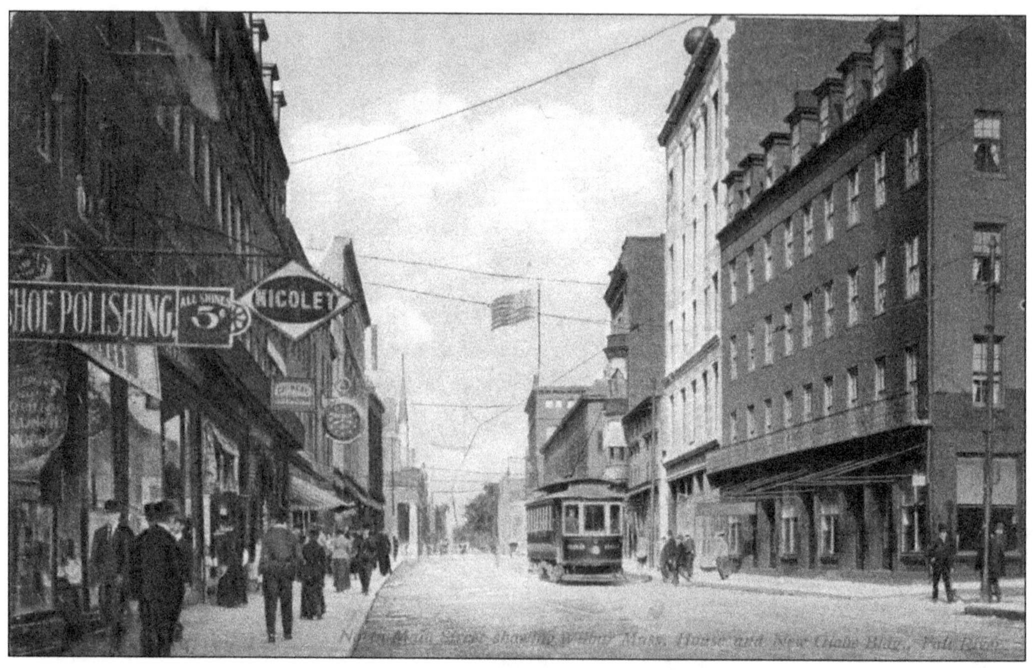

In 2009, while the City of Fall River was digging up the roads to replace some water lines, workers happened to excavate some old trolley tracks on North Main Street, near what was known as French's Hill. The workers at the job site had believed that all of the trolley tracks had since been removed when that mode of transportation had become obsolete, but apparently, this was not so. In fact, there are places in the city where one can see the indentation of the tracks just below the surface of the asphalt. (Both, courtesy of Michael Brimbau.)

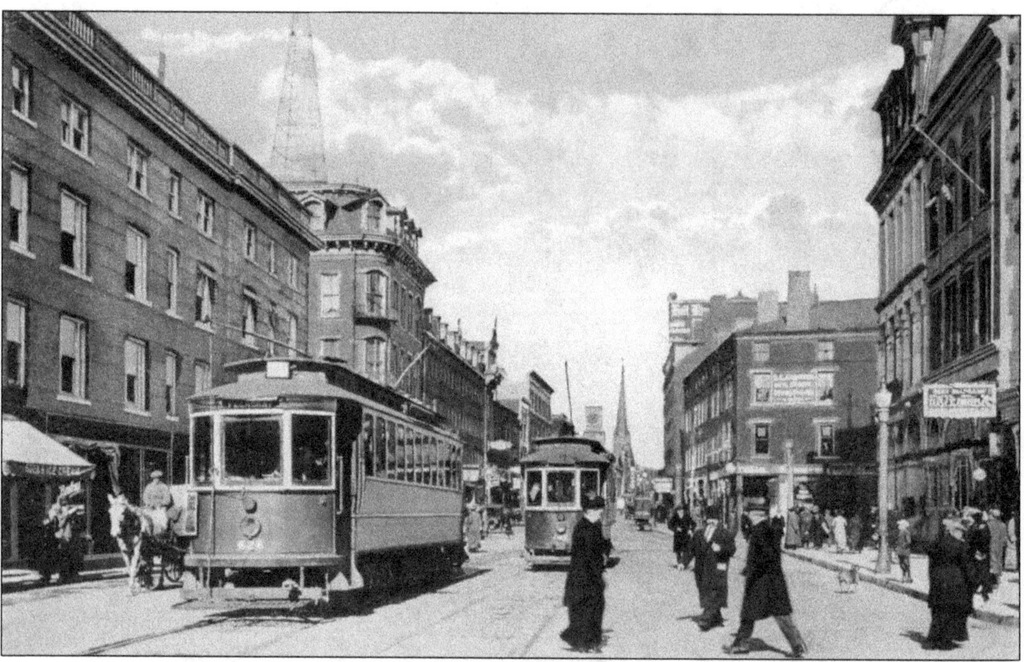

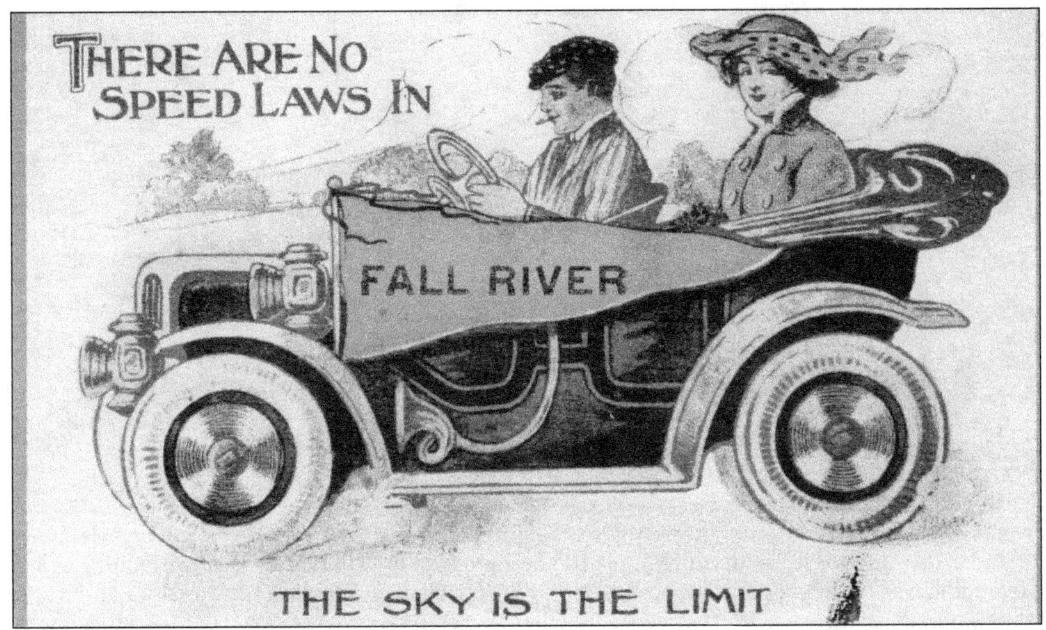

These types of mass-produced novelty cards were very popular with tourists who were looking for a humorous expression of friendship to send to folks back home. Fall River postcards are very collectible, and older ones in pristine condition—especially of a rare scene or a real photograph (one of a kind) that has been made into a postcard around the turn of the 20th century—can fetch a pretty penny. (Courtesy of Michael Brimbau.)

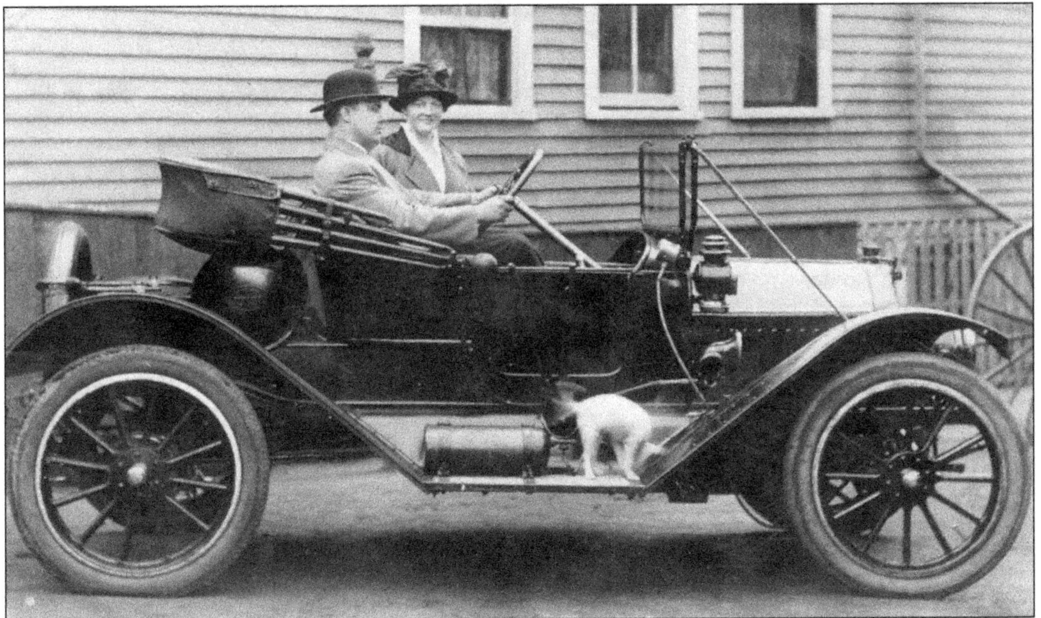

Edmond and Emerilde Parent, the owner of Parent's Hardware located on Brightman Street in the North End of Fall River, sit in their automobile around 1920. To be able to afford a motorized vehicle like this one was a sign of success and enabled the owners to travel beyond the train or trolley routes. The automobile is credited with causing, or at least assisting in, the demise of the Fall River Line. (Courtesy of Kenneth M. Champlin.)

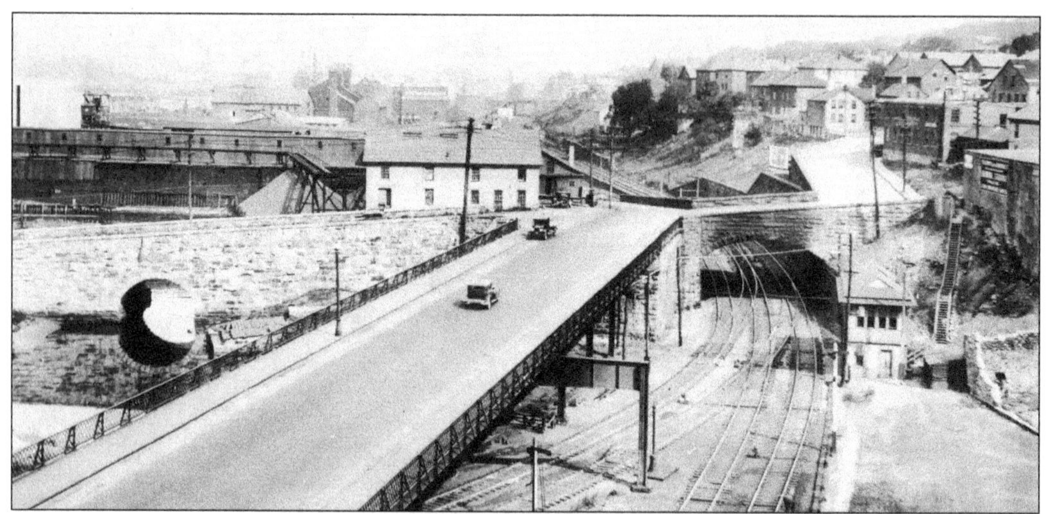

America's love of the automobile changed medium-sized cities, like Fall River, in ways that can never be measured but are definitely felt in the here and now. The newfound mobility aided the middle classes, who no longer had to depend on public transportation timetables and route selection to determine where they went and when. Once the residents of cities began to explore the world around them via the freedom of the open road, it can be said that a new great migration was on the horizon, and this one was to the suburbs, dispersing the urban geography and creating sprawl. The 1929 image above is looking northward from the top of Metacomet Mill. The below image is looking south down South Main Street from Anawan Street. (Both, courtesy of the Fall River Historical Society.)

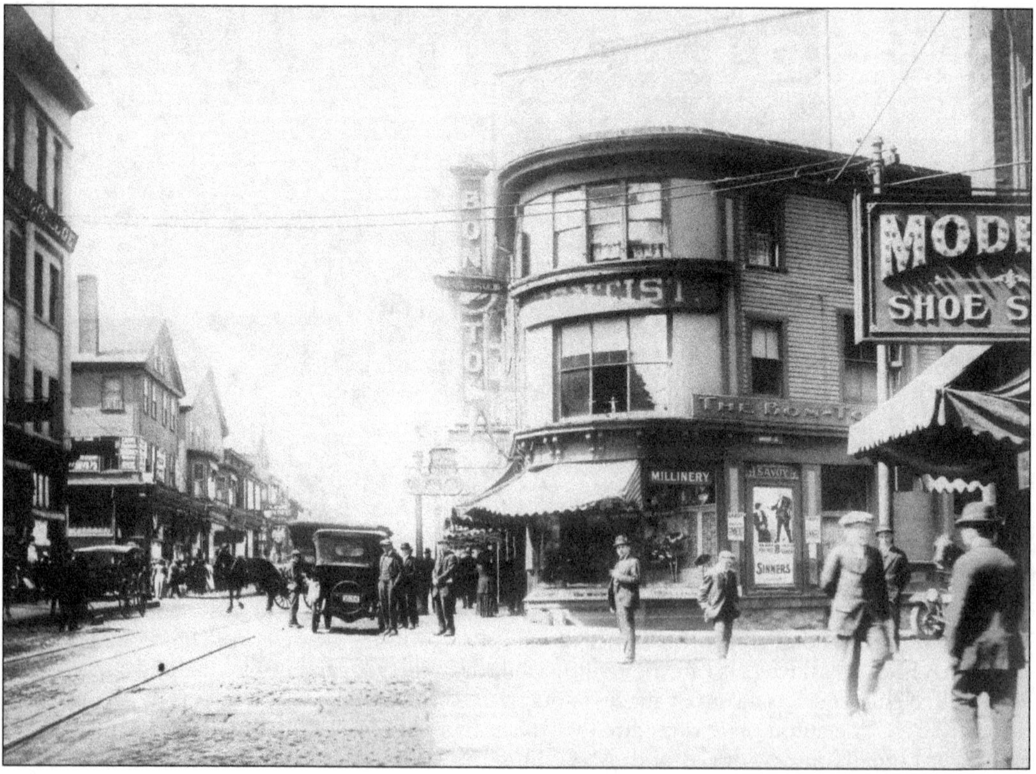

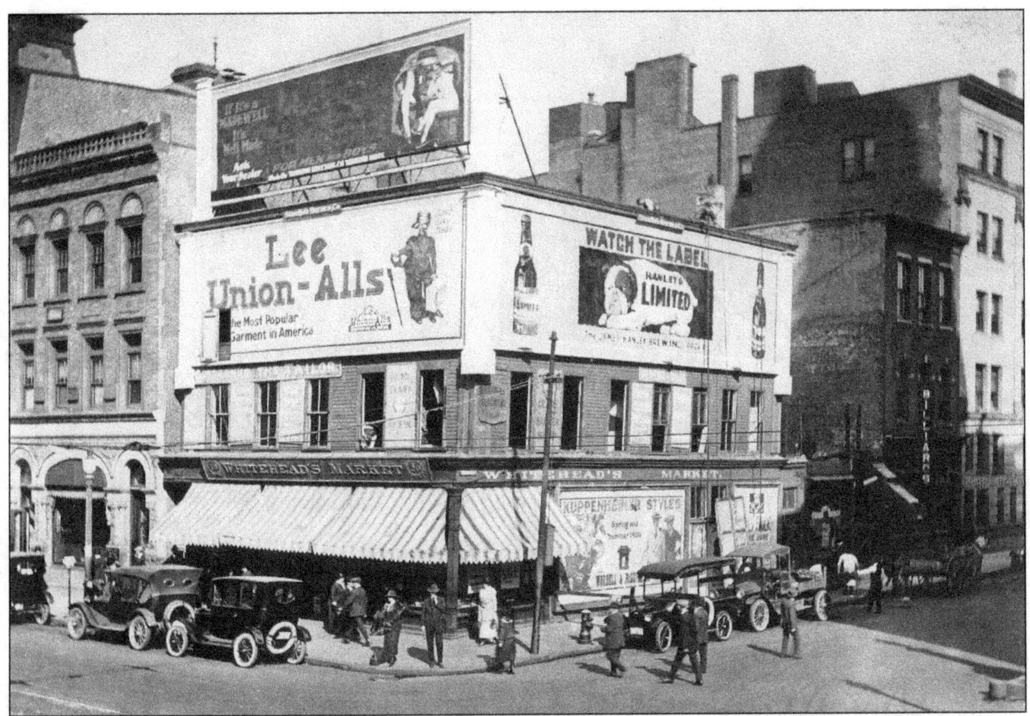

With the decline in the economy of Fall River even before the Great Depression and the diversity of ways in which people could travel, without the restriction imposed by transportation boundaries, the population of the city has suffered. From a peak population in 1920 of 120,485, Fall River has seen a steady decline until 2010, when the city's inhabitants numbered 88,857. The photograph above is of the northeast corner of Main and Market Streets in 1920. The below image is of the southwest corner of South Main and Pocasset Streets. (Both, courtesy of the Fall River Historical Society.)

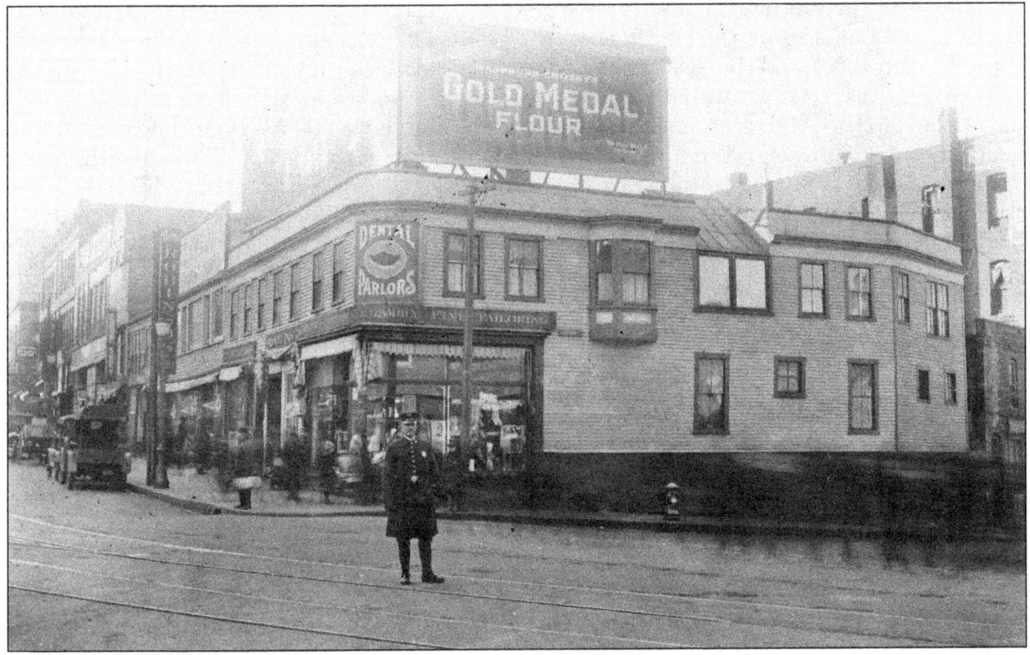

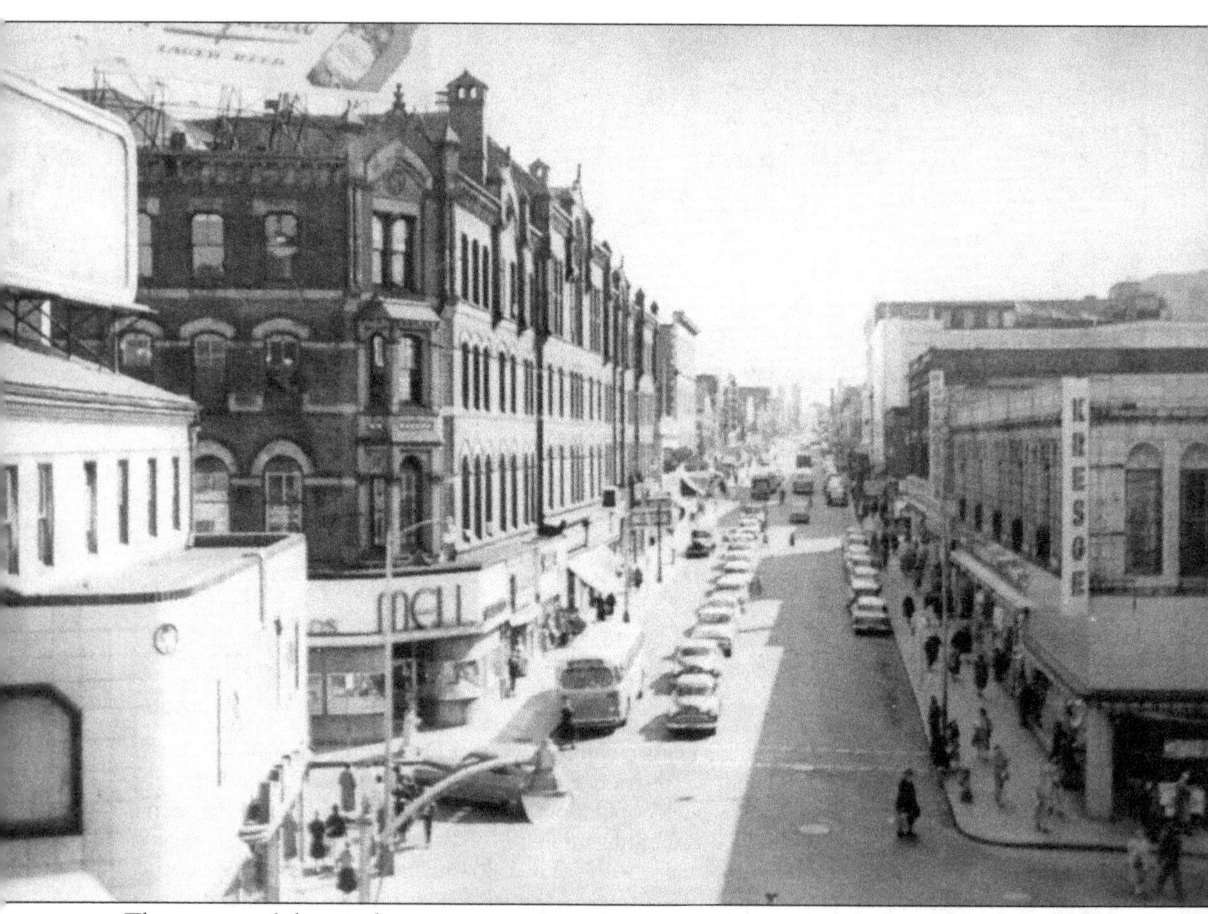

This image of the southwest corner of South Main and Pocasset Streets gives a good view of the Academy Building, on the left, in the early 1950s. The Academy Building was also known as the Borden Block and the Academy of Music. Like the Central Congregational Church on Rock Street, it is styled in Ruskinian Gothic. It was constructed in 1875, modernized in 1946, and restored in the 1980s and converted to senior housing above the first floor. The theater was demolished at that time. Some notable stars who graced its stage include Edwin Booth, Lotta Crabtree, Sarah Bernhardt, Joseph Jefferson, Maude Adams, Fannie Davenport, Mrs. Fiske, Otis Skinner, all of the Barrymores, Lillian Russell, and Nance O'Neil. (Courtesy of the Fall River Historical Society.)

Six

SUNDRY CITY SIGHTS

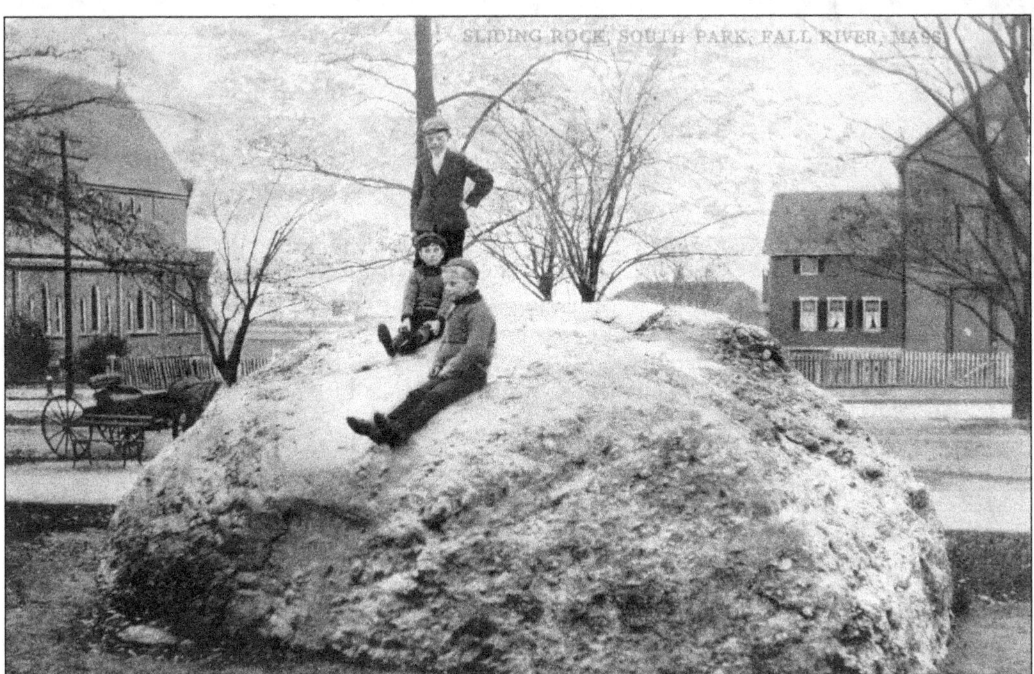

Sliding Rock is located on the north side of Kennedy Park along Bradford Avenue. In this image, the old St. Louis Church, now the site of an empty lot, is across the avenue at the left, and the house and former location of Thom's Barbershop, located on the corner of Fountain Street, can be seen on the right. (Collection of Stefani Koorey.)

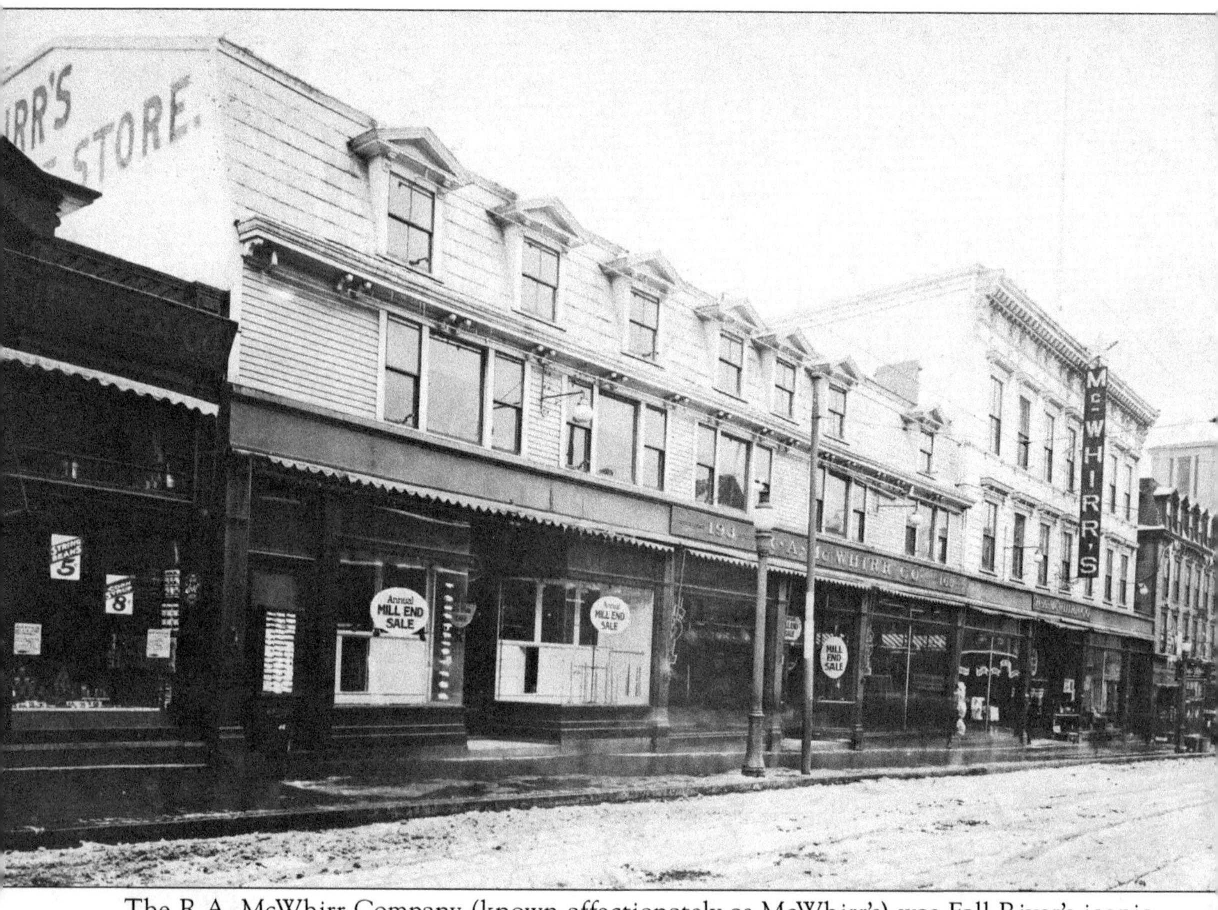

The R.A. McWhirr Company (known affectionately as McWhirr's) was Fall River's iconic department store. Pictured here in 1915, it was located on the west side of South Main Street (Nos. 163–193) near Borden Street. Unique in its day, the store boasted its own US post office branch, a private lending library, and its own radio studio, which broadcast a midday program over local radio station WSAR. McWhirr's survived both the devastating 1916 fire to its south and the massive 1928 conflagration to its north. According to the *Herald News*, "In its familiar, final configuration, the five-story, white terracotta-fronted building comprised 166 feet of frontage housing more than 120,000 square feet of floor space." Much to the chagrin of loyal customers, McWhirr's closed its doors forever in 1975. (Courtesy of the Fall River Historical Society.)

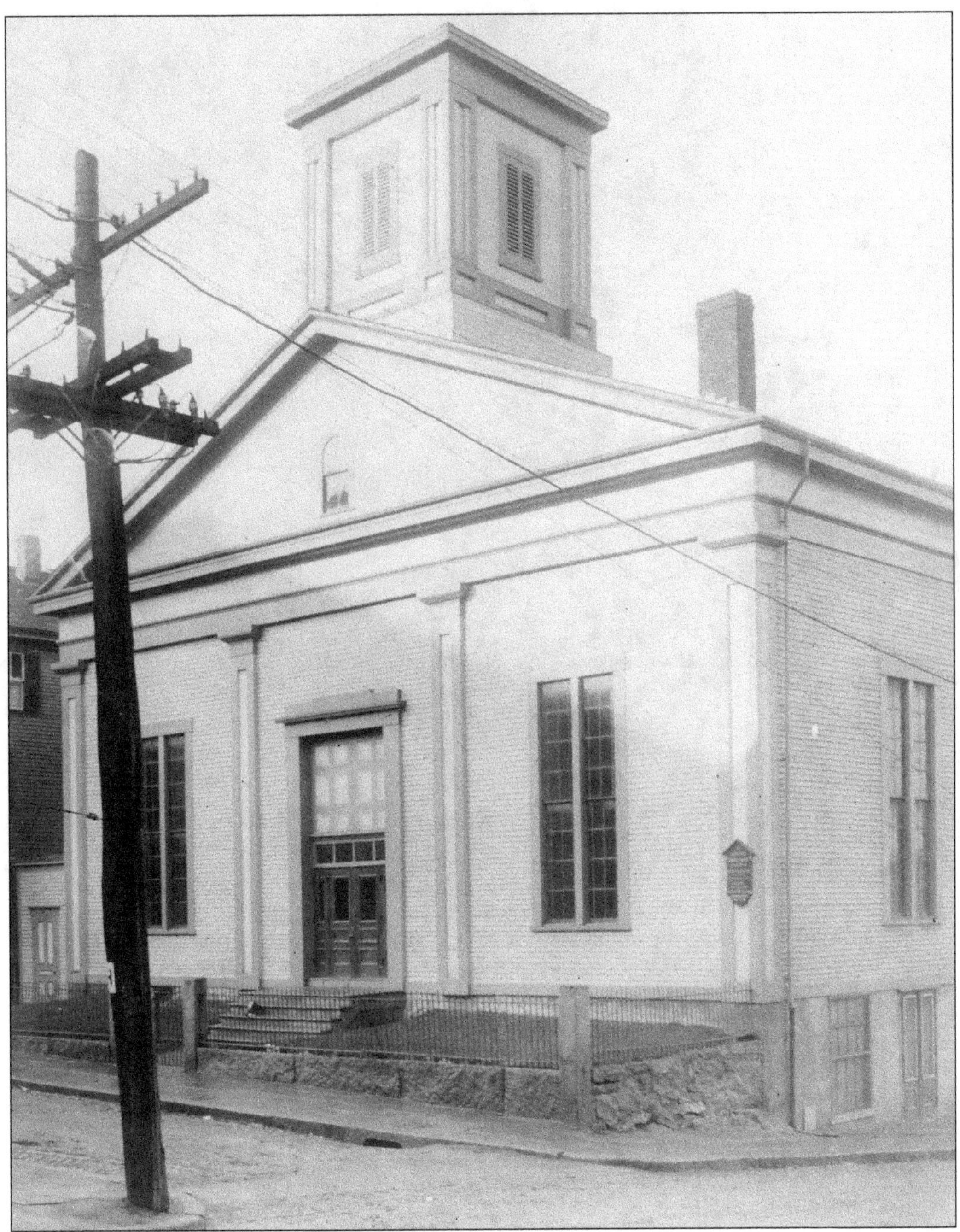

The Presbyterian church on the corner of Anawan and Pearl Streets was built in 1851 and served as a place of worship for over 75 years. In March 1926, the congregation moved to Rock and Walnut Streets, and the old church was abandoned. The area is now a parking lot. (Courtesy of the Fall River Historical Society.)

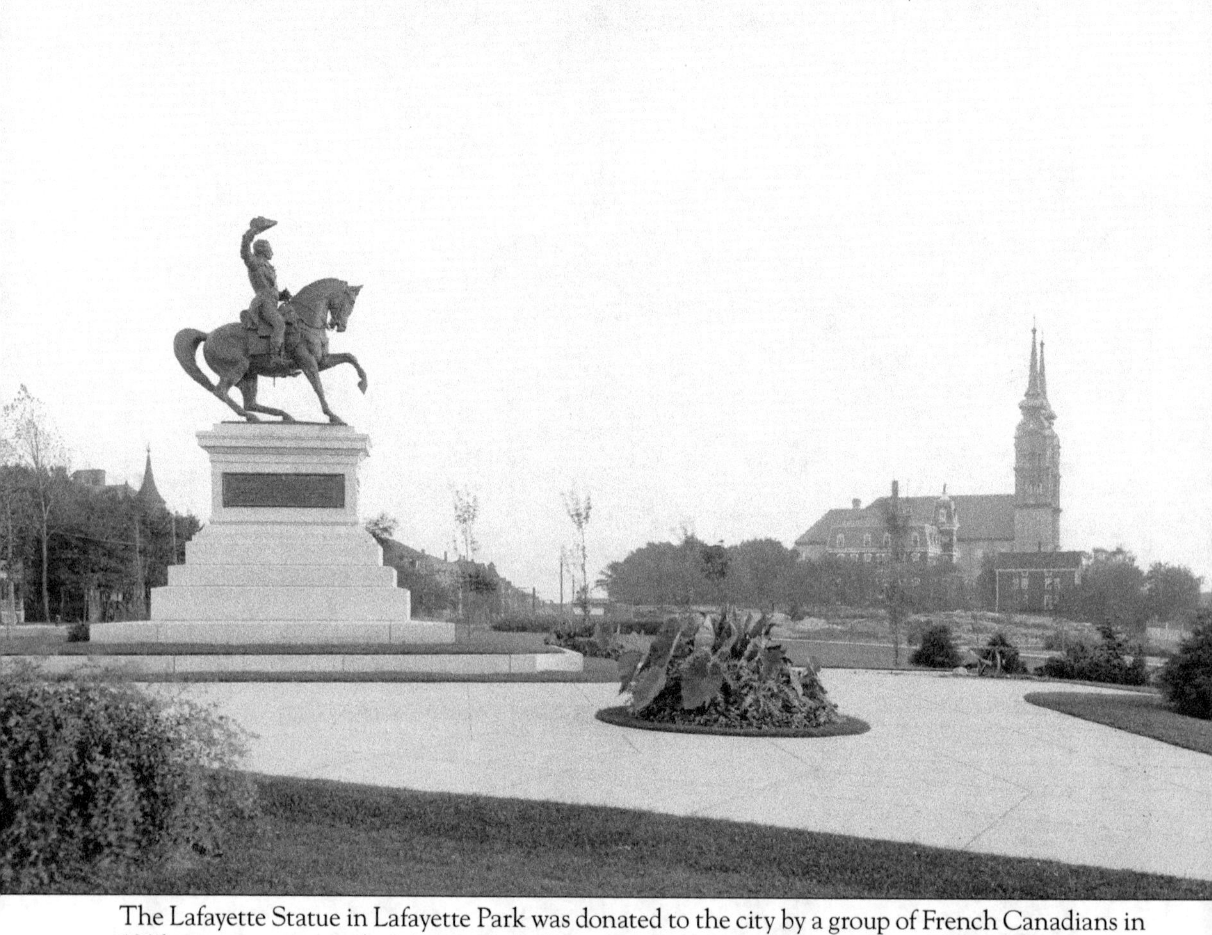

The Lafayette Statue in Lafayette Park was donated to the city by a group of French Canadians in 1916 to commemorate the Marquis de Lafayette passing through the area during the Revolutionary War on his way from Newport to Boston. Many stories surround the "mystery" of why and when the statue was turned around to face in the opposite direction. No one seems to remember exactly what happened, but the least conspiratorial suggests that the statue was originally erected to face the center of Fall Fiver, but when Eastern Avenue became much more important and Pleasant Street east of Eastern Avenue became irrelevant due to Interstate 195, the Lafayette Statue was turned at the time it was refurbished and rededicated. The most commonly shared explanation is that members of the French Canadian community, which lived in the Flint section of the city, were not pleased with the original placement with the rear of the horse facing them. The statue was turned around when a cleaning was conducted, and it now faces Eastern Avenue instead of to the west. The towering spires of Notre Dame de Lourdes are seen on the right. A fire completely destroyed the church and part of the Flint section of the city in 1982. (Detroit Publishing Company photograph, courtesy of the Library of Congress.)

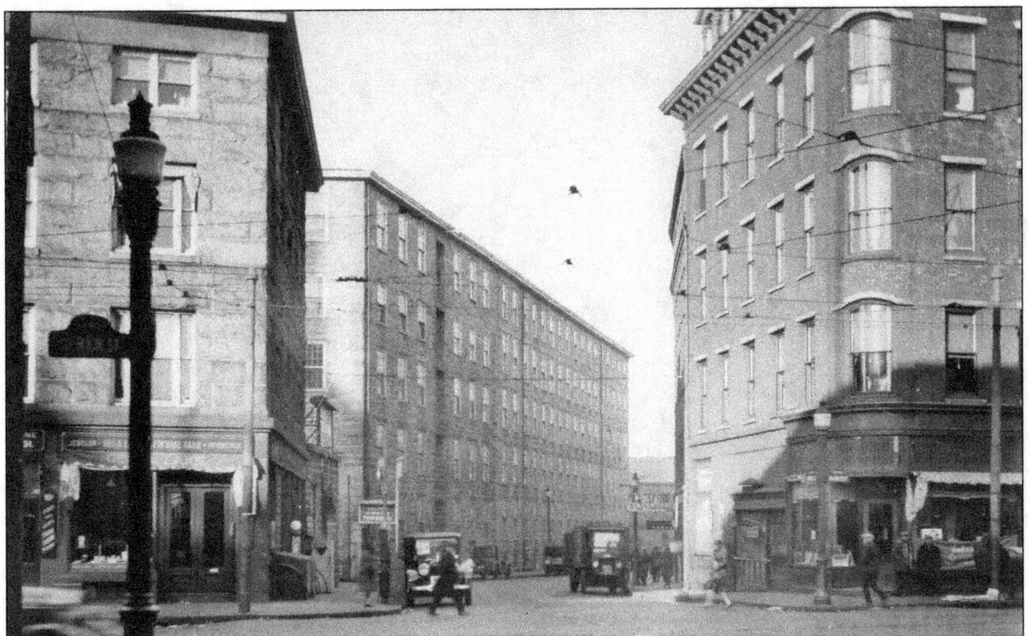

What makes this image rather unique is that all of the buildings in it were destroyed in the 1928 fire that had such a devastating impact on the business district of Fall River. Here, in a westward view across Main Street, one can see Central Street from Bedford Street. The photograph shows the Granite Block, Pocasset Mill, and the Durfee Block, the site of the Mohican Hotel. (Courtesy of the Fall River Historical Society.)

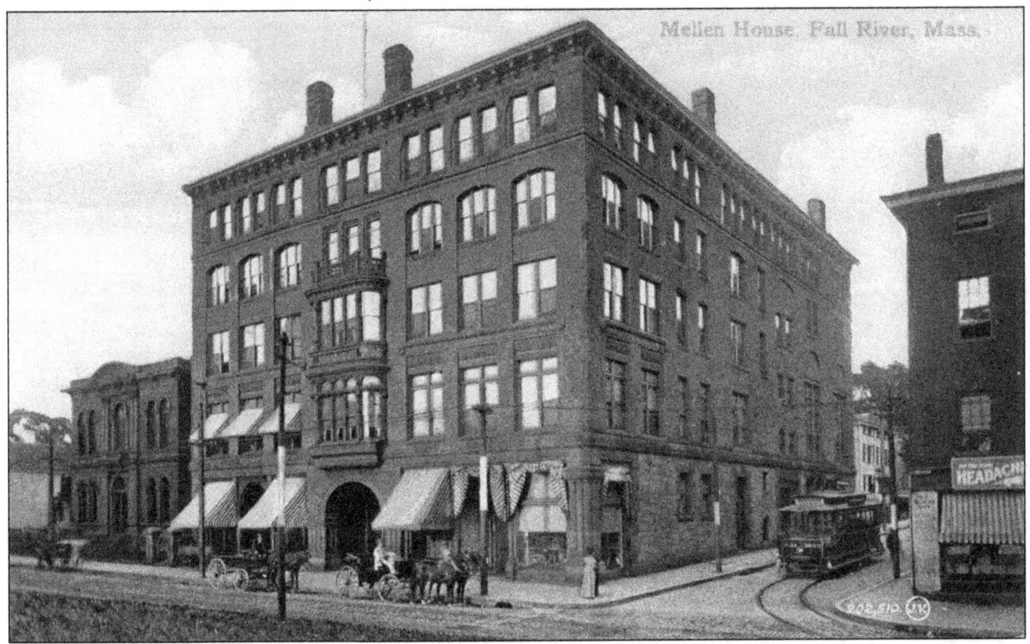

The Mellen House, located on the corner of North Main and Franklin Streets, across from the Fall River Public Library, was named after the hotel's president and chief promoter, George F. Mellen. Once a leading hotel in the city, it was gutted by a fire on September 27, 1943. (Collection of Stefani Koorey.)

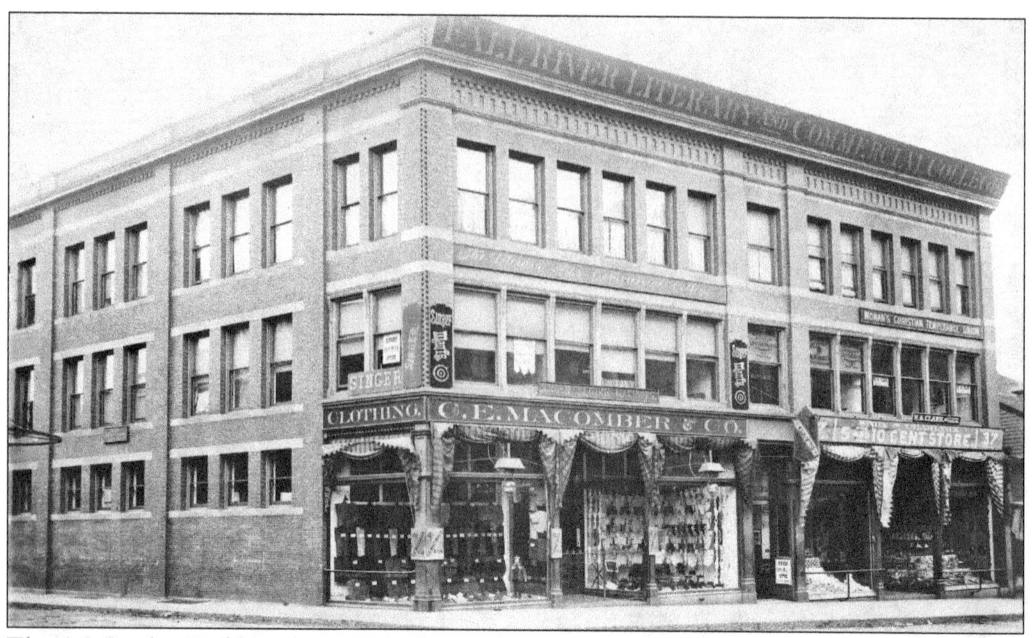

The A.J. Borden Building, located on the northwest corner of South Main and Anawan Streets, was built by Andrew Borden, the father of Lizzie, as a tribute to his self-made status as a prominent businessman. When it opened, it housed all manner of companies, including Charles E. Macomber & Company, Knox & Charlton Five and Ten Cent Store, the Fall River Christian Science Institute, Gay's Gallery of Art, and Mr. Beno Brodkorb, music dealer and teacher. (Courtesy of the Fall River Historical Society.)

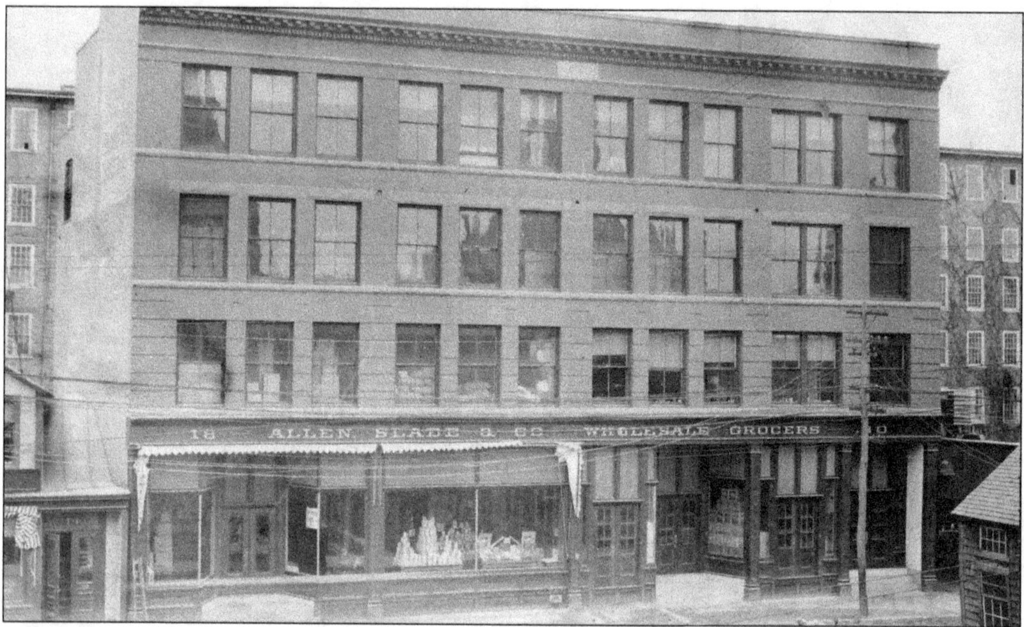

Built in 1906 on the east side of Third Street, the "new" Allen, Slade & Co. Building provided a much-needed expansion of its wholesale grocery business as dealers in teas, flour, butter, cheese, lard, oils, and hay, as well as agents for Bush & Denslow's Premium Safety Oil, fire- and burglarproof safes, and oil tanks. (Courtesy of the Fall River Historical Society.)

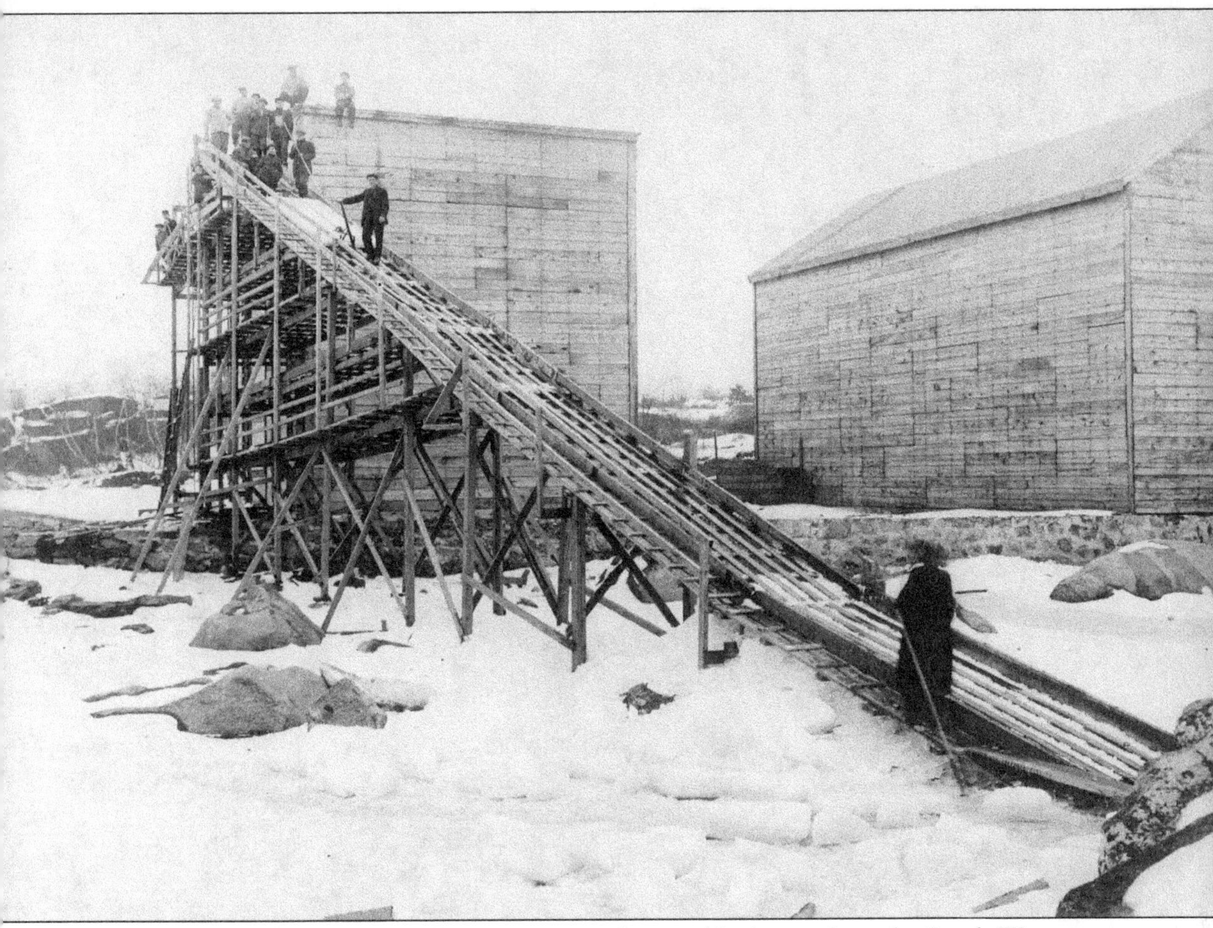

These workers for the Payette Ice Company are guiding ice blocks, cut from the South Watuppa Pond, up a conveyor belt for storage around 1920. Once inside, the 22-inch square blocks were fitted together on the floor of the icehouse, insulated from the walls by paper and sawdust. According to Fall River ice industry historian Bill Goncalo: "Icehouses had only a ground floor, and ice was stacked in layers from the floor nearly up to the roof. Doorways spanning the entire height of the house were closed up incrementally as the stacked ice rose. When the whole house was filled, it would be sealed until ice was needed in the warmer months (May through October). Then it would be delivered throughout the city by wagon to both homes and businesses. The stored ice easily kept through the summer, and a well-packed and insulated icehouse could preserve ice through two summers if needed. In fact, when icehouses occasionally caught on fire and burned, it wasn't uncommon to have the ice remain stacked and intact long after the house around it had burned to the ground." (Courtesy of Kenneth M. Champlin.)

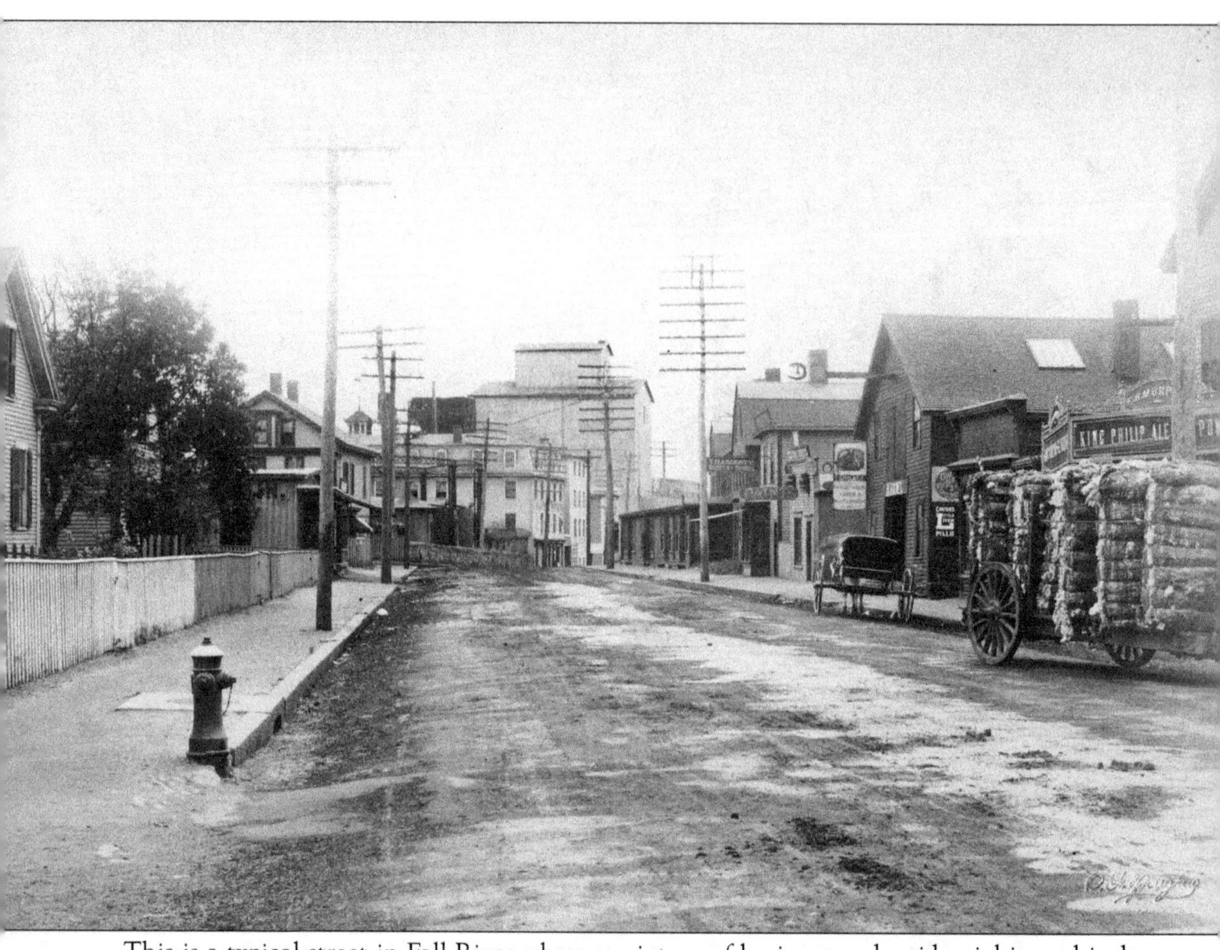

This is a typical street in Fall River where a mixture of business and residential is to this day more the norm than the exception. On the left side of Davol Street (seen in this view looking south from Baylies Street) are homes with white picket fences, followed by industrial property and what appears to be a grain elevator. Directly across the street on the right from the residences is a wide variety of businesses—T. Haggery, Boots and Shoes; a store with the sign "Paints;" E.G. Holmes, Horse Shoer, Jobber, and Wheelwright; and E.H. Murphy, selling King Philip Ale. Note the large cotton wagon in front of this last location, parked by the side of the road, perhaps bringing in a day's load of raw material, just off the boat from the South, to the cotton mills. (Courtesy of Bill Goncalo.)

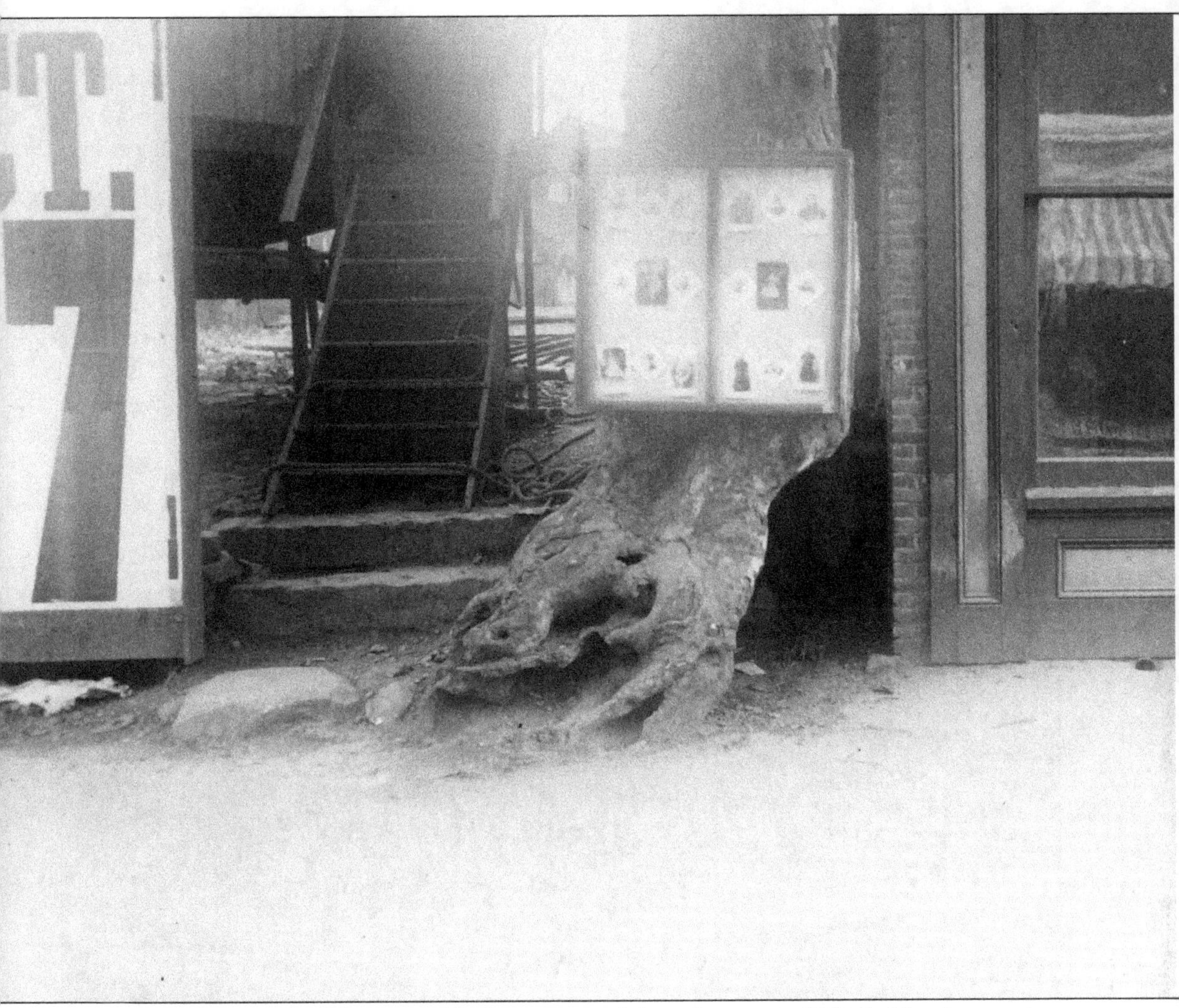

At one time, the city of Fall River straddled two states—Massachusetts and Rhode Island—creating a boundary dispute that would take the Supreme Court of the United States to resolve. The only point of reference for the dividing line was a buttonwood tree, located on the east side South Main Street opposite No. 286, near Columbia Street. Fall River, Rhode Island, was set apart from Tiverton, Rhode Island, by an act of the Rhode Island General Assembly. However, it was not until 1861 that the long-awaited boundary decision was handed down by the United States Supreme Court to take effect on March 1, 1862, when the town of Fall River, Rhode Island, was annexed to, and became a part of, the city of Fall River, Massachusetts. And so, after serving its purpose, the lowly buttonwood tree sat forgotten for many years, until it was cut down by the city of Fall River on April 9, 1896. (Courtesy of the Fall River Historical Society.)

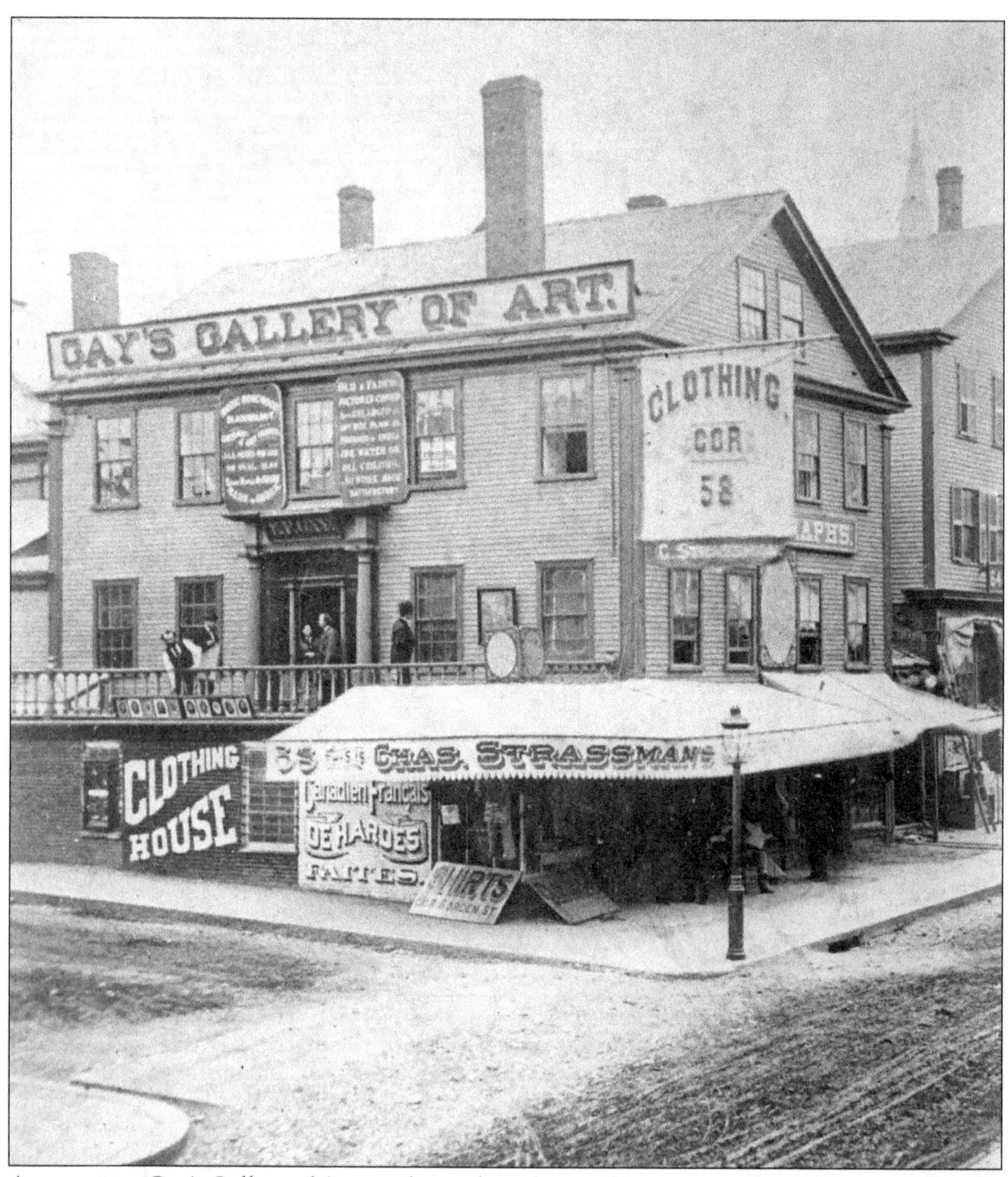

At one time, Gay's Gallery of Art was located on the southeast corner South Main and Borden Streets, at 52 South Main Street (pictured here in 1860). By 1882, it had moved across the street to the A.J. Borden Building and relocated to 44 North Main Street by 1921. Gay's was perhaps Fall River's best-known photography studio. Emily (Mrs. Edwin Forest) Gay ran the business after the death of her husband on April 6, 1879. Their daughter Winona Marian Gay, a photographer and retoucher, also managed the business after her mother. The Gay family was the photographer of choice of Fall River's elite. Where this building once stood is now the new Fall River Division of the Bristol County Superior Court. (Courtesy of the Fall River Historical Society.)

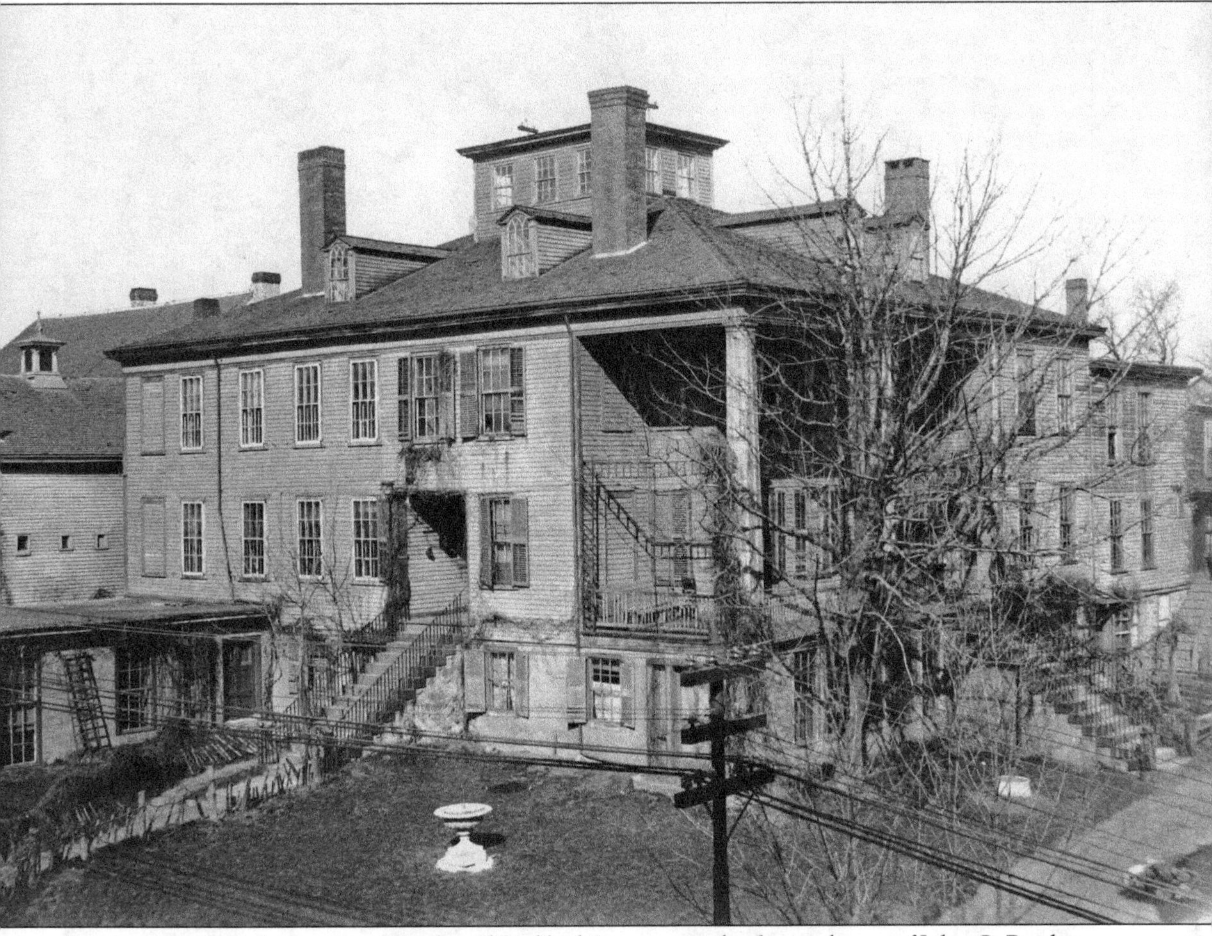

On this parcel on the corner of Rock and Bedford Streets was the former home of John C. Borden, who died in 1833. Borden had constructed what can only be described as the most colossal mansion ever built in Fall River. Later, this building was known as the Exchange Hotel, and in its last days, it would be known as the Gunn Mansion. Horatio Gunn purchased the entire property in 1844 and continued to employ it as a hotel. Eventually, Gunn used the building as a private residence until his death. It was still standing in an increasingly dilapidated condition until 1910, when it was torn down, and the former Second District Courthouse was erected. Benjamin Buffinton stated that the Gunn House was a remarkable structure in its day—with 55 rooms, hand-carved mantels and window casings, floors, ceilings, and doors of heart pine, and walls decorated by landscape artists. (Collection of Stefani Koorey.)

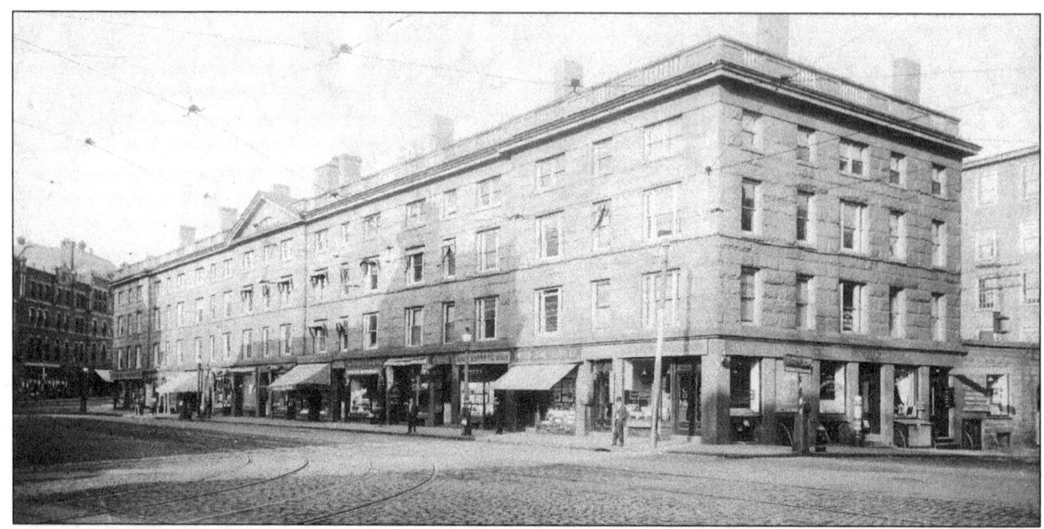

The Granite Block, once located on the east side of Main Street, from Central to Pocasset, actually had two incarnations. The first structure was erected in 1843 and was used for law offices and tenements on the second and third floors, with stores on the first. It was destroyed in the 1928 fire, and a second Granite Block was constructed on the same site. It survived until the 1960s, when it was demolished to make way for the new interstate highway. (Courtesy of the Fall River Historical Society.)

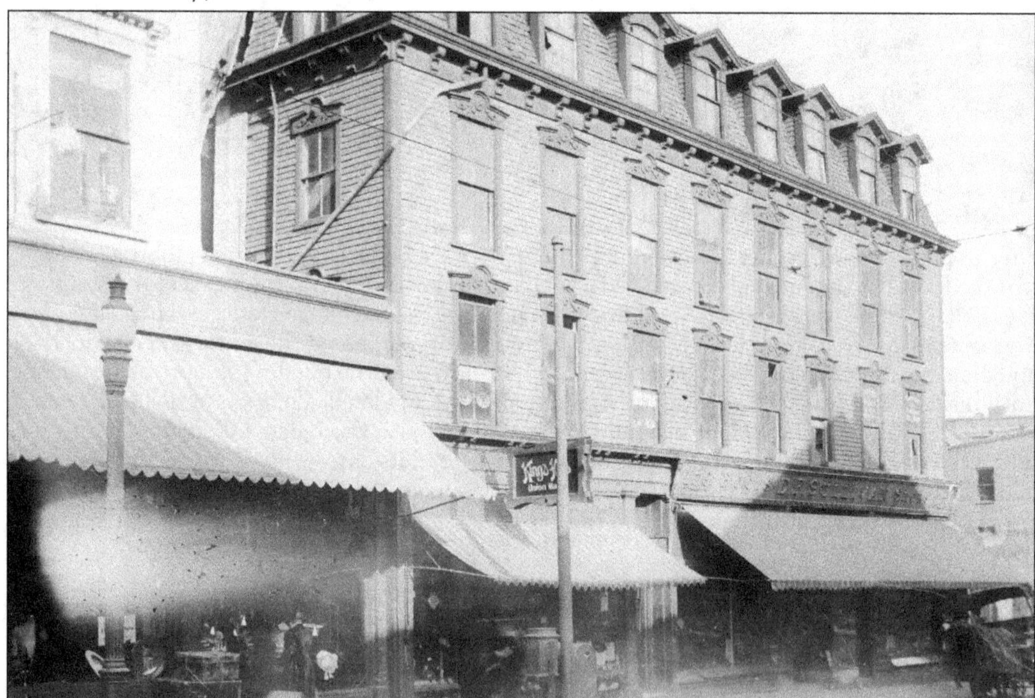

Whether due to fire, benign neglect, or choice, so many of Fall River's early buildings are no longer standing. One such structure is the D.F. Sullivan Block, which stood just south of Borden Street on the west side of South Main Street. Across the street in 2012 is the new Fall River Division of the Bristol County Superior Court, a 153,000-square-foot concrete, metal, and glass structure. (Courtesy of the Fall River Historical Society.)

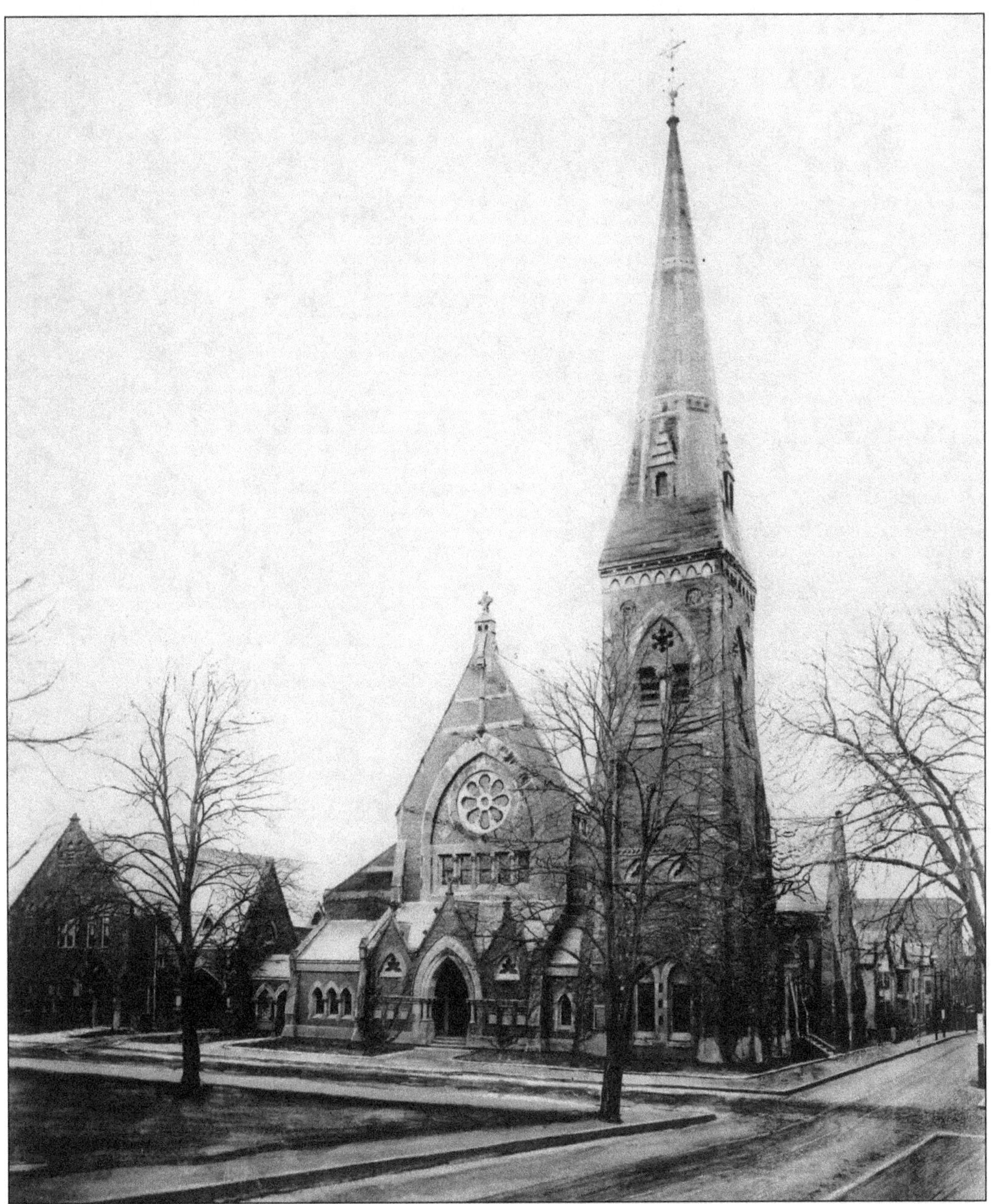

The Central Congregational Church was first organized in 1842, with its first church edifice dedicated in 1844. By 1870, the church had over 300 members and was in need of a new house of worship. The present Central Congregational Church structure is of Ruskinian Gothic design and was dedicated in 1875. The chapel was first occupied in 1892. Once the church of Lizzie Borden, it boasts a Hook & Hastings organ with 48 stops and 3,196 pipes, the largest of which is 16 feet long and the smallest equal in size to a lead pencil. In 1983, the structure was placed in the National Register of Historic Places. In the 1990s, the chapel and great hall were converted into the International Culinary Academy and Restaurant, which, after running into financial problems, closed its doors in 2009. The now abandoned building is still located on the southwest corner of Rock and Franklin Streets. (Courtesy of the Fall River Historical Society.)

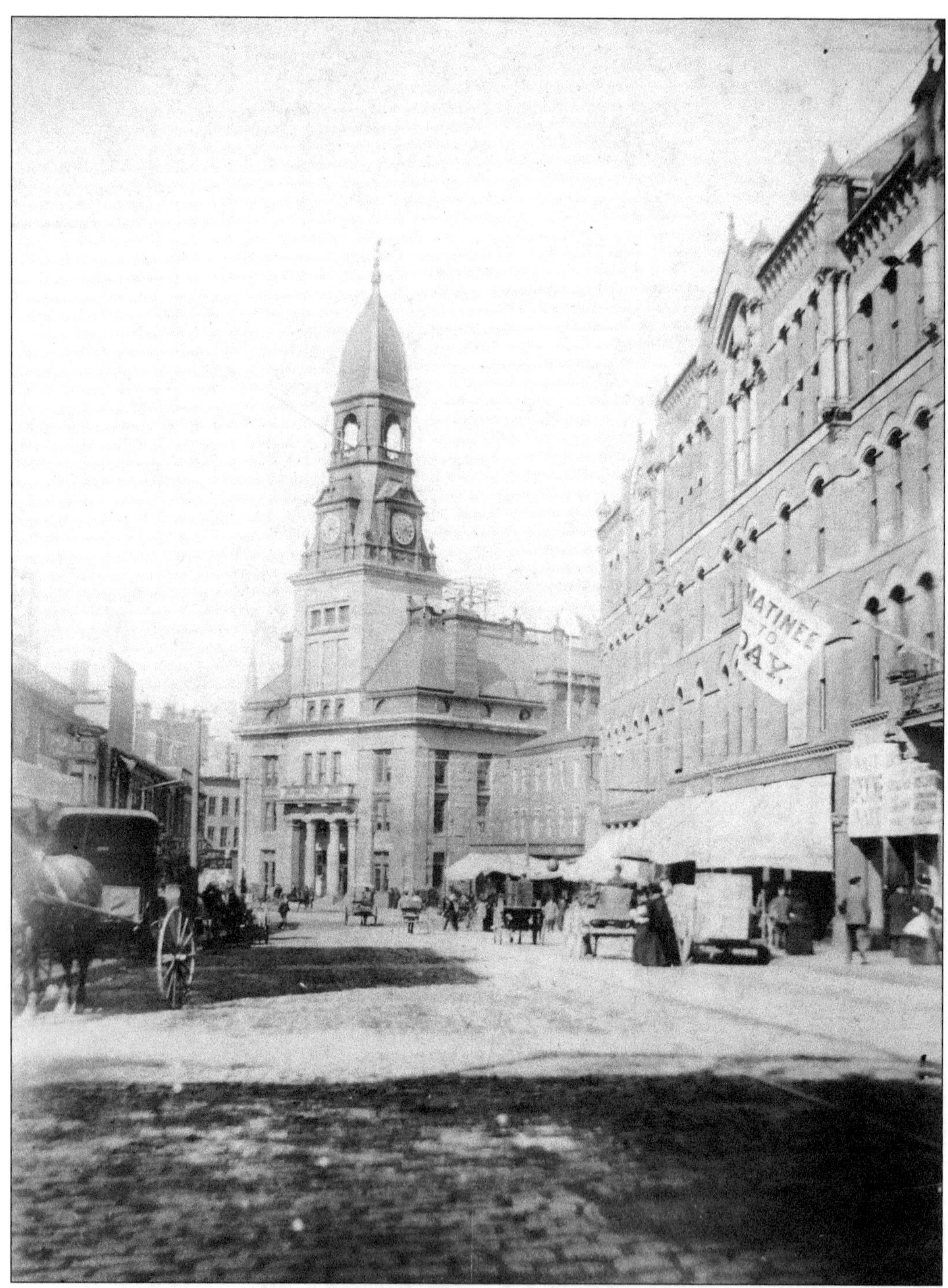

The Academy Theater, seen here on the right, was the principle theater in Fall River and, at the time of its opening in 1876, the second-largest stage in the state of Massachusetts. Housed in the Academy Building, also known as the Borden Block, it was removed in the 1980s when renovations to convert the upper floors into senior housing were approved. (Courtesy of the Fall River Historical Society.)

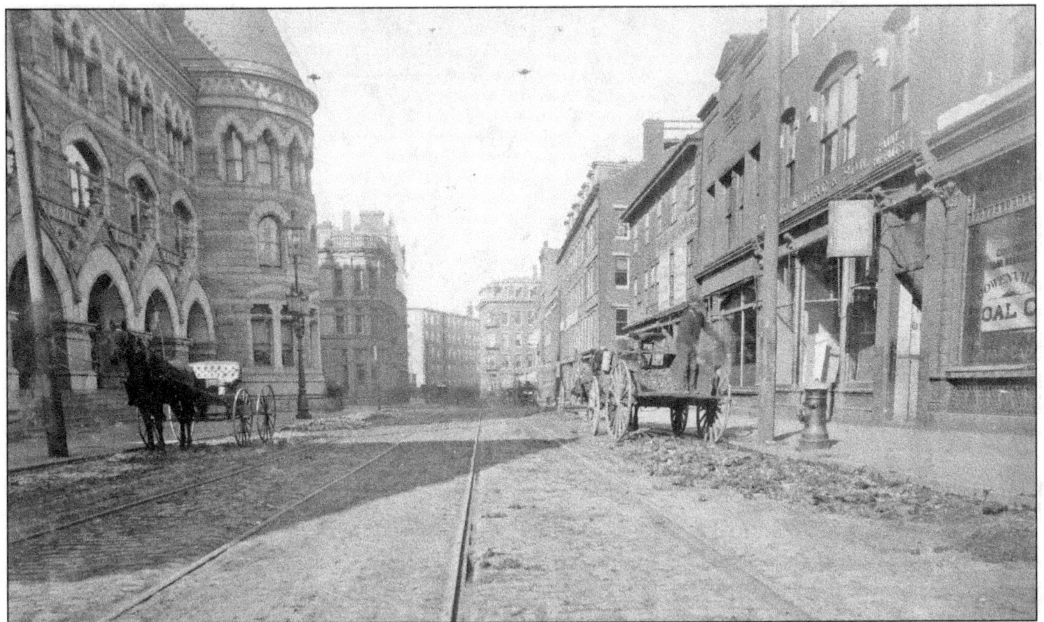

This scene showing Bedford Street from Rock Street dates from before the fire of 1928. On the left is the federal post office and customhouse building, which was untouched. At the end of street are the Pocasset Mill (left) and the Mohican Hotel (right). The Granite Block is the next building past the post office. All three of these massive structures—the mill, the hotel, and the block—were destroyed by the blaze. (Courtesy of the Fall River Historical Society.)

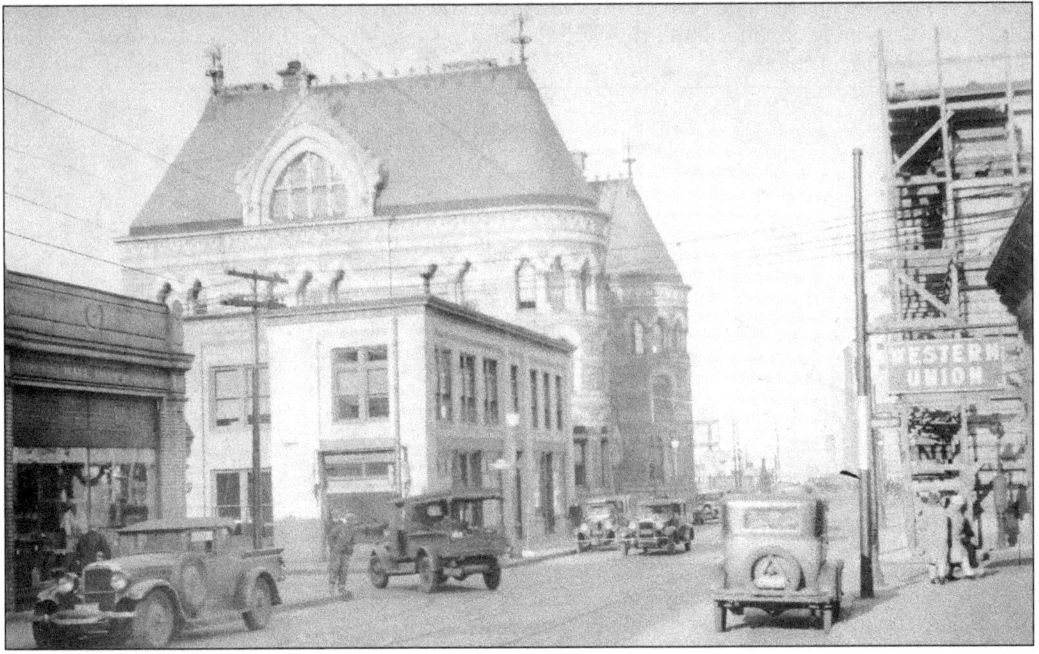

The federal post office and customhouse building, located on Bedford Street, is seen in this view from Third Street to Main Street in 1928. The skyline beyond the customhouse is missing because this is the area of devastation from the 1928 fire. Note the construction on the right as the rebuilding process has already begun. (Courtesy of the Fall River Historical Society.)

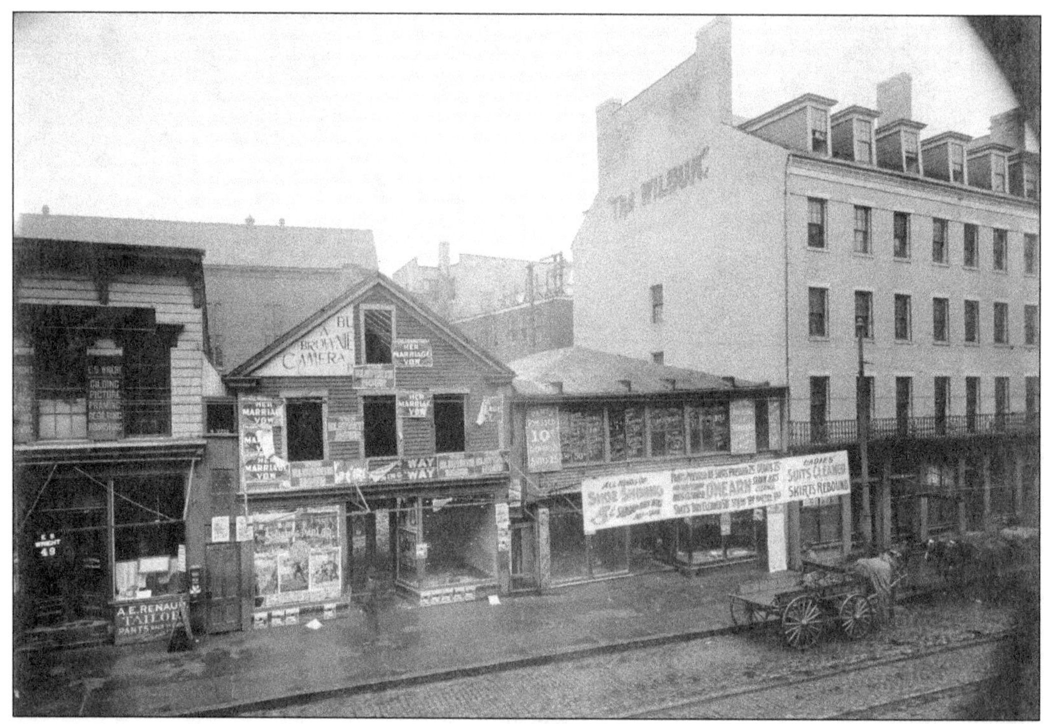

The Wilbur Hotel, located on the corner of North Main and Granite Streets, was once Fall River's leading hotel. In 1869, Darius Wilbur operated a small restaurant on the ground floor and leased tenements on the upper floors. He slowly converted the entire building into the Wilbur Hotel. Like the 500-room Mohican Hotel, the Wilbur was destroyed in the 1928 fire. (Courtesy of the Fall River Historical Society.)

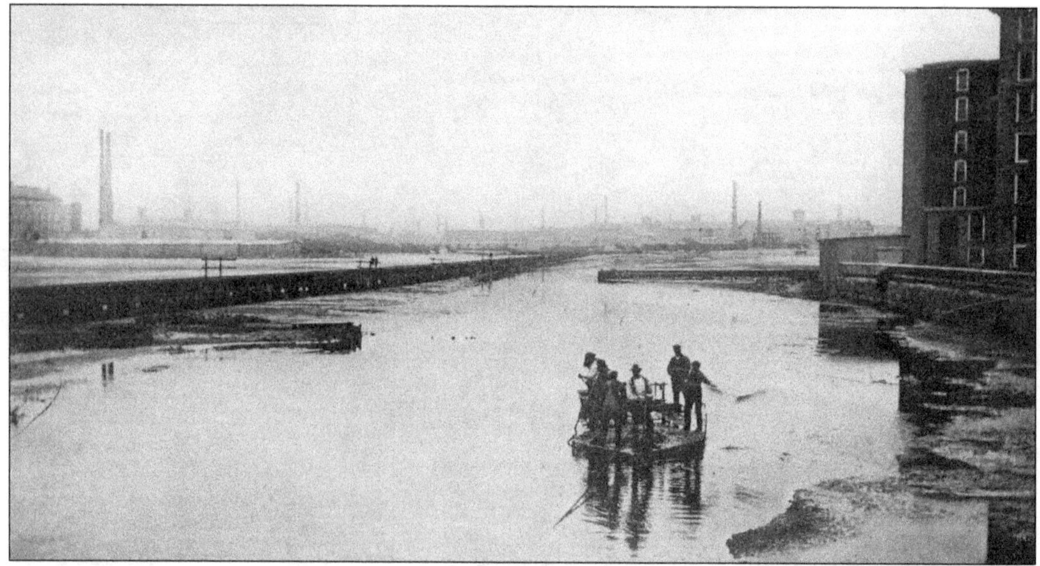

This 1909 view is from the Quequechan Street Bridge near Quarry Street, and looks west down the Quequechan River with Barnard Mills on the right. While the image may resemble a group of young men rafting on the Mississippi River, it is not. Rather, it is a photograph of men who are employed by the American Print Works Company dredging the channel. (Courtesy of John Friar.)

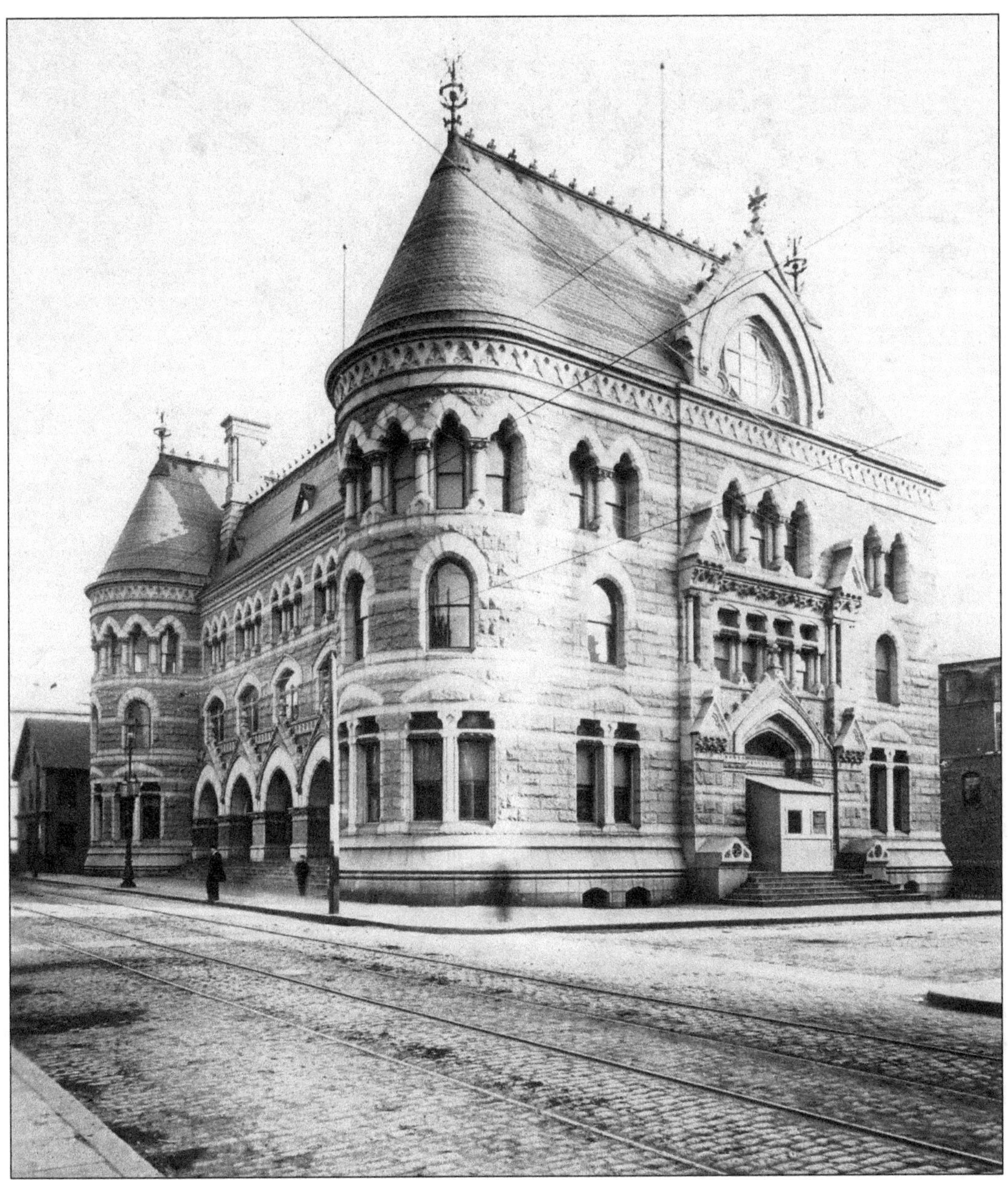

Opened in 1880, the ornate federal post office and customhouse sat on the corner of Bedford and Second Streets, facing Bedford, and was constructed at a total cost of $518,000, of which $132,000 was for land. Two of the supports for the arcade arches of the front are now the pedestals of the Spanish-American War Monument at the north end of Plymouth Avenue and the *Prince Henry the Navigator* statue, which sits at the junction of Eastern Avenue and Pleasant Street and was presented to the city by the citizens of Portuguese extraction. When the present post office building was in the process of construction in the early 1930s, the old building and the fire stations east of city hall were demolished, and Pocasset and Third Streets were widened. Third Street had previously been extended across the Quequechan River by an iron bridge to Bedford Street. The river was confined within a conduit, and the bridge was eliminated. (Courtesy of the Fall River Historical Society.)

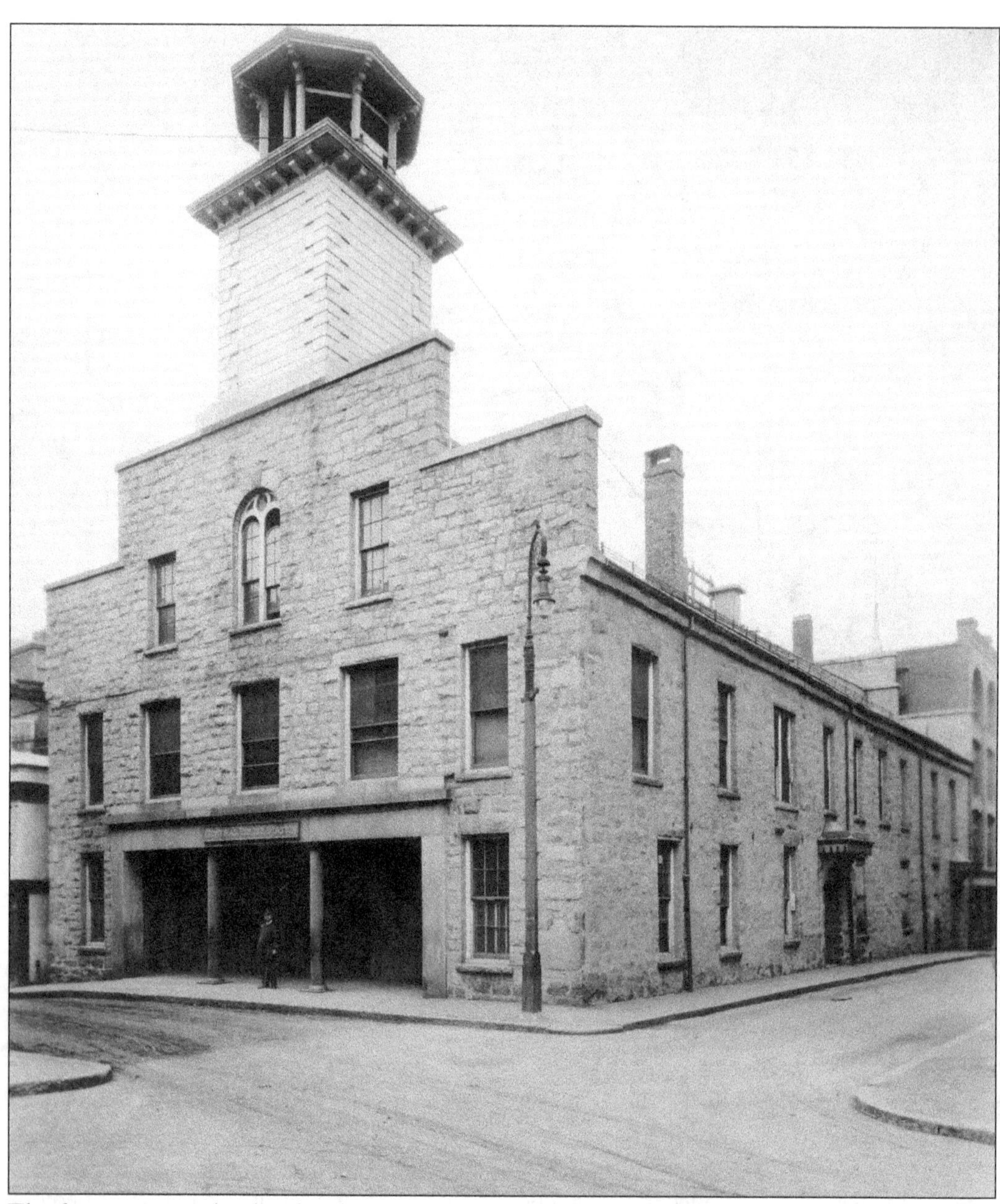

The first city-owned police headquarters was located on Central Street at the old town house. Later, its were relocated to the basement of the new city hall on North Main Street, between Market and Bedford Streets. From 1857 until 1916, Central Station (pictured here) was a sizable granite building on Court Square, on the corner of Purchase and Granite Streets. Built in 1843, the former Richardson House had a large stable that made it suitable for city purposes, as this station was to house the police force, the engine house for the Fall River Fire Department, and a courtroom. The figure standing in front of the police station is Marshal Rufus Hilliard, who figured prominently in the inquest upon the deaths of Andrew and Abby Borden in 1892, which was held at this location. In 1916, the police headquarters was again relocated to the corner of High and Bedford Streets, and this granite building was torn down with the widening of Purchase Street. (Courtesy of the Fall River Historical Society.)

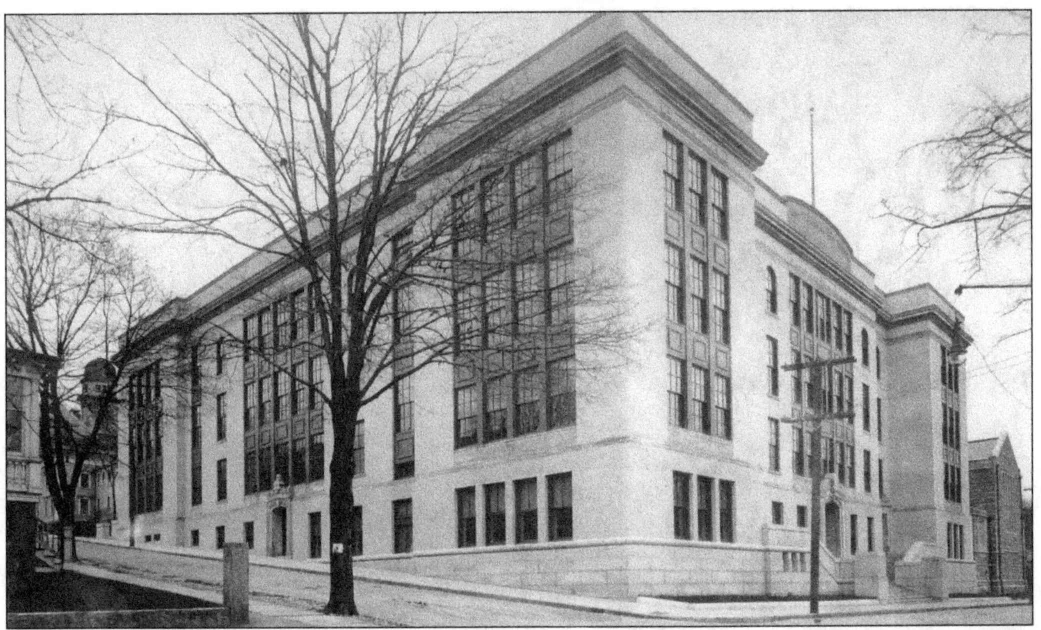

This is the Durfee Technical High School; the building is still located on the corner of June and Locust Streets but currently serves as a middle school. In 1936, the Works Progress Administration commissioned John Mann to paint murals depicting Fall River's history on the walls of the auditorium. There are four sets of murals: Indian history; the history of Fall River; the cotton mills; and the workers in the cotton mills. (Courtesy of the Fall River Historical Society.)

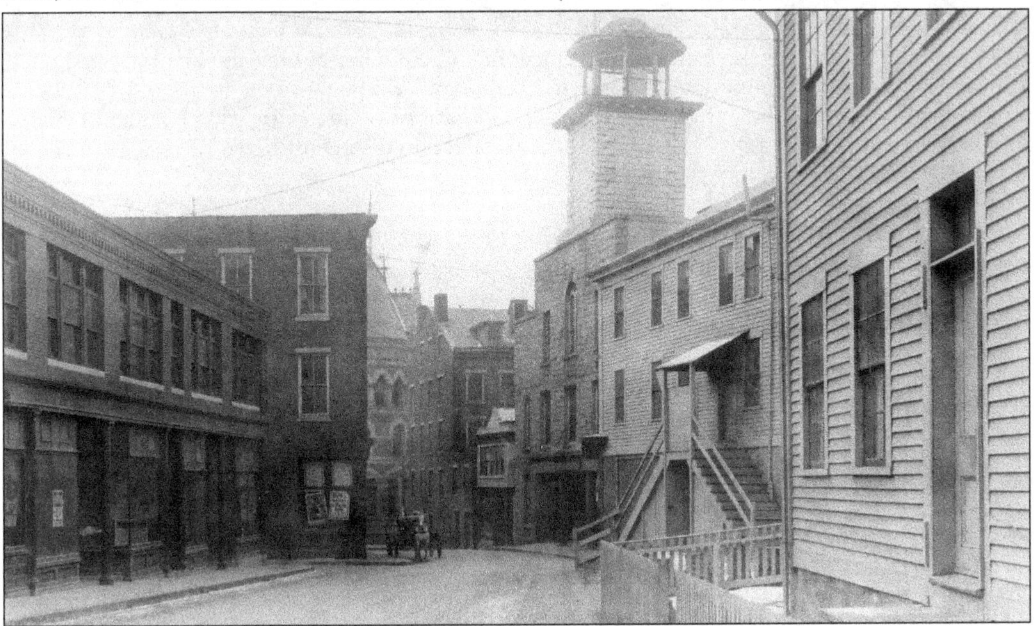

This is a view of Central Station of the Fall River Police Department on Purchase Street, as seen from Granite Street. In 1854, the police force consisted of 15 watchmen (paid $8.50 a week), a chief constable (paid $10.50 a week), and a chief of the night watch. By 1874, the force had increased to 70 people, and the city was divided into five districts with smaller stations located throughout. (Courtesy of the Fall River Historical Society.)

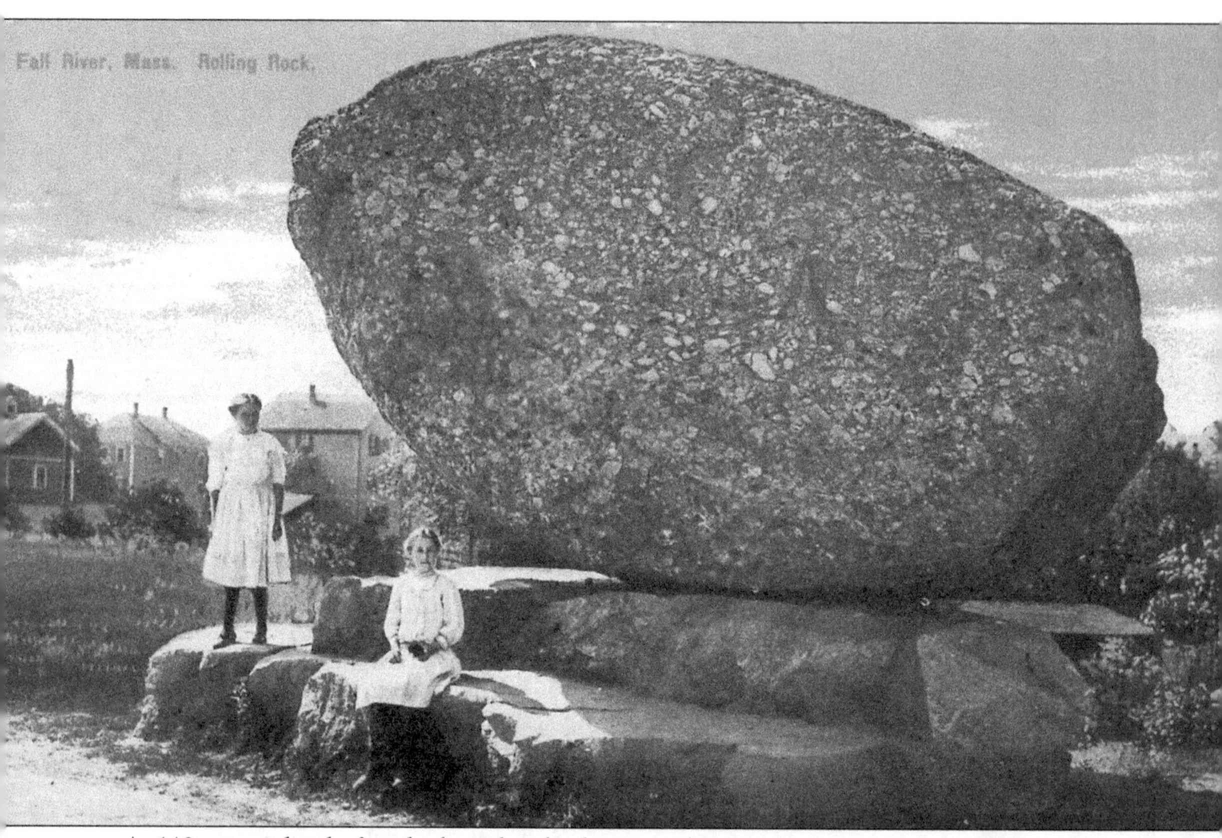

At 140 tons and eight feet thick, and with a horizontal circumference of 58 feet, Fall River's famed Rolling Rock sits at the junction of Eastern Avenue and County Street. In 1860, when locals feared that it would tumble off its perch from the vibrations of quarrying, this boulder of coarse conglomerate was forged to its ledge of granite. (Collection of Stefani Koorey.)

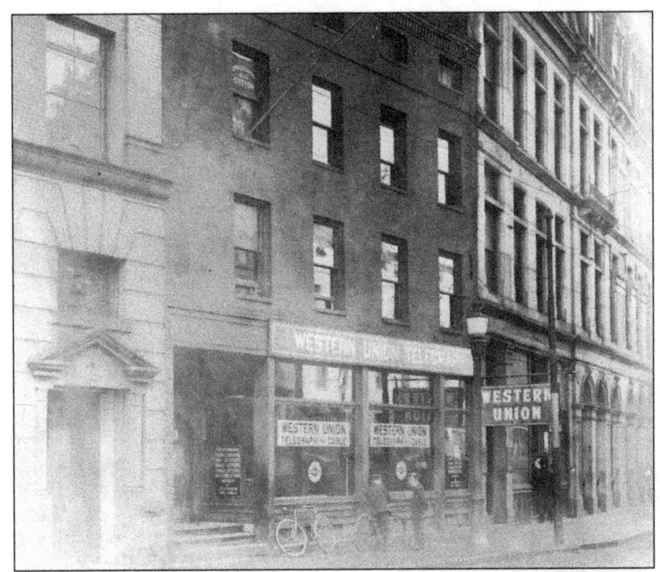

Until 1877, and the invention of the telephone, the telegraph was the primary means of rapid communication, and telegraph offices, like the one shown here in 1925 on Bedford Street, were commonplace. In 1919, the rate was 60¢ for a 10-word message from New York to Chicago, while a three-minute telephone call the same distance was $4.65. Once long-distance telephone rates became less expensive than the telegram around 1970, the service lost its popularity and began a steep decline. (Courtesy of the Fall River Historical Society.)

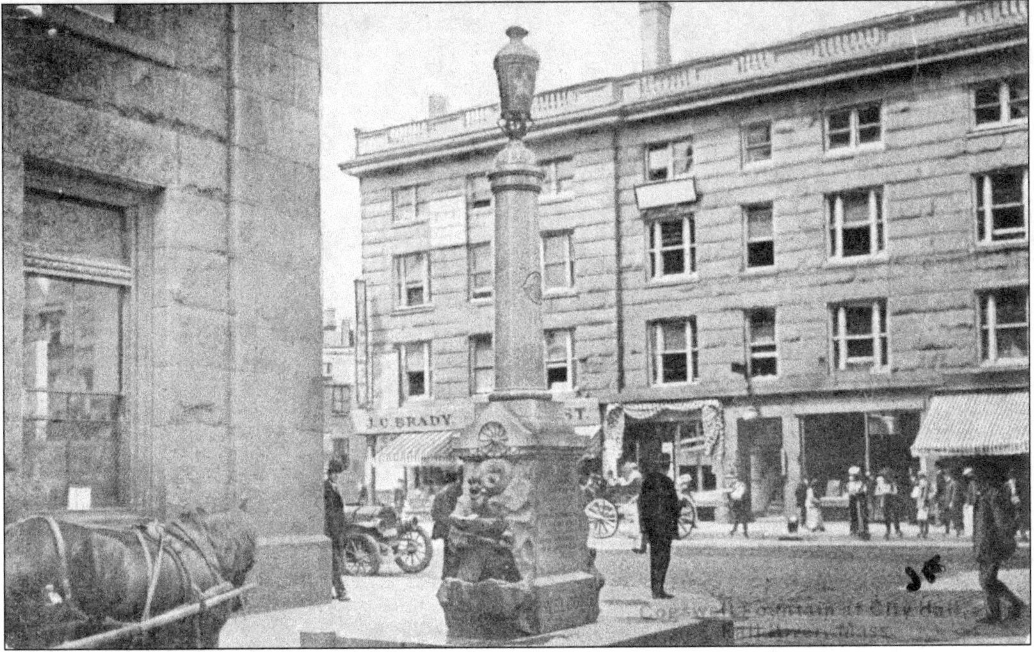

Dominating the image on this postcard is the Granite Block, which was located across from the old city hall on North Main Street. In the foreground is the Cogswell Fountain, made, ironically, from New Hampshire granite. A gift to the city by temperance accolade and San Francisco dentist Henry Cogswell, it was installed in the summer of 1884 on Market Street at a cost of $2,500. In 1962, city hall and the Granite Block were both demolished to make way for a new highway. At that time, the 26-foot-high fountain was dismantled and stored at the city's public works property on Rodman Street, where it deteriorated for the next 10 years. Eventually, the fountain was rescued by the Fall River Historical Society and erected on its property in the fall of 1972, where it sat until plans were made in the later part of the 1970s to move it back to Main Street. Today, Henry Cogswell's dry fountain sits less than a hundred feet from its original location, on the southwest corner of Central and Main Streets, across from city hall. (Collection of Stefani Koorey.)

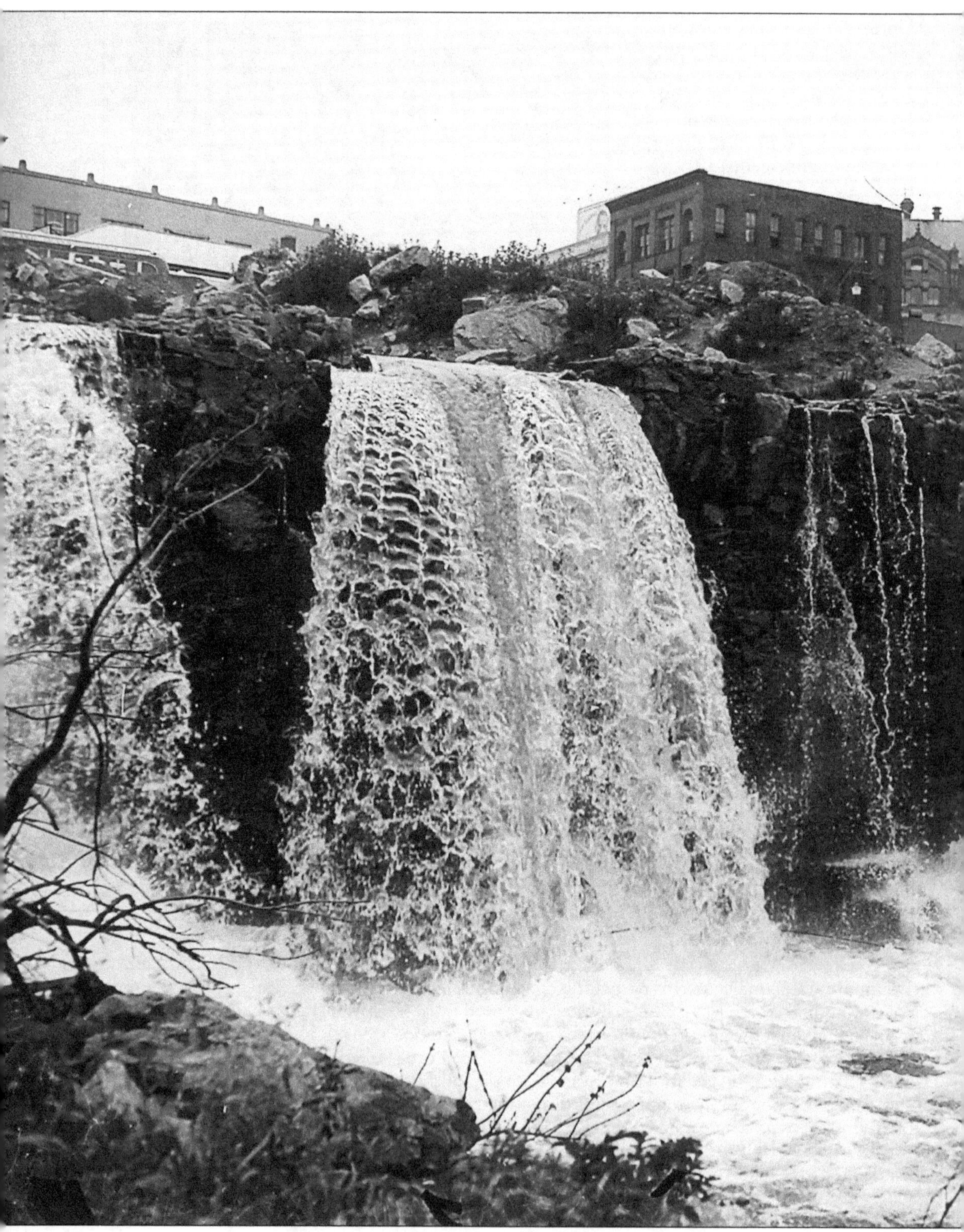

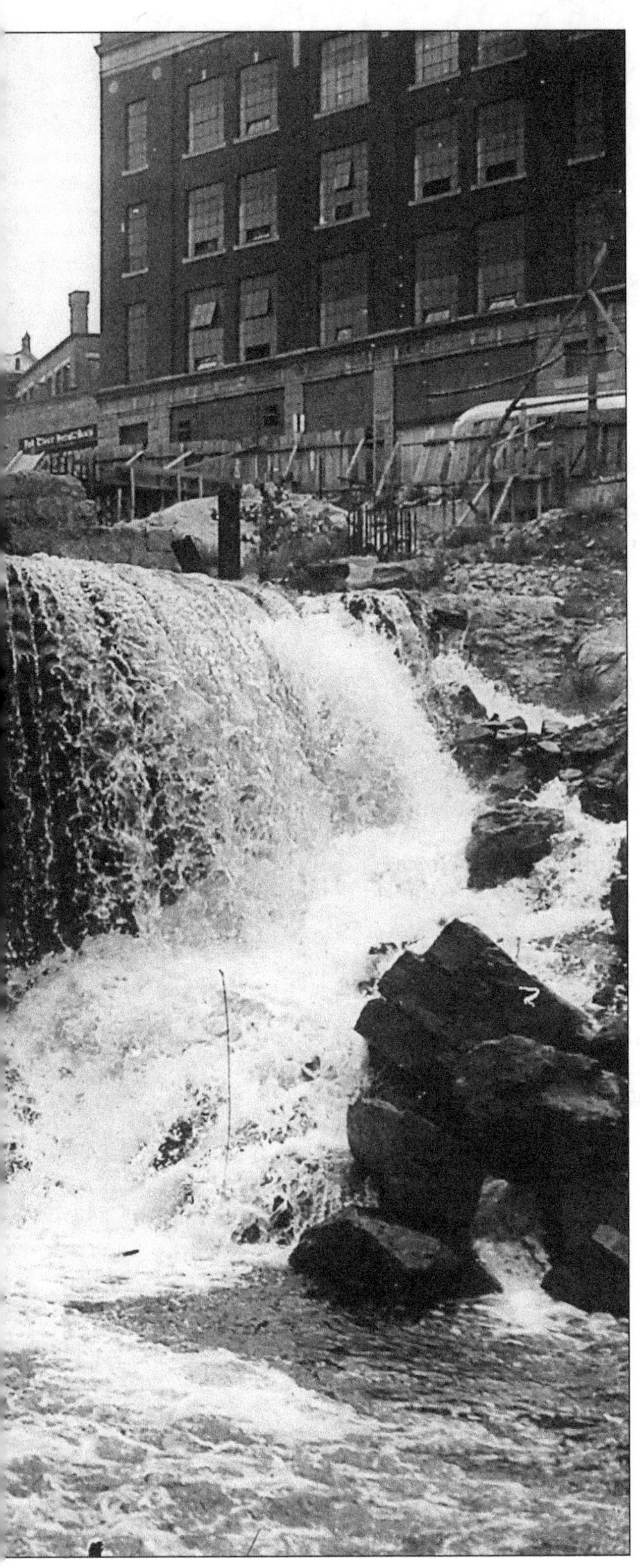

The history of the Quequechan River is fraught with instances of man's interference with its natural course for the sake of commerce. There is little to no evidence or description of the river's pristine state, and now that a great deal of the stream is underground, one can only look to photographs of man's impact upon it for insight. With a drop of 21.67 feet, this is the tallest of the eight falls that the river eventually sported. The Quequechan made it possible for the industry of cotton textile manufacturing to proliferate, as the cotton mill's power was, at least for a time, derived solely from the horsepower generated by the dropping of the water. (Courtesy of John Friar.)

Bibliography

Champlin, Kenneth M. "The Granite Quarries of Fall River." In *A River and Its City: The Influence of the Quequechan River on the Development of Fall River, Massachusetts* by Alfred J. Lima. Fall River, MA: Green Futures, 2007.

Clarkin, Harold E. *The High-Ball and the Iron Horse*. Fall River, MA: Fall River Historical Society, 1954.

Conforti, John J. *Fall River's First Italians, 1872–1914*. Fall River, MA: privately published, 2003.

The Cost of Living Among Wage-Earners, Fall River, Massachusetts, October, 1919. Research Report Number 22, November, 1919. Boston: National Industrial Conference Board, 1919.

Dunwell, Steve. *The Run of the Mill: A Pictorial Narrative of the Expansion, Dominion, Decline and Enduring Impact of the New England Textile Industry*. Boston: D.R. Godine, 1978.

Earl, Henry H. *A Centennial History of Fall River, Mass.: comprising a record of its corporate progress from 1656 to 1876, with sketches of its manufacturing industries, local and general characteristics, valuable statistical tables, etc.* New York: Atlantic Publishing and Engraving Company, 1877.

Fenner, Henry M. *History of Fall River, Massachusetts: Compiled for the Cotton Centennial by Henry M. Fenner, Under the Direction of the Historical Committee of the Merchants Association (1911).* Fall River, MA: Munroe Press, 1911.

Lima, Alfred J. *A River and Its City: The Influence of the Quequechan River on the Development of Fall River, Massachusetts*. Fall River, MA: Green Futures, 2007.

Living Conditions of the Wage-Earning Population in Certain Cities of Massachusetts. Commonwealth of Massachusetts, Bureau of Statistics. Boston: Wright & Potter, 1911: 277–293.

Phillips, Arthur Sherman. *The Phillips History of Fall River*. vols. 1–3. Fall River, MA: Dover Press, 1944–1946.

Report of the Watuppa Ponds and Quequechan River Commission to the City Council, City of Fall River. Boston: Fort Hill Press, 1915.

Silvia, Philip T. Jr., ed. *Victorian Vistas: Fall River*. Vol. 1, *1865–1885*; Vol. 2, *1886–1900*; Vol. 3, *1901–1911*. Fall River, MA: R.E. Smith, 1987, 1988, 1992.

About the Fall River Historical Society

Founded in 1921, the Fall River Historical Society's mission is to preserve and protect all manner of artifacts relating to the rich and varied history of the city of Fall River, Massachusetts.

The historical society is housed in a granite mansion, built in 1843 in the Greek Revival style for Andrew Robeson Jr., a prominent businessman. A onetime station on the Underground Railroad, the house was to change hands several times over the next quarter century.

For information on membership or research requests, please write to the Fall River Historical Society, 451 Rock Street, Fall River, Massachusetts, 02720, attention: Michael Martins, curator; or visit the society's website at LizzieBorden.org.

Visit us at
arcadiapublishing.com

www.ingramcontent.com/pod-product-compliance
Lightning Source LLC
LaVergne TN
LVHW081541100826
845153LV00004B/284
* 9 7 8 1 5 3 1 6 5 0 8 8 9 *